T0285702

IRON MIKE

IRON MIKE

MY LIFE BEHIND THE BENCH

MIKE KEENAN
WITH SCOTT MORRISON

Random House Canada

PUBLISHED BY RANDOM HOUSE CANADA

Copyright © 2024 Mike Keenan

www.penguinrandomhouse.ca

Random House Canada and colophon are registered trademarks.

All photos are courtesy of the author, except for the cover of *Amerk Magazine*, reprinted courtesy of the Rochester Americans.

Library and Archives Canada Cataloguing in Publication
Title: Iron Mike : my life behind the bench / Mike Keenan and Scott Morrison.
Names: Keenan, Mike, 1949- author. | Morrison, Scott, 1958- author.
Description: Includes index.
Identifiers: Canadiana (print) 20240350863 | Canadiana (ebook) 20240350901 |
ISBN 9780735281851 (hardcover) | ISBN 9780735281868 (EPUB)
Subjects: LCSH: Keenan, Mike, 1949- | LCSH: Hockey coaches—Canada—
Biography. | LCGFT: Autobiographies.
Classification: LCC GV848.5.K43 A3 2024 | DDC 796.962092—dc23

Jacket design: Emma Dolan
Text design: Emma Dolan
Typesetting: Erin Cooper

Image credits: (Mike Keenan) New York Daily News Archive / Contributor,
(crowd) Image Source / both Getty Images

Printed in Canada

2 4 6 8 9 7 5 3 1

Penguin
Random House
RANDOM HOUSE CANADA

To my loving family and many friends, thank you.
And to those I pissed off or disappointed, I meant well.

CONTENTS

FOREWORD

SAY WHAT YOU want about Mike Keenan—and many have said a lot—but in the past 84 years the New York Rangers have won the Stanley Cup only once, in 1994, and Mike was the head coach behind the bench when it happened.

Mike Keenan is a legend for a reason. Simply put, he was one of the best bench coaches I have ever played for. He had a great feel for the team, for individual players and, of course, for what was needed to counter the opposition every night. I also loved Mike's innovative approach to fitness and the fast-paced practices that he ran.

When I was growing up, like a lot of kids I thought coaches were gods. As I got older, I became aware that coaches make mistakes, just like everyone else. But they are also a key part of the process of winning, and Mike was undoubtedly crucial to the Rangers winning the Stanley Cup in 1994.

What Mike did best was to get the most out of his players. From 1985 to 1994, he led teams to the Stanley Cup final four different times. When I was with the Edmonton Oilers, we played Mike's Philadelphia Flyers twice in the final, beating them in five games in 1985 and, two years later, winning in seven games after the Flyers were down 3–1 in the series and battled back. In 1992, Mike led the Chicago Blackhawks to the final, where they were swept by the Pittsburgh Penguins. He was out-gunned twice by the Oilers when we were historically dominant, and by a

Penguins team led by the great Mario Lemieux. Mike coached the heck out of those underdog Flyers and Blackhawks teams with his signature style and plenty of heart, grit and determination, getting every ounce of effort from his teams along the way.

I became familiar with Mike's coaching through those two springs when the Oilers played the Flyers, but I really got to know his style well during the 1987 and 1991 Canada Cup tournaments, when he coached Team Canada and I was fortunate enough to play on that team. We won those two tournaments together for Canada, and we participated in some of the greatest hockey ever put on ice.

Mike did an excellent job bringing Team Canada together, and I knew from that experience that he was the right coach for the Rangers and what lay ahead for the 1993–94 season. He was firm enough, tough enough, and confident enough to handle the New York market. He was the right guy at the right time.

Throughout that season—with me as the Rangers' captain and Mike as coach—we were able to talk about anything that happened on and off the ice. He always listened. We played good cop/bad cop very well. He'd tear into a teammate for falling short on some aspect of the game; I'd talk the player through what he needed to do to get the coach off his back. We thought through the game very similarly. We believed in the same principles required to win.

Although some of his methods can be described as controversial, Mike always knew how to hold his players accountable. I know he rubbed some guys the wrong way, and he could be a hard-ass, but many of those guys who were pissed at him still performed at the highest level of their careers. You don't have to like your coach, but you must respect your coach. If you're on good terms all the time, then he's probably not pushing you hard enough. Nobody on Mike's teams was on good terms with him all the time, but he made sure his players were always paying attention. I liked that he was not afraid of confrontation if it was going to make the team better.

Mike had an unwavering belief in our team and an unwavering willingness to stand up for his vision for success. At no point was that more evident than at the trade deadline in 1994, when he pushed hard to make a series of moves that ultimately made a huge difference in our championship run. We were sitting in first place as the trade deadline approached. What first-place team makes wholesale changes at the deadline? But Mike knew we were missing key ingredients that we needed to go all the way. Credit to general manager Neil Smith for making the deals, but credit to Mike for identifying the players who would make a difference and pushing the organization to acquire them.

Entering the NHL playoffs in the spring of 1994, the Rangers faced an unbelievable amount of pressure. We'd finished the regular season first overall and won the Presidents' Trophy. Expectations in the New York market had never been greater, and we couldn't shy away from those expectations. We had to "slay the dragon." Anything less would be a failure.

As for how it ended for Mike in New York with the Rangers—well, he will tell his side of the story. But whatever was going on behind the scenes was not a distraction to the players in the room. For me and the other players, it was very simple: "Stay focused and finish the job." And we did.

With almost every championship team, the leadership group has a good relationship with the coach, and you see it in the celebration and embrace afterwards. In 1994, you saw it when I skated to the bench and handed Mike Keenan the prize he'd been working so hard for so long to get his hands on: the Stanley Cup. For obvious reasons, he calls it one of the favourite moments of his whole career. Handing Mike that trophy was one of mine.

—Mark Messier

1

I REALLY AM A BASTARD: FAMILY AND HOCKEY

I REALLY AM a bastard. There, I said it. Over my six decades as a coach and general manager, in a variety of leagues, from high school to junior to the pros, in several countries and continents, players have referred to me in many different languages, using many different terms, most of them not terribly flattering. And, no doubt, I deserved most of them. But it was my good friend, Jay Greenberg, who summed it up best.

Jay, for those not familiar, was the hockey beat writer for the *Daily News* in Philadelphia when I got my first job as a head coach in the National Hockey League, with the Flyers in 1984. He was a great guy and great writer, with a quick wit, and he was honoured by the Hockey Hall of Fame in 2013. Jay was originally going to write this book with me, but he passed away at the age of 71 on August 12, 2021, of complications from, of all things, West Nile virus. So very tragic and sad.

Jay once said to me that of all those names the players had muttered and sometimes screamed, "One is correct by dictionary definition."

Jay was right. I was born out of wedlock on October 21, 1949. Yes, I was a bastard. Still am. Of course, for many of those players, I was also a bastard of a coach. But more about that later.

I was born in Bowmanville, Ontario, to Thelma Chatterton, who was 19 at the time and previously married, and Ted Keenan. Bowmanville is about a one-hour drive east of Toronto. And it was a stone's throw from Oshawa, where my parents had lived until the pregnancy, which was not a proud moment for a very Catholic family! Anyway, after I came along they moved back to Oshawa, and over time along came my sister Marie, two years younger, then brother Patrick and sister Catherine. All my siblings came after Thelma and Ted got married.

Dad, like so many in Oshawa and like most of his family, including two uncles and my grandfather George, worked at the General Motors plant. Once Catherine started school, my mom worked in the men's department at Eaton's, a famous department store that is no longer around. Because our family didn't have a lot of money, it helped that Mom was able to get us clothes at a discount.

Sadly, when I was four, Patrick passed away. He was born prematurely, and at just two months old he died from complications from pneumonia. I was too young to really comprehend the tragedy, but I do remember when the police officer came to our home to tell my parents about Patrick's death (he was in hospital and we didn't have a phone). My mom was, understandably, crushed and hysterical. My dad, too. I remember at the funeral kneeling beside my father in front of Patrick's casket. Even at that young age, it's something you don't forget. I'm sure that tragedy somehow pulled my sisters and me together. We got along well growing up and still do.

The year Patrick passed, my dad took me skating for the first time, outside of course. I fell in love with hockey at that early age, playing day after winter day on a frozen patch of Lake Ontario, which was only a few miles from our apartment. Because our family had limited means (we ate a lot of hot dogs or ketchup sandwiches for lunch), my grandmother, Helen Chatterton, bought me my first pair of skates. For a long time, we didn't have a television, so I would watch *Hockey Night in Canada* on Saturday nights at her home. She was a special woman, very street-smart, a huge influence on me growing up. My grandfather had solid carpentry skills, and the two of them turned a condemned three-storey building near downtown Whitby into apartments, which eventually housed all their children. My grandmother was also responsible for getting the grandkids involved in sports. Sadly, when I was in grade eight, Grandma was diagnosed with multiple sclerosis. It was agonizing to watch her decline, and I did my best to help my mom look after her. Grandma died at age 54, far too young, but she had a profound impact on me. My other grandmother, May, passed at the age of 69, far too young.

Because money was tight, you took good care of your hockey gear and your sticks. I was allowed two sticks a year. So, if one broke or cracked, it was nailed or taped back together. Play on. I was a good skater from a young age and played both defence and forward. My first season in organized hockey in Oshawa, at the age of seven and playing against kids two years older than me, I was named the most valuable player. I once scored 16 goals on 16 shifts, if I remember correctly, and the coach benched me, saying I had embarrassed everyone. I had a confident personality.

Someone who had a big influence on me as a young player and person was my coach and mentor Doug Williams. He had played for the Whitby Dunlops senior men's team and was a high-school principal. Many times he talked with me about leading the other kids because they looked up to me. His influence helped to build my confidence even more. Two of my father's cousins, Tom and Ted O'Connor, helped teach me the game as well. Tom was a winger, Ted a defenceman with the Dunlops when they won the world championship in 1958. Harry Sinden, who went on to become a legendary coach and general manager and would one day hire me in Boston, was a teammate of theirs. In Oshawa and Whitby in those days, mentors were plentiful, and happy to help a talented young player. This included my uncle Bob, who coached me.

Both my parents had finished school after grade nine. Despite their lack of formal education, my parents were smart. And perhaps because my mom didn't get far in school herself, she was determined that I would, and she made it clear that if my marks suffered the hockey (and other sports) would stop. This happened once and caused another fight between my parents, who probably married too young (but you know why!) and argued a lot. Anyway, I respected what she was trying to do, got my nose back into the books, and I was playing again a month later.

And I was doing well. At various times, I was playing baseball (catcher), box lacrosse (centre), basketball (point guard) and hockey. When I was in grade nine at Archbishop Denis O'Connor Catholic High School, I was voted athlete of the year. But I always made sure my marks were just good enough that I could keep playing. On top of all that, I was working both part-time and summer jobs. At age 14, I was cutting grass and even hired kids to work for me. Because my dad and others in his family worked for General Motors, I was able to get a summer job in the plant. I also worked one summer in the Coca-Cola plant, and the next year on a delivery truck. When I was in grades nine and ten, I worked for the printer of the local newspaper and had a delivery route for the *Globe and Mail*.

As for hockey, at 15 I was playing for my high-school team, but also for the junior B Whitby Lasco Steelers. I was still splitting time between forward and defence, and playing well against kids two or three years older than I was. That lasted two seasons before I was cut by the team, which was a very painful learning experience, the first time I had really failed as a hockey player. It was humbling. But I managed to earn a spot with their rivals, the Oshawa Crushmen.

Back when I was 13, the Boston Bruins had signed me to what they called a C-form. Before the NHL introduced the amateur draft, teams could sign players at a young age and essentially own their rights. The Bruins' junior A team was the Oshawa Generals—the same team the great Bobby Orr played for—and it was coached by future Bruins coach Bep Guidolin (and a few seasons previously by Doug Williams). During my grade 12 year, the Generals called me up from my junior B team for a few games. The plan, or hope, was to play for the Generals during the 1967–68 season and hopefully get a scholarship to an NCAA school.

That was the path my mom wanted me to take. To clarify, back in the day, playing a few games with a junior A team, even though the players were paid a few bucks, didn't prevent me from playing in college. And back then, high school went to grade 13.

Anyway, the best laid plans . . .

One of my Whitby junior teammates, Kevin O'Shea, earned a scholarship to St. Lawrence University in Canton, New York. I knew about the school through a girl I had dated, who was the stepsister of Brian McFarlane, an All-American at St. Lawrence who would one day become an announcer with *Hockey Night in Canada*. Although Kevin had accepted the scholarship, he and another player, Jimmy Adair, were invited to join the 1968 Canadian Olympic team, meaning two scholarships at St. Lawrence were available. I applied and took the SATs and the school sent out a scout named Buck Moore to watch me in the junior B playoffs. My coach, Bob Dionne, played me heavy minutes. Moore was impressed, and I got the offer.

Talk about mixed emotions. It was a feather in my cap to be offered a scholarship by a really good hockey school, a prestigious school, but my dad and I were both keen on me playing for the Generals. Back then, junior hockey was the best path to the NHL, not college hockey. But, despite another argument between my parents, Mom ruled the day. All along she was determined that her kids get an education.

It wasn't what I wanted to hear, of course, but part of me was smart enough, mature enough, I suppose, to realize that the road to the NHL was long and without any guarantees, so school was probably the better way to go. And believe it or not, I had it in my head that if I wasn't going to be a hockey player, I wanted to be a doctor!

While all that was happening, life off the ice was moving along pretty well, too. I guess you would say I was falling in love. Her name was Rita Haas. I first saw her at a basketball tournament at Henry Street High School, where she was in grade 12. I was at Archbishop Denis O'Connor, and we won the tournament. I was happy to win the tournament, but all I really wanted was to win her over. The interesting dynamic, of course, was that I was a good Catholic boy and Rita was a good Jewish girl, the granddaughter of a Hungarian Jew killed at Auschwitz, and hers was one of very few Jewish families in Whitby. It was a different time.

We talked a little at the post-tournament celebration. A few days later, I called to ask her out on a date. Her father, who was a smart business man and a hobby farmer, answered the phone and told me she had gone swimming. But fate being what it is, that night I was with some friends at the local Dairy Queen, getting some ice cream, when Rita and a girlfriend walked in. With some strong urging from my pals, I wound up talking to Rita, who did remember me from the tournament and, it turned out, liked me.

We might have had wildly different faiths, but neither Rita nor her wonderful parents, Olga and George, were going to allow that to interfere in her life. After eight years serving as an altar boy at St. John's Catholic Church, I had sworn off religion, so it wasn't an issue from my end. Rita's family were impressive and welcoming. There was a calm with them I didn't have all the time at home. They were a very close and well-educated family, and I quickly saw how intelligent Rita was—despite falling for me.

2

CATCHING THE BUG: FROM PLAYER TO COACH

WHEN I ARRIVED at St. Lawrence University for the first time in the fall of 1968, dropped off by my parents, it felt like a special place. My friends and teammates and I absolutely loved it, from the girls to the atmosphere to the opportunity. The Oshawa Crushmen were in the playoffs when my scholarship offer came through. I had to write the SATs and ended up finishing high school at grade 12, which was enough for admission to university in the United States.

I had enrolled in pre-med, so there were a lot of science, physics, biology, chemistry and math studies. On top of that I was trying to play hockey. I actually adjusted pretty well to university life in general. If anything, it was nice to be away from home and all the battles between my parents, who had separated several times over the years but didn't get divorced until 1977. The population of Canton, New York, where St. Lawrence was located, was probably 5,000 or so, and there wasn't a ton to do. And on campus, there were lots of restrictions—no booze, no co-eds in your room, dorm curfews. But life there was still pretty darn good.

My only real problem was that I couldn't decide whether to be a doctor or dentist, if not a hockey player, and pre-med studies were intense. Too intense. At that time, you couldn't play varsity in your first year: you had to play junior varsity. The idea was that freshmen needed more time to study and get acclimated. Were they ever right about that! Our hockey schedule was light; we didn't play too many games, all of them exhibition games. But we practised almost every day. Combined with schoolwork, it was too much.

On any given day I had three labs—physics, biology and chemistry—and then I'd go to practice. I simply wasn't ready for that kind of workload. My teammates would come by the labs and tease me. After the first year, my marks were insufficient and I flunked a few courses. The school said, "You have to go home and get yourself organized and see if you want to come back." Of course I wanted to come back, and I asked for another chance. The dean said to me, "Okay, you have to sit out a semester in your sophomore year, and when you come back prove to us that you are serious about your studies." Needless to say, my mom was not happy.

I went home and worked at the General Motors plant through the fall, spot welding on the assembly line. It was one of the worst jobs you could have, tough and gruelling. But I had to work long hours to pay my tuition, get back to school and earn back my scholarship. At the end of the day, my shirt was burnt, my skull was burnt, my face was burnt. It was a really dirty job, but I think that was the message my dad was sending: smarten up, literally, or this could be your future. My family was big in GM. My grandfather was a general foreman; he served 50 years. My older uncle, Bill, was a union steward and served more than 35 years. My uncle Bob was there 38 years. My father was there for 30 years working as an electrician. My dad's oldest sister, Lorraine, worked there and my sister Marie did as well. But when I was leaving in late November, I said to the guys at the plant, "You will never see me here again." And I ran to the exit.

When I returned to St. Lawrence, I met with the dean and changed my studies to a bachelor of science degree in health and physical education. My secondary was geology. I worked hard and became a better student. I didn't want to blow this opportunity. I was on the dean's list after that. He said to me, "I guess you proved you could study." I was prepared to study, but that first year I had been in over my head. To be studying medicine and playing hockey was really tough as a freshman. Years later at the University of Toronto, when I coached, I had mature students who were in dentistry and medicine, but as a freshman it's tough to balance all those responsibilities. Anyway, I really enjoyed the studies, and understanding more about how the human body worked; it was something that would serve me well in the years ahead.

I also really enjoyed playing Division I NCAA hockey, mostly playing Ivy League teams, the arena full every night. My sophomore year I made the varsity Saints, but my season started slowly. The coach, George Menard, wasn't a big fan in the beginning. He could be as tough as Iron Mike ever was, sometimes much tougher. One game, I turned over the puck and he accused me of throwing the game. I couldn't believe it. He told me I would never play again. I ended up sitting two games, but I battled through and kept myself in incredible shape, running five miles every day, doing whatever I could. By my senior year, under coach Bernie McKinnon, I was one of the captains.

I stayed for a couple of summers in Canton and worked hockey schools. I stayed for two reasons: I wanted to accelerate my academics, so I would graduate in three and a half years, and I was also a lifeguard on the river that ran through campus. Rita was studying at York University in Toronto, and she would visit from time to time. My parents each made the occasional visit, too. You could hardly use a telephone back then to call home, either. There was one phone on the whole dorm floor. My dad and I had a signal we used on Sundays. I would call him, but because he didn't want to spend money, I would call collect. He would say, "I'm not accepting the call," which meant that everything was okay. Goodbye. When Rita visited, she would take the train to Brockville, and I would pick her up in a car I borrowed from a couple of buddies. Being so far apart certainly wasn't easy on our relationship. We would call it off and then call it back on—typical university kids.

I made a lot of great friends during my time at St. Lawrence, guys I hung out with who are still friends. Mike Barnett played hockey at St. Lawrence, and he played football as well. When the coach said Mike couldn't play football anymore, he left for the University of Alberta in Edmonton, where he could continue playing both. Of course, he went on to become Wayne Gretzky's agent. I knew Mike long before anyone in hockey circles knew him. He was from Calgary. I remember asking him, after his freshman year, how he was getting home. He said, "I'm going to hitchhike." I said, "That's a long way to hitchhike," and he said,

"It's not too bad." He would go the airport and ask if anyone was flying west on a small plane. He went from plane to plane to plane, back to Calgary. Smart guy.

Tim Pelyk—God bless his soul; he passed away in August 2022—was the brother of Mike Pelyk, who played defence for the Toronto Maple Leafs. Tim bought an old Cadillac limousine for $50. It was a stretch limo, seated eight, and was an old one from the late '50s. Heat was optional or non-existent on some rides. We would take the tire out of the front wheel well, put it in the trunk and off we'd go, driving to Montreal to watch the Leafs play the Canadiens. A bunch of us, a full limo load, would go, and when we were crossing the border we'd all buy duty-free 40-ouncers of booze and hide the bottles in the wheel well. Mike would ask his Leafs teammates if they wanted some 40-ouncers in exchange for their two complimentary tickets that night. That's how we got into the games.

My senior year, a bunch of the hockey players, including Peter Brennan, Mike Flanigan and Al Howes, all lived on campus. We approached a guy in town named John Smith. He owned a grocery store and a big warehouse with a two-storey apartment in it. He wasn't doing anything with the apartment, so we asked him if we could make an addition. He said okay. So, we built two more bedrooms, a kitchen, a living room and a big patio. It was next to the most popular bar in town, the Hoot Owl. We had a big, big common room that we painted black, with a grey floor. We had black lights (which we didn't know would allow us to see through the ladies' blouses), and we always had a keg on tap. We would have these parties—girls were admitted free, and guys had to pay a dollar to help cover the beer.

We also had a rehearsal room on the third floor for our band—Nik and the Nice Guys. The genesis of it was Gary Webb, a winger on our team and a very bright guy. He started playing the accordion at a very young age, and as a 14-year-old he once sang back up for Harry Belafonte at Expo 67. That's how good a musician he was. With us, he played lead guitar. Another winger, Eric Sandford, was a talented drummer. He came from Whitby, lived in the same dorm building as me, and was on a scholarship as well. Another guy, Ron Harris, could play the drums. If Ron was there, Eric would play the bass guitar upside down. He was self-taught, a left-hander, so he flipped over the guitar to play. In 1971, the band was born. And then they recruited a few of us to sing.

That was my junior year. After the games on the weekend, we would go to frats, sororities, the student centre or our apartment and we'd play. The places would be packed. Students would go from the hockey games to the rock-and-roll show. After a while we played local bars. The band's name came from Eric, who on date nights would announce he would be Niky Nice Guy! I didn't play an instrument, but I loved singing on stage. My big song was "I Want to Take You Higher" by Sly and the Family Stone. I'd get everyone down on the beer-soaked floor on their knees, rolling around, and then I'd get them to rise back up. What can I say? Maybe it was some early coaching skills shining through. Another of the singers was our backup goalie, a freshman from Ottawa I've known since graduating from St. Lawrence: Jacques Martin.

AFTER I GRADUATED, I had some decisions to make. Rita and I had decided to get married, although my mother wasn't convinced it was the right time to do it because I had been invited to the training camp of the NHL expansion Atlanta Flames. I didn't think I would make the Flames, of course. My big intention, apart from marrying Rita, was to go to university back home and get my teaching certificate. I could have gone to Queen's or Western, but the University of Toronto was close to home for both me and Rita, who needed another degree herself, and with any luck I could play for the Varsity Blues and coaching legend Tom Watt.

Rita and I got married on June 22, 1972, at Toronto City Hall. We didn't want a big wedding, just something small and simple with a party to follow, which we held at Rita's parents' farm. As an aside, we got married on the 22nd because 22 was my sweater number at St. Lawrence. It was an exciting day, to say the least, and the start of a very loving and interesting marriage, which would not end well. But more about that later.

Next up was the Flames camp. Back then it was a long, long shot for a college player to make the NHL, but just attending would be a good experience, and would hopefully put me in good stead to make the Varsity Blues, a Canadian university powerhouse. I arrived at the camp in Drummondville, Quebec, in tremendous shape. Back in the day, most players used camp to get in shape and burn off the summer beers, but I had been working out like a fiend, running every day, lifting weights, skating as much as I could, although ice could be hard to find in the summer.

Pat Quinn—who had earned legendary status of sorts for his mammoth hit on Bobby Orr in the 1969 playoffs, and who would go on to become a great coach—was there, along with goaltender Phil Myre, who would later play for me and who coached with me in Rochester, and Keith McCreary, who became Atlanta's captain. I had a good camp, got through it unscathed, and when it was over general manager Cliff Fletcher wanted to send me to the Flames' farm team in Omaha, Nebraska. I said thanks but no thanks. It might have been fun to give it a try, but Rita and I decided it was best to go back to university in Toronto.

When I got back, I went to the Blues' offices in Hart House near Varsity Arena in downtown Toronto and went to see Tom Watt. There was a lady by the name of Phyllis Lea who was the secretary for Tom as well as the football and basketball coaches. I asked her if Tom was available. A few minutes later, Tom came out and I introduced myself. I told him I had just graduated from St. Lawrence University, that I had just gotten back from the Atlanta Flames' NHL training camp, and that I would like to try out for his team. Tom asked what position I played, and I said, "What position do you need?" He said, "Defence." I said, "I play defence," which I did. I had actually played forward and defence at St. Lawrence, depending on what injuries came up.

Tom called Bernie McKinnon, my coach at St. Lawrence, to get a reference. Who is this Keenan kid? I guess the reference was good, because Tom invited me to try out. There had to be a hundred guys trying out and not too many open spots on a very good roster. At the end of each day, Tom posted a list—either of the guys staying or the guys going. He didn't have time to talk to everyone. After practice, after you got changed, the first thing you did was look at the list. Well, I ended up making the team, and my first game playing for the Blues was an exhibition game against St. Lawrence. We beat them, so that was a good trip.

We had a great team that season. Not just really good players, but excellent students. There were seven of us in grad school, including Gary Inness, one of our goalies, who was looking to get his teaching degree and went on to play for the Pittsburgh Penguins. Bruce Durno, our other goalie, played for and graduated from Harvard, was going to law school at U of T and went on to become an Ontario Superior Court judge. Bobby Munro was a really good centre and played in the Montreal Canadiens' system. He and Al Milne, my defence partner, were studying dentistry, while Rick Leroy also became an Ontario Supreme Court judge. Warren Anderson, Rick's defence partner, went on to play for the 1980 Canadian Olympic team. Kent Ruhnke played a couple of games with the Boston Bruins, a few with Winnipeg in the World Hockey Association (WHA) and had a long career in Europe. Gord Davies was our captain. He'd been captain with the Toronto Marlboros and was drafted by Boston. Winger Neil Korzack was a Buffalo draft pick.

Rita and I lived downtown, a short walk from Varsity Arena, in assisted housing for students. It was a great year. I played a lot on defence, and Tom played four defencemen most of the time. I was on the power play and penalty kill and taking a regular shift. I probably had the most ice time of anyone on the team. I had a couple of goals and 26 points in 17 league games. And we won a national championship. How good is that? Tom Watt was a huge influence in my life, and also as a coach. When I walked into that dressing room I was afraid to have a bad practice. He had won so many championships, you couldn't and wouldn't goof around. You had to take it seriously. As I said, most of the guys were grad students, in law school or med school or dentistry school all day. Then we'd practise at 5 or 5:30 p.m. And they were tough practices but good practices—always fast-paced, not a lot of standing around—and there was a purpose to them. Winning was an expectation; there was no alternative. We had lots of fans, a full building, the Lady Godiva Memorial Band playing. If you made that team, you were expected to win the national championship. In the fall, the football and hockey teams would eat together at the arena with our own chef.

When I wasn't in class or spending my day teaching as part of a student placement at Jarvis Collegiate or Danforth Tech, I would go to the rink and skate for an hour on my own. When I was teaching, Tom would lend me his orange Volkswagen—it was the only way I could get back from teaching in time for practice. He endeared himself to his players doing things like that. Tom would just take transit, since he lived in midtown.

One of the highlights of that season arrived at Christmas, when the team travelled to Poland. For almost all of us, it was the first time in a Communist country. As we walked across the airport tarmac into the terminal building, I looked up to see soldiers standing on the balcony with machine guns. I said to myself, "Oh my God, if one of them is trigger happy, we're done."

In Warsaw, it was like the Second World War was still on. Nothing had been fixed. The food wasn't good, and a lot of guys got sick while we were there and lost weight. The day after arriving we drove to the city of Katowice, which had an arena where we were going to play some senior teams. It took us all day to get there because the bus driver kept turning off the engine and coasting down hills to save gas. We practised one night on the huge European ice, and the soot in the air was so thick we thought it was the roof. But there was no roof on the arena. There also weren't any seats, and the rink could hold 10,000 standing fans.

I remember one game, we had a brawl. Rick Cornacchia got in a fight, and he was beating the crap out of a Polish guy. I went over to him and said, "Let him up, he doesn't know how to fight, you're going to kill him." The fans were not impressed. They weren't used to fighting in the European game and they let us know, with whistles (their form of booing) cascading down.

We were there a couple of weeks, and one day when I was walking around the city I found a nice hotel that catered to Brits and Westerners. It was a beautiful place. Everywhere else, the food had been terrible, but there you could sit down and have a wonderful meal for four or five bucks. Delicious. The next day I took a few of the guys with me. We traded money on the black market, traded blue jeans. It was a different world, a different lifestyle than we were accustomed to.

One very poignant and jarring moment came on our first night when we slept in the Warsaw Ghetto and later visited the Auschwitz concentration camp. I knew a little bit about that because Rita was Jewish. Rita's mother, Olga, and two aunts had survived, along with her grandmother, but Rita's grandfather was killed when they arrived at Auschwitz from their home in Hungary. Olga had told me her bunker number and I went to see it. There were still bloodstains on the walls. We saw the gas chambers where the Nazis had killed hundreds of thousands of people. I saw all of that. It was an incredibly emotional experience.

We also went to an old cathedral in the city of Kraków, near where Pope John Paul II was born. There was a roped-off chair in the middle of the church, where I presume the pope or a king or both had once sat. For whatever reason, I jumped over the rope and sat in the seat and told the guys to take my photo. All of a sudden, military guys came running into the church with guns. I'm thinking they're going to throw me in jail, but luckily all they did was march us out of the church. My nickname thereafter was, you guessed it, the Pope!

On another day they took us to a coal mine, and we went down 5,000 feet. We're crawling on our hands and knees, and we can hear them blasting. Right beside me I see this flash of white—it was a guy smiling at me. I hadn't even known he was there. When we got out of the mine, we walked into a big bathhouse. Two at time we jumped in a tub to wash off the soot. That was an experience.

One of the highlights and lowlights of the trip came on New Year's Eve, when our hosts threw a big party for us. The team got there early and started partying. They had a couple of bottles of champagne and vodka on each table. There was supposed to be food, but all I remember is the booze. At one point, Harry Sems, who spoke German, asked the waitress if we could get some orange juice to mix with the vodka, but the best they could do was bring us a bunch of oranges. We quartered them and passed to them each other, but the lack of mix didn't prevent us from getting pretty inebriated. Hammered, actually. At some point, Bobby Munro and I went to the men's room. When we came back out, everyone from the team had gone. A military truck had taken the team back to the baza, which was basically a university dormitory. Bobby and I had to figure out how to get there on our own. Somehow we did it.

Fifty years later, at Christmastime—the same time of year—I was scouting a junior tournament and went back to Warsaw and

Katowice. They in no way resembled the dilapidated places we saw during that visit with the Blues. I didn't go back to Auschwitz, however; the memory of what I saw that day will never leave me.

That season playing for Tom Watt and the Blues was a great experience. Our team went undefeated, 17–0, during the season (16–3–3 in non-league games) and won a national championship— another one for Tom, who was a great coach. He eventually went on to coach in the NHL, earning Coach of the Year honours with the Winnipeg Jets. The big star on his team that year was Dale Hawerchuk, who I coached when he was a teenager. Small world. Tom also coached in Vancouver and Toronto, and has had a long scouting career. In 2022, he was inducted into the Ontario Sports Hall of Fame. Given his amazing university record and NHL accomplishments (he also coached with me on two Canada Cup–winning teams), I think he should be in the Hockey Hall of Fame.

Tom taught us from the start of training camp that we were working every day towards winning a national championship and reminded us of the work ethic and commitment required to be champions. I didn't know at the time that coaching was in my future; I thought I was going to be a teacher once my playing days were done. But I never forgot what I learned from Tom.

But for now my playing career wasn't over—it was just over with the Blues. Although I graduated with my teaching degree, I had been drafted in the second round of the World Hockey Association's 1973 professional draft by the Vancouver Blazers, who had just moved after a season in Philadelphia. Note the word *professional*, not *amateur*. Essentially, from what I have been told, the "pro" draft allowed the upstart WHA, in just its second season, to select players who hadn't been drafted the previous year or signed with any NHL or WHA club. Apparently, the main purpose of the professional draft was that it allowed the Houston Aeros to draft Mark and Marty Howe, who had been playing junior with the Toronto Marlboros, as pros, not juniors, and opened the door to signing their dad, the legendary Gordie. Whatever. I played all the pre-season games with Vancouver and did well enough. Colin Campbell—who played junior with the Peterborough Petes and went on to have a nice NHL career, and was an assistant with me in New York and worked for the league in hockey operations after—was drafted by the Blazers. Jimmy Jones, another Petes junior who later played for the Maple Leafs, was also there, along with Les Jackson, who went on to become a long-time scout and assistant general manager.

I was one of the final cuts, along with Jones, and was assigned to their farm team in the Southern Hockey League (SHL), the Roanoke Valley Rebels. Phil Watson was the general manager and the coach was Gregg Pilling, a career minor leaguer. One of my first interactions with Watson happened after an exhibition game when he came to me and said, "Nice game, Jack." Johnny "Pie Face" McKenzie, who had played with the Boston Bruins, was on the Vancouver team and a real character. We would get on the bus and Pie Face would be sitting there, wearing a bowler hat. We'd put money in the hat and take out a bingo card, so we played bingo on the bus. I'm thinking, this is pro hockey? Holy shit!

The Roanoke experience was interesting, to say the least. I was serious in my approach, trying to be a professional. I worked hard. Back then, guys would practise, go for lunch, drink beer all afternoon, go home for a nap and do it again. I started the year on defence. I hurt my knee early on, tearing my MCL, and missed 22 games. While the other guys were going to the bar after practice, I would rehab and go to the gym every day.

When I returned from the injury, I played right wing on a line with centre Denis Meloche, who was the brother of California Golden Seals goaltender Gilles, and left wing Michel Plante. The league was just like *Slap Shot*, with all the fighting. We were the only team that wasn't allowed to wear helmets. And most of these displaced former junior players didn't like college players. We had so many brawls, and you were expected to fight. In my first game, we were playing in Charlotte against the Checkers. I got into a scrap with a guy named Dale MacLeish, whose brother Rick played for the Philadelphia Flyers. He was pissed because he had been playing for Roanoke but was cut and he blamed me, thinking I had taken his job. We had a fight and went to the penalty box. Back then you sat beside each other. We're sitting there and, all of a sudden, I feel this tap on my shoulder. I turn around and see his fist four inches from my face. He breaks my nose, a brawl starts, the players jump into the box, we're fighting—welcome to pro hockey. And a lesson learned: never turn your back or let your guard down.

Another lesson I quickly learned was that it was better to be proactive. I was already an aggressive player, but I got even more aggressive. There was one guy, Perry Miller, who played for Charlotte but went on to play in the NHL, who was always taking out guys' knees. He tried it on me. I told him, "Do it again and I will spear you in the face." He did, and so I did. I had a similar incident where I promised to break a wrist and did.

I had a pretty decent year, scoring 25 goals and 61 points in 58 games, along with racking up 94 penalty minutes playing forward and defence. I made a colossal $6,000 tax free, paid in cash, and we got bonuses. If we won on the road, there was a $200 pot to share among the players, $100 for a road tie. Every little bit helped. We had some guys making good money, upwards of $100,000 if they were signed by the big team. George Gardner, a goalie who had been sent down to play with us, was always borrowing money from me. He was making $80,000 or $90,000, but he was broke because he was going out every night with different women.

We ended up going 53–19–0 and won the SHL championship. It was a good year. But as good as we were, the playoffs were a challenge. We had a bunch of injuries, but we battled through and found a way. At the end of the year, Watson got fired and Pilling desperately wanted me to come back. But Rita said, "Let's go home." She was right. And not too long after, I got the coaching bug.

It started, of all places, in a midtown Toronto high school. And it wasn't hockey, it was box lacrosse. But I got the bug big time.

Upon our return to Ontario, neither Rita nor I had a job or a place to live. Her parents had sold their farm to a developer and moved to Oshawa. I asked the developer if we could rent it until he was ready to build. He agreed and gave us a good price. Meantime, Rita landed a teaching position at her old high school, Henry Street, in Whitby. I didn't have a job yet, but I was busy in hockey.

A bunch of us, guys like Bruce Durno and Tim Pelyk and several others, had a desire to keep playing, so we decided to start an Ontario Hockey Association (OHA) senior A team in Whitby, which was just opening a new arena. Tom Fitzsimmons, who was my math teacher in high school and was heavily involved in the community, spearheaded a small group of businessmen and, after some wrangling to reach a lease agreement, the Whitby McDonalds were born. All the players kicked in $1,000 each and a fellow named Bob Beal, who owned three McDonald's restaurants, came on as our sponsor, hence the team name. I had done some marketing work for McDonald's, so there was a connection.

I was eventually the playing coach, in part I suppose because I had a teaching background and had played for Tom Watt with the Varsity Blues. I was actually a co-coach with Gary Milroy, who had played for the Marlboros and was a great, smart player. He ran the bench when I was on the ice, and I ran the practices. We had a pretty darn good team, too, with the likes of Durno and Pelyk. We recruited a lot of U of T guys, a few from St. Lawrence. Over the years, we had retired NHL players join us, guys like Carl Brewer and Eddie Shack. We had a defenceman named Ken Desjardine, who played in the WHA. Pete Vipond, a winger and my teammate in minor hockey, had played for California in the NHL.

It was in December of that first season when I finally got my first teaching job, at Don Mills Collegiate, a high school in the midtown Toronto suburbs. Once again, my U of T connection served me well. One of Tom Watt's ex-players wanted to take a leave of absence, and he and the principal asked Tom if he knew of a potential replacement. That's how I got the job. I was hired as a phys. ed teacher for the remainder of the school year. A starting salary for teachers was about $9,000, so between Rita's salary and mine, we were making more money than we ever had before.

The box lacrosse team at Don Mills needed a coach, so I took it on. I had played box lacrosse as kid in Whitby, where the sport is pretty big, so I knew the game. I really, really enjoyed it. The kids were great; they were working and they were winning. I would leave the farmhouse at 5:30 every morning so I could take the team for a 7 a.m. five-mile run through the Don Valley ravine. We would practise at the local Don Mills arena. It was fun. And we won the North York championship.

After that school year, the job ended and I faced an uncertain future. The next fall, I was reading the classifieds in the newspaper and saw an ad for a phys. ed teacher at Forest Hill Collegiate Institute in Toronto. I went directly to the school and met with the principal, Whitey Clayton, who, as it turned out, was a U of T grad. After that, I met with the head of the phys. ed department, Irv Salsburg, and I was hired. I was soon behind the bench for the Forest Hill hockey team, and when I wasn't coaching hockey I was coaching the girls' swim team and even some basketball. Again, I really enjoyed it. As an aside, one kid who played on the hockey team for me was Ken Daniels, who went on to become an NHL broadcaster with *Hockey Night in Canada*, and then with the Detroit Red Wings.

My days were long: leaving home at the crack of dawn, driving in to Toronto, then hockey practice, games after school—and I was still playing-coaching the senior team at night. I was lucky I became the commissioner of hockey for the Toronto Board of Education, so I could finesse the school team's schedule to mesh with mine. As for the senior team, which became known as the Whitby Warriors in its second season, after our sponsor pulled out, I played for three seasons, but my playing career ended badly. During a game in Barrie, I got run by two guys at the same time, one from the front, one from the back, and my shoulder exploded into the boards.

I had to have a six-inch pin put in. My right arm was immobilized. I couldn't lift it, and atrophy was setting in. I went back to the surgeon and told him something was wrong in there. He insisted nothing was wrong. I finally convinced him to take out the pin. The next day he did and I could move my arm again.

My coaching career went to the next level in 1977, when at the age of 27 I was hired by the junior B Oshawa Legionaires. I had played junior B and junior A in the area, so the team knew me. They knew what I had been doing with the high-school and senior teams, and they recruited me. I'd never taken any assignment lightly, and I hated losing at any level, but I was suddenly taking coaching much more seriously. These were predominantly 16- and 17-year-old kids who were hoping to either make it to major junior or land a university scholarship. We won two Metro championships. The first season, we went 27–4–5 and finished in first place overall. We then proceeded to run the table in the playoffs, though we lost in the provincial semifinals.

In the summer of 1978, just when I thought my playing days were over, I accepted an invite to try out for Canada's 1980 Olympic team, which was being run by the legendary Father David Bauer, Tom Watt and university coaches Clare Drake and Lorne Davis. The camp was held in the summer at Upper Canada College (UCC) in Toronto. I played defence and my partner was Tom Laidlaw, who ended up playing with the Los Angeles Kings. For part of the time we stayed in a hotel, and then they moved us into the dorms at UCC. They roomed me with Greg Millen, who was a hotshot goalie in junior. In practice, Tom and I would come back in our zone to get the puck and Millen would fire it up the ice, right past us. *What the fuck are you doing? Just leave it or pass it to us.* One night, likely after too many drinks, he came into my room—I was very disciplined, I didn't party, I was serious—and threw a bucket of cold water on me when I was in the middle of a deep sleep. Well, I jumped up and screamed at him. He ran out and never came back. I could have had a heart attack. Next time I saw him, I said, "If you ever do that again I'll beat the shit out of you." Fast-forward several years and our paths would cross again.

I was on the bubble at the Olympic camp. The coaches liked me, but unfortunately I didn't make the first cut. Father Bauer thought I was too aggressive and would take too many penalties. It was disappointing, but at least I had the Legionaires and my job at Forest Hill, and I was enjoying coaching as much as playing.

That Oshawa team became like a farm team for the University of Toronto and Tom. We developed and sent a bunch of kids to the Blues and other schools, while Tom would send us top cuts, guys like goaltender Dave Henderson, who is the father of Canadian professional golfer Brooke Henderson. Another guy was defenceman Mike Pelino, who has been with me throughout my coaching career. The kids would finish their day at university, meet me at Forest Hill, and we'd drive out to Oshawa for a game or practice. Quite often, they would stay at the house with Rita and me because the commuter GO trains had stopped running back to the city by the time our games were done.

One kid on the Legionaires was a special player. His name was Dale Hawerchuk, a gifted 15-year-old who was our leading scorer, already a star. He got drafted off my team to Cornwall major juniors and went on to have a Hall of Fame NHL career with Winnipeg and a few other teams. Our paths would cross again at the 1987 Canada Cup.

We had great support in Oshawa, out-drawing the major junior Generals by the end of the season. We got deep into the playoffs and they didn't. That's where I started chewing ice behind the bench. The arena was new, dry and dusty. I asked for water, but the trainer gave me a cup of ice cubes. They became a habit for most of my career.

Coaching the Legionaires was a great experience. I enjoyed teaching at Forest Hill, but I had the coaching bug big time, and I was developing my skills as a coach—including picking up some of the intensity that earned me the Iron Mike moniker later in my career. And life was about to take another turn.

3

MEMORIAL CUP MADNESS: WE DID NOT TANK

TO SAY MY world changed dramatically—and for the better—in June 1979 would be a major understatement. A few major junior teams had taken notice of my work with the senior Whitby Warriors and my two championship seasons with the Oshawa Legionaires, and I was looking to build on that experience.

With Tom Watt taking a leave of absence from the University of Toronto to assist with the 1980 Canadian Olympic team, I had expressed an interest in filling in for him. Meanwhile, Sherry Bassin, who was the general manager of the Oshawa Generals, had fired his coach, Bill White. He was very familiar with my coaching and was interested in me. But then I got a call from Gary Green, who had been the GM-coach of the Memorial Cup–champion Peterborough Petes and was leaving to coach the Hershey Bears, the American Hockey League (AHL) farm team of the Washington Capitals.

Gary had seen me at the 1980 Olympic tryouts, and he had seen me coach in Oshawa too. He was out scouting a lot, recruiting players, and he came to a lot of our games, mostly to see Dale Hawerchuk. Greener liked what I was doing behind the bench. He asked if I was interested in the Peterborough job—I was, of course—and he recommended me to the hiring committee. Bassin, who wound up hiring Paul Theriault as his coach, also recommended me and told Peterborough, "You'll be making a mistake if you don't hire this kid." I was offered the job, talked it over with Rita, and then talked to my principal at Forest Hill, Whitey Clayton. I told him I wanted to give the Petes job a try and asked if I could take a leave of absence for a year, because I wasn't sure if it would work out. He said yes.

The other big event happening in our world was that Rita was pregnant and expecting in July. Complicating matters was that she'd had a previous miscarriage, at six months, so we were anxious—and even more so when she went into labour five weeks early, although the doctors were confident all would be fine even with a premature birth. Turns out they were right. Into the world that June day came Gayla Roseanne Keenan, at a slight five pounds. Although she was in an incubator for a couple of weeks, everything turned out fabulously well.

The Petes offered me the job of coach and GM at $22,000 a year. Rita and I had been making $9,000 each teaching, and then $12,000 each. Rita wasn't going to be working for a while, so the money would be a wash. Two days after Gayla was born I signed with the Petes, at the age of 29.

I was told that other candidates for the job included Dick Todd, who was the Petes' trainer and equipment manager but also pretty much an assistant coach. He would stay in that role with me, proving himself invaluable, and he would be with me again later in my coaching career. Another candidate was Bryan Murray, who had been coaching junior B in Pembroke, Ontario, and wound up getting hired by the Regina Pats of the Western Hockey League. As fate would have it, our paths would cross later in the season, and many times after that—and not in a pleasant way.

The Petes were a well-respected organization, with a great tradition for developing players and coaches. Two legendary coaches, Scotty Bowman and Roger Neilson, preceded me. And there was Greener, who had been an assistant to Roger, who went to the Memorial Cup in both his seasons with the Petes and won it all in 1979. I didn't really know Greener or Roger or Dick at the time, but I got to know them very quickly.

While Greener and the Petes had just won the Memorial Cup, the team was facing a lot of turnover. We had lost good players such as forwards Keith Crowder, Tim Trimper and Bob Attwell, goalie Ken Ellacott, defenceman Greg Theberge and a few others—five of our six leading scorers. But we still had a good group of returning players, including future Hall of Fame defenceman Larry Murphy, who wound up being drafted fourth overall the next spring, and our second-leading scorer, centre Bill Gardner, a Chicago draft pick. We also had the late Mark Reeds play forward, God bless his soul, and thanks to Tom Watt we were able to get winger Andre Hidi, a late cut at U of T.

There were a few other good ones, too: defenceman Jim Wiemer, who went on to play for Boston and other NHL teams; defenceman Dave Fenyves, who landed in Buffalo; forward Dave Morrison, a Los Angeles pick and the son of former NHL defenceman Jim

Morrison (Dave went on to have a long scouting career with the Maple Leafs); defenceman John Beukeboom, a Detroit pick and brother of Jeff; winger Carmine Cirella, another Detroit pick; and a young Tom Fergus, who went on to play for the Leafs.

I worked the group hard. I was always very well prepared, and I held them to a certain level of expectation and accountability. And there was no wavering on work ethic. In many ways, we were kind of ahead of our time. We had aerobic skates every day for the first part of the year. We got hooked up with the local radio station and we'd skate to music in the mornings. The DJ would say, "Here's one for the Petes this morning, for their morning aerobic skate." We'd do that every morning before school. After school, we'd come back to practise. We had a few big guys who needed to learn how to skate better.

Fitness was part of the culture there. Another part—and this was probably due to my teaching background—was that I would call the high school every single day to make sure of attendance. The players were supposed to check in with the guidance counsellor when they arrived. If they weren't there, Dick or I would call their billets or the rooming house. If they were sick, they had to see the team doctor. Otherwise, get your ass out of bed and get to school. And there was a 10 p.m. curfew every night. The guys were usually pretty good about it, but boys will be boys. I remember one night I called one of the guys, I think it was Murph, and the landlady said he was just on his way home, she'd get him to call. Two minutes later he calls me. I said, "Murph, that's funny you called because I said I was busy and *I* would call *you* back." He admitted he wasn't at home; he was calling from his girlfriend's. Another time, with another kid, I called and he said he had spent the night at home. I went by the house. It had snowed that night, but the snow had melted off the hood of his car. It was still hot. Of course, with the early morning aerobic skates and long days, late nights weren't advisable.

I was a bit of a hard-ass at times, yes, but I felt I was responsible for these kids, especially the ones from out of town who were not living at home. There were a lot of temptations, and my job was to help get these kids to the next level, to understand the commitment that was required and that winning was the goal. And I felt quite confident handling the players off the ice and behind the bench. There were a few times when I bag-skated the team, once after a road loss. There were times when I got involved in drills. I did that with Oshawa as well, and sometimes there would be physical contact. I wasn't shy about getting in their faces if I thought that was what was required. As a player, I had been a student of the game. The student in me was now learning how to be a teacher and coach.

Without teaching, my days revolved around hockey in ways they hadn't before. I was an intensely focused person, and I started a routine after lunch of lying on the wooden floor in our apartment. I would turn the music on, lie beside the speaker and completely go to sleep with that noise in my ear. A little while later, I'd wake up and know exactly what I was going to do that night. It was kind of freaky, actually. A psychologist would call it a super-focus routine. I continued doing it throughout my career.

Around the rink, Dick Todd was a really good buffer with the kids. He would give me information I needed, off the ice and on the bench. We worked very well together. Quite often after practice, Dick and I would drive all over the area to watch kids we might recruit. I had a big station wagon, and he would jump in the back and sleep while I drove. We took turns.

The kids, by and large, were great. They were eager. We had to mix in the veterans, mould the team, bring the kids along and win. I set attainable goals for them, and they got better. Remember the band called the Village People? They came out with a song "Go West." From the very beginning we knew the Memorial Cup was out west that year, in Regina, Saskatchewan, and Brandon, Manitoba. So we used that as our theme song. I said to them, "A lot of you guys won last year. The only standard we're going to accept this year is winning the Memorial Cup. You veterans have to establish that standard of winning." Greener was a players' coach; I was more demanding and tougher than they were accustomed to. We ran a very tight ship, a very disciplined environment, but they embraced it. Go to school, do your homework, pass your courses, practise hard, play and win.

And so we did.

As defending Memorial Cup champions, the Petes were to represent Canada at the 1980 World Junior Championships, which were being played in Helsinki, Finland. Back then, club teams, bolstered by some additions from other teams, represented the country. That's how I got to coach. I decided I wasn't going to play the rookies on the Petes because they weren't part of the Memorial Cup–winning team, though we brought them on the trip. And we wanted to be—we knew we had to be—a better team to compete on the world stage. So I recruited winger Dino Ciccarelli from the London Knights, as well as the big line of Jim Fox, Sean Simpson and Yvan Joly; defencemen Bill Kitchen and Doug Crossman from our rival Ottawa 67's; and defenceman

Rick Lanz from Oshawa. They were all really good additions, all among the best players in our league.

We played the host Finns in our first game, on December 27. It got crazy. The officiating was lopsided, and not in our direction. We had a slew of penalties. I was not happy. We battled and were tied 1–1 in the third period, already down a man when we got another penalty called on us. So I called for a stick measurement, which was unheard of. I was right with the call, though, so the Finns were given a penalty. A while later, with guys once again in the penalty box, I called for another measurement, and even though we were right we were given a delay of game penalty. I went berserk. Down two players, we gave up a goal and ended up losing 2–1.

We played the Soviet Union the next day and were beaten 8–5. Still very angry, I said at the post-game press conference that Canada should not send teams to the World Junior Championship if the tournament is being played in Europe, because of the incompetent officiating. That was not an exaggeration. We beat Switzerland 9–5 to finish the preliminary round. In the consolation round we beat the United States 4–2 and Germany 6–1 to finish first, but fifth overall. We returned home with nothing but hard feelings.

We had a strong end to the regular season, finishing with a 47–20–1–0 record for 95 points, two more than Ottawa, with the race for first place in the Leyden Division coming down to the final day of the season. In the first round of the playoffs, we met the Sudbury Wolves, who had beat Kingston in the preliminary round. We did not start well, blowing a two-goal lead and losing 4–3 in overtime against a team that had 27 fewer points than us. The playoff format back then was difficult, to say the least—home, then road, home, then road, et cetera. With the drive to Sudbury roughly five hours, that was a lot of travel, especially with overtime games. Anyway, we bounced back the next game with a feisty 6–2 win, but two nights later the Wolves beat us in our rink, 6–5 in double overtime. We won again in Sudbury, 5–4, then flexed our muscle and won the final two games 9–4 and 5–1.

It was a tough, nerve-racking series, but it might just have slapped us to attention, because we went on a roll, winning our next eight straight. Next up was Ottawa, and that was a legendary series. We were the better defensive team, allowing 50 fewer goals than the 67's, but they were a great offensive team, scoring 402 goals, 86 more than us. The media coverage of the series posed this question: Can the best defensive team beat this offensive powerhouse? Well, we did. Defence wins championships, right? We felt we had enough scoring and our special teams would help us to prevail. We took the opener 4–1, then went into Ottawa and won 2–1 in overtime on a goal by Gardner. By the end of the four-game sweep, the defensive team had outscored the offensive team 17–10.

We had a nine-day break before we played the Windsor Spitfires in the final, and the rust showed early, but we managed a sweep to extend our winning streak to 11 and earn a return visit for the Petes—and my first—to defend the team's title in the Memorial Cup. The Regina Pats, coached by Bryan Murray, were the Western champions and a very strong team, with the likes of centre Doug Wickenheiser, who would be the first overall pick in the 1980 draft, and defenceman Darren Veitch. They also had a defenceman named Barry Trotz on the roster. The Cornwall Royals, coached by Doug Carpenter and led by Dale Hawerchuk, were the Quebec champions. The tournament format was a bit flawed, with each team playing each other twice in a round robin to determine the two finalists. Ultimately, the 1980 Memorial Cup is remembered as one of the most controversial ever—and in the eyes of many, it was all my fault.

We opened the round robin against Regina and started strong, but blew a 3–0 lead. We managed to get back on track and won, 5–4 in overtime, with Murray unhappy about our physical play. We were a big, fast, physical team that rolled four lines. But Bryan was always complaining. Regina lost its second game as well, this time 5–3 to Cornwall, which put them in a tough situation. We fell behind the Royals by a couple of goals in our next game, but again bounced back to earn an 8–6 victory. Next up was a rematch with the Pats at their rink in Regina, in front of 6,000 home fans. This time we had to overcome a 3–0 deficit. I didn't earn any friends when I asked the referee to inspect Wickenheiser's gloves, which had holes in the palms. The referee wouldn't do it, so I called my guys to the bench and refused to send them back out, which prompted the ref to give us a bench penalty. But I convinced him to check the gloves, and he called a penalty against the Pats. Hey, the rules are the rules. Anyway, we overcame the three-goal deficit with four in the first eight minutes of the third period and rode that home for a 4–3 victory, punching our ticket to the final with our 14th consecutive victory. Of course, afterwards Murray was pissed about the gloves call and said it was "classless." Whatever. Like I said, the rules are the rules.

The Pats blew out Cornwall, 11–2, to keep their slim hopes alive, but Regina needed the Petes to beat the Royals to get in. We win, we play Regina; we lose, we play Cornwall. That was the scenario, and Bryan fuelled the flames by saying we could determine who we played in the final, the self-proclaimed underdog Royals or the home team Pats. We were the favourites going into that game, but people were quick to forget we had fallen behind Cornwall by a couple of goals in our earlier game and had needed to battle back. We had done the same against Regina. It's not like we had been playing perfect hockey. Having said that, we took a 4–1 lead on the Royals and were up 4–2 after two periods, but then the bottom fell out. Cornwall scored three third-period goals, two on the power play, the winner at 9:48.

With a couple of minutes left to play, and with Cornwall ahead 5–4, it got ugly in the Agridome. Many of the 5,823 in attendance were, of course, Regina fans. Realizing their Pats were about to be eliminated because of our loss, they started yelling "Petes go home!" and "Throwing the game!" They threw crap on the ice and at our bench—pop, toilet paper, programs, anything they could find. The officials had to stop the game for 15 or 20 minutes. It was brutal. Even the Pats players in the stands were hollering at our bench. Bryan Murray was screaming at us. We had words. The whole rink was accusing us of throwing the game.

A couple of our players, some of our top guys, were getting their skates sharpened in the third period. Back then it took forever, so we had those players sitting on the bench without skates. It wasn't intentional. They were getting their skates sharpened because there was so much crap on the ice. But it looked intentional to the frustrated Pats fans, and it fuelled their anger, escalated the rage. After the game, I had to lock the kids in the dressing room until the police got the crowd out of the building. Then we went out to the bus and there were hundreds of fans outside. We had an escort, but we thought they were going to tip the bus over. It was nuts.

Afterwards, Bryan Murray had a lot to say: "This is a real disappointing day to be involved in junior hockey. It wasn't a hockey game. Peterborough made sure they didn't win . . . It was a mistake that Peterborough was ahead by the third period but they soon corrected it. They stopped moving the puck out of their zone. They weren't shooting the puck in the third period . . . It's a very obvious fix. The Peterborough coach should be suspended and put out of hockey for a year . . . They should be fined and the Pats and Cornwall play in the final, but I know that won't happen because no one has the guts to do it. They've destroyed the national championship and everything it stands for."

I get his frustration and disappointment and being pissed off, but accusing a team of throwing a game is pretty strong stuff and unfair. He also conveniently forgot that his team had lost to Cornwall in their first meeting, and their slow start to the tournament was the result of having too many days off after winning the Western title. Murray did finally admit they lost three games, "so maybe we don't deserve to be there, but Cornwall doesn't either."

Anyway, it's not in my DNA to lose, period. At first, I refused to speak to the accusations, but eventually I said they were garbage, which they were. If we were going to tank, why would we have taken a 4–1 lead? I wondered how we could have collapsed the way we did, but I don't think anyone did anything intentional and certainly nothing was ever discussed. They were kids playing a game that didn't matter to us. We were going to the final either way. It was our first non-important game in weeks, while it was life and death for Cornwall. It's not surprising our guys couldn't match Cornwall's intensity. Murray, by the way, predicted we would win the final "by five goals."

The final, two days later, was uglier than the Cornwall round–robin game. Just 3,500 of the sellout crowd turned up for the game, but they were a hostile bunch. Between games, we were bombarded at the hotel with crank calls. There were cars and trucks in the parking lot honking horns and making noise all night long. Somehow, most of those fans were able to get into the arena armed with eggs. One person even brought a live chicken. Yes, a live chicken, which got tossed over the boards and landed on Bill Gardner's shoulder. The game was stopped sixteen times to clear debris from the ice.

I was literally ducking eggs on the bench. They were spattering the glass behind me. Fans were throwing food, rolled-up tape, eggs, pop, tomatoes, anything sold at the concession stands. Some were throwing pucks at us. My goalie, Rick LaFerriere, had a beer bottle thrown at him while he was standing in his goal crease, and he said it was from a Pats player. He figured he got hit by 20 eggs. And all of this was happening on national TV. Mike Brophy, who was the sportswriter with the *Peterborough Examiner*, asked a police officer why they weren't doing anything; he was told he would be arrested if he didn't move on. The security was non-existent.

Despite all that, we played hard and twice led, but we couldn't score another and wound up losing 3–2 in overtime. Defenceman Robert Savard, who had four goals all season, scored the winner. It was a soft goal, a tough one to take, but under the circumstances, our kids played their hearts out. Every one of them was assaulted by eggs and garbage and had the stains on their sweaters to prove it.

When it was over the players were heartbroken, and I was angry. The hostile surroundings no doubt had an impact on the outcome of that game. We played well. I couldn't complain about our guys' effort.

"Certainly, the crowd affected our players, there's no question about it," I said to the press after the game. "These are people 18 and 19 years old, and there's only so much you can expect from them. It wasn't just a small group of individuals who were abusing us tonight, it was most of the arena, and that is a reflection of the people from this city. The conduct of the people of Regina was deplorable, disgraceful to their city and the province. The management of the Regina Pats prompted the whole incident, suggesting we would throw the [previous] game. If they had a complaint . . . they should have directed it to the CAHA [Canadian Amateur Hockey Association], not the Peterborough Petes. It's been insinuated time and time again we threw the game. It was never in my mind, never an instruction given to the players. Complete nonsense. Garbage."

The organizers came to me after the game, and I told them we couldn't have this format again. A couple of years later, they changed the format for the tournament. A "host" team was added, and a single round robin was played among the four teams. The winner of the round robin would advance to the finals, while the second- and third-place teams would meet in a semifinal to determine who would go on to play for the Memorial Cup.

That wasn't the last I would see of Bryan Murray. The following season we were both coaching in the American Hockey League, him with Hershey, me with Rochester. Then, in the NHL, he was with Washington and I was Philadelphia; later he was with Detroit and I was Chicago. Bryan didn't want to talk to me for years. One day in Florida, when we were both general managers, we met up for a beer. We started laughing about where our rivalry had started. We had some real brawls in the American league. He had one of the foulest mouths, and a little bit of a lisp. When I was coaching Chicago—Bryan was always yelling at me or the players on our bench—Duane Sutter stood up and started mimicking and mocking him. Bryan almost lost it. I told Duane to sit down, and not to do that. Despite all we had been through, I respected Bryan. But we never talked about the Memorial Cup.

4

LEARNING TO WIN: ROCHESTER AND THE VARSITY BLUES, 1980–84

WHEN THE DUST finally settled after the Memorial Cup debacle—and despite the bad press and accusations—three AHL teams were pursuing me with head coaching offers. The Rochester Americans, farm team of the Buffalo Sabres, was one of them, with a strong Peterborough connection at play. Roger Neilson, who had coached the Petes for ten seasons and was something of a junior hockey legend, had worked a season with the Sabres as an associate coach with the great Scotty Bowman, who had also coached the Petes for three seasons back in the late 1950s. For the 1980–81 season, Scotty was going to focus on his general manager job and Roger was going to take over as head coach. Down on the farm, in Rochester, coach Bill Inglis was about to be fired.

While I was coaching the Petes, Roger and Scotty came to watch us play when we were in Niagara Falls, and, knowing a coaching change was likely coming, Roger recommended me to Scotty, saying, "We've got to talk to this kid." After the game, Scotty came down to the coach's room, and—typical Scotty—asked me all sorts of coaching questions. Why I did this, why I did that.

A second team pursuing me was the Hershey Bears, farm team of the Washington Capitals, and another Peterborough connection. Gary Green, who preceded me with the Petes, had been hired to coach Hershey the previous season but was promoted to the Caps job after only 14 games. The third team was the New Haven Nighthawks, farm team of the New York Rangers. The Rangers flew me down to New York and I met with coach and GM Fred Shero and his assistant GM Mickey Keating. It was May 24, and we met at Madison Square Garden at 10 in the morning.

And then I met with Scotty and the Sabres owners, Seymour and Northrup Knox. Again, typical Scotty, lots of questions. As I found out years later, Scotty saw a lot of himself in me. We had similar backgrounds in terms of our coaching careers, and there were similarities in how we coached as well. When he was young, Scotty had suffered a head injury playing junior. Later, when he was working as a paint salesman, he would watch the Montreal Canadiens practice during his lunch hour. He caught the eye of legendary GM Sam Pollock, who eventually gave Scotty his coaching start in junior hockey. The rest, as they say, is history. I'd worked my way up through the ranks, too—coaching high school, senior A and junior B. Beyond that, Scotty and I could both be hard-asses and demanding. And we won.

Rochester was the most appealing job for a few reasons, starting with Scotty and Roger but also because of the location. I talked things over with Rita. She would be able to drive home, just four hours away, to see family. She was really connected to her family, and Gayla was only a year or so old. Rochester made sense.

When I met with Scotty, I was pretty direct. I told him I appreciated the opportunity to coach his AHL club, but I needed a three-year contract and some security, because I was going to be giving up my teaching position and the Petes job. He said no problem. He offered me $35,000, $37,500 and $40,000 a year, plus bonuses. I was making $22,000 as coach and GM with Peterborough, so this was a great opportunity. And it was in American dollars, with health insurance, a car and a travel budget. On June 3, I signed and let the Petes and the principal at Forest Hill know I was leaving and hopefully wouldn't be coming back any time soon.

It actually took a bit of time after I signed the contract to get my work visa, which was unsettling. There were a lot of American coaches who were trying to stop Canadians from taking jobs in the United States at any level under the NHL. The Sabres hired a lawyer for me and looked after it, but it took several weeks for US Immigration and Customs to approve me.

My first training camp with the Sabres organization was in Lake Placid, working with Scotty, Roger and the other assistant, Jimmy Roberts. Scotty ran the main camp with his assistants, but I was on the ice, too. After the first wave of cuts, I returned to Rochester and Scotty kept sending me players who didn't make the big team.

I had just turned 31 to start the season and a few guys on the roster were just about the same age. I wasn't coaching kids anymore. At least half the guys I had in senior A had played professionally, some in the NHL and WHA, some in the AHL. In Whitby I had dealt with Eddie Shack, Carl Brewer and a few others who were well-known. That experience of dealing with men as a playing coach helped me gain the respect and confidence of the veterans in Rochester.

That first year was a real adjustment for me, because the roster was in constant flux. We had affiliations with the Sabres, of course, because they owned the team, but also with Los Angeles, Calgary and Quebec. Needless to say, they all wanted their players to get lots of ice time. During that season, we had 50 players dress for at least one game. All four GMs would come to Rochester to ask about their players, and they would want me to play them more. Dealing with four GMs is not easy. I told Scotty how tough it was to manage the bench with so many players coming and going, and he understood, but we had obligations to our affiliates and their players.

The chaos this caused began right on opening night. A 22-year-old player named Ron Carter was sent to us. He arrived during the warm-up and I didn't see him until he got to the bench in his gear a few minutes into the game. I said to him, "I have no idea who you are or how you can play, but good luck." It got even more bizarre a few games later. Prior to our seventh game, Ron Chipperfield, who was a talented centre, the 17th overall pick in 1974 and now property of Quebec, walked through the concourse of the rink, through the fans, from the dressing room to my office wearing just his shin pads and his jock strap. That's it. He said, "Mike, I quit." I said, "You can't quit, you're making $150,000 a year," which at the time was a lot of money. He said, "I can't take it anymore." He had been in the pros, in the WHA and then in the NHL, and six games into his minor league career he had had enough. He said he was going to Europe, and he did. He was there for 25 years—not playing all that time, of course. He went to Bolzano, Italy, where, oddly enough, our paths would cross again. But that's another story.

I was hard on the guys, no question. And, of course, none of the players were really happy because they didn't want to be in the minors. Still, I was a young coach who had to prove myself at the next level, whether the players were happy or not. One situation that came to a head was in the case of Bill Stewart, a defenceman who had been a fourth-round pick of the Sabres. He had played parts of two seasons in Buffalo; he's an NHLer, so he's pissed off he's in the minors. One day, after practice, I go in the dressing room and he's gone, but his equipment and underwear and sweater are sitting in the middle of the room, in front of his locker. There was a big bin in the middle of the room for players to toss in their sweaters and underwear. I said to our trainer, Jim Pizzutelli, "If you pick that stuff up, I will fire you." Next day, Stewart comes in and everything is still lying there. He says, "What's the story?" I said, "You're like everyone else. Walk three steps and throw your stuff in the laundry bin. Your option today is to wear that wet, dirty underwear or not. You're not doing that again." He never did. And that's not the way we treat the trainers.

Jim Pizzutelli was an unbelievable trainer and a great asset and ally for me. "Pizza" served in the Vietnam War as a medic. He's one of the main reasons why Clint Malarchuk is alive today. Jim eventually moved up to the Sabres with my recommendation, and he was working the night Clint got his throat cut by a skate blade. As a medic in the war, Jim had been involved in a lot of critical situations and knew exactly how to handle them. He was a great sounding board for me, and he knew how to deal with

forceful men. He was also a guy who could break the ice. The
players loved him. I remember one day, there was some tension
around the team and I was in the room addressing their discipline, being very firm with the group. All of a sudden the door to
the dressing room bangs open and there's nobody there. I'm
thinking, *What just happened?* A few seconds later, Jimmy—in his
goddamn battle fatigues with his rifle—is crawling on his belly
through the door, and he says to the team, "Where the fuck is he?"
Meaning me. Everybody just started to laugh. It was unbelievable.
And it broke the tension. His timing was perfect.

We didn't make the playoffs that year, finishing with a 30–42–
8–0 record, although we were close, just missing the final spot. It
was the first year I had ever coached that I didn't make the finals,
never mind the playoffs. That was an education for me. I did a
lot of yelling and kicking water buckets and garbage cans. I hated
losing, and when the season was over I had no idea if I would be
fired or invited back, regardless of the three-year deal I had
signed. But I think Scotty knew the challenges I had been facing.

It was really interesting working for Scotty, I learned so much.
He would come to games and would leave a few minutes early to
avoid traffic for the drive back to Buffalo. He would call from his
car right after the game and grill me about the game, how I handled situations, matchups, lines. He would ask how certain players were performing. If he needed to call someone up, he would
ask for recommendations. He called often, sometimes at one or
two in the morning! One night, Rita finally said, "You've got to
go in the other room." I'd be talking to him for an hour about
hockey. He wanted to know everything about every player we
had: strengths, weaknesses. He would second-guess me at times,

but it was an education. I had the greatest professional hockey coach ever holding my feet to the fire almost every day.

Scotty and I became good friends. I wasn't intimidated by him. I was always respectful, but I'd go right back at him when he challenged me, and I think he enjoyed my self-confidence. But I was thorough in my preparation for each practice and game. Sometimes he'd acknowledge a good move I'd made. One time, he came to a game and was sitting with my agent, Rob Campbell. That night I jumped on the boards and started yelling at the referee. Scotty just got up, turned to Rob and said I was crazy, and left. I took losing very personally. It was something I had to adjust to over the years. It was during the 1987 Canada Cup that the Edmonton guys—Gretzky, Messier, Anderson, Coffey and others—taught me to embrace winning. Yes, losing is tough, but take time to enjoy the wins.

Late that summer Hockey Canada and the International Ice Hockey Federation invited me to be a coaching observer at the 1981 Canada Cup. There were six of us—including Clare Drake, Tom Watt, Tim Taylor, who coached Yale, Pierre Pagé and George Kingston. I was assigned to the Czechoslovakian team. I went to every practice and game, rode the bus with them, stayed at the same hotel. As part of our involvement, each of the observers wrote a chapter for a coaching book, and we exchanged coaching methods and practice routines. It was a great experience, and the Czechs advanced to the semifinals, losing 4–1 to the Soviet Union. Scotty, of course, was coaching Team Canada, and he was not a happy camper when they lost 8–1 to the Soviets in the final. I was right in the hallway when the game ended, and Scotty came down from the bench and said, "Do you believe that? Do you

believe that [goalie Mike Liut] couldn't stop a fucking thing?"
Scotty didn't like losing, either, especially on such a grand stage,
with our country's hockey supremacy threatened.

The second season with Rochester felt a lot better. Scotty took
care of my biggest problem, and we became the farm team exclu-
sively for the Buffalo Sabres. No more juggling guys from four
NHL organizations. And that also meant I had only one GM to
deal with—Scotty—not four.

Still, part of life in the AHL is players going up and down.
I was still adjusting to this, but I had learned to tone down my
tirades. Well, at least a little. Which is not to say that I didn't have
a few conflicts. One was with winger Randy Cunneyworth, an
eighth-round pick of the Sabres in 1980 from the Ottawa 67's.
He'd had a taste of the NHL, playing 20 games with the Sabres,
but got sent down to the Amerks. Over time he and I became
great friends, but as a youngster, he was furious about being sent
down. And that led to us having our share of heated exchanges.

Every month or so, our rink, the War Memorial Auditorium,
had a concert or some event, so we would go to our other practice
rink, the Lakeshore Hockey Arena. There were six or seven rookies on the team, and I had a rule that the rookies had to bring the
pucks to practice. We would change at War Memorial, then bus
to the practice rink. So a rookie would only have to bring the
puck bag once every few months, if that. Well, when it was his
turn, Randy didn't want to take the pucks. I said to him, "Randy,
three or four guys have already done it." He reluctantly took the
pucks, but when the practice was over and I was about to leave,
Pizza said to me, "We've got a problem." He said, "When I told
Randy to pick up the pucks at the end of practice he refused to

pick them up." So I made Randy pick up every puck. When we got back to War Memorial, I saw him in the medical room, and he threw the bag at me. I asked everyone to leave, closed the door, and said, "If you ever do that again, I will beat the shit out of you." I was young and in good shape. I could have held my own. I never would have done it, but he had to learn some respect for the team. He wound up playing well for us and had a good NHL career. Just not with Buffalo.

That second season in Rochester wasn't just easier, it was better. For one, we had better players. Also, I had a year of pro coaching under my belt, and I had some help. A young fellow named E.J. McGuire had offered to help in any way he could. I met E.J. at Roger Neilson's coaching clinic, which he ran every summer in Windsor, Ontario. E.J., who was from Buffalo, was coaching the team at SUNY Brockport State University, which was about 20 miles west of Rochester. One day during my first season, we needed a rink to practise in and I called him to see if we could get some time at the school. After that, he became a part-time assistant and showed up when he could. In the second season he was with me more often. He was into statistics and video and was a great help. E.J. and I often drove to other cities so we could pre-scout an upcoming opponent. We'd leave after practice, watch a game and drive home. And some of those rides weren't short.

When we weren't scouting, we spent a lot of time watching video and breaking down tape, using it to show players things they were doing well or not so well. Roger was the pioneer with this technique, but we certainly tried to make it a key part of our program. I would give our bus driver 25 bucks to tape our road games; he would drive us to the game, tape it and then drive us home, no break. E.J. was a really bright hockey mind. I felt bad that I couldn't afford to pay him for his efforts, but the experience ultimately worked out well for his career—which included future stops working with me. Sadly, he passed far too soon, at the age of 58, in 2011.

That second year we finished with a 40–31–9 record and made the playoffs. We beat New Haven three games to one, including two overtime games—one that went seven periods, the longest game in AHL history at the time. Our goalie, Tim Bernhardt, was amazing that night. I had ordered pizza and beer for the bus ride home, but between overtime periods they ate the pizza and drank the beer. That was the game we lost. We still won the series, of course, but then lost 4–1 to the Binghamton Whalers in the second round. That was disappointing, but I was still encouraged because we had made progress from the previous season. We made the playoffs, won a round. We were moving in the right direction.

Any feelings of contentment I was experiencing as we headed into summer didn't last. A pregnant Rita, Gayla and I were driving back to Whitby after the season when Rita started to have issues in the car. We drove straight to the hospital in Toronto, where she had a miscarriage—the third. Obviously, the mother sees the baby in the delivery room, but after I had dropped Gayla off at her grandparents' and returned to the hospital, they brought the fully developed boy, about five months, out to me so I could see him and, they suggested, have some sort of closure. That was fucking awful and incredibly sad.

IN MY THIRD season, I was given an assistant coach of sorts. Phil Myre, who played goal for the Montreal Canadiens and a handful of other teams, landed in Buffalo but was going to quit playing. He had an interest in coaching, so Scotty said, "Go help Mike as an assistant coach and be the goalie as well." He appeared in 43 games and played well. I was grateful to have Phil, because E.J. had left to study kinesiology at the University of Waterloo and was going to be an assistant coach on the school hockey team, although he did return for our playoffs. Even though he was an assistant, Phil also brought some leadership to the dressing room.

As a team, we had a slow start to the season and were struggling in November: 8–9–3 out of the gate. We had quite a few young players, and after Scotty sent them to the minors it took a while for me to get them focused. They're disappointed, upset—for some it was disturbing. Oftentimes I'd say, "You're here, let's make the best of it. I'm going to be demanding, but let's improve your game so you can get back to play for someone else who is very demanding. Show them you deserve to go back up." But it takes time. I was starting to feel the heat a little. One day during that slow start, Scotty sent me a memo from U of T, which said they were looking for a coach for the following season. Interesting. And his assistant, Bucky Kane, came to Rochester to remind me how poorly we were playing. To this day, I don't know if Scotty was thinking of making a coaching change or just sending a message. Whichever, we did get things turned around.

One day at practice while the team was in New Brunswick, I gave them a bag skate, no pucks, no water. Some guys got physically sick. It became known as the Moncton Massacre. But they got the message about hard work and discipline, and in some ways they came together as a group because they hated me for those gruelling skates. I became the common denominator. And we did start to play much better. I also had a strong leadership group on the ice with Phil, who would be my foil, and a veteran named Yvon Lambert, who had won four Stanley Cups with Scotty in Montreal.

Yvon was one of the hardest-working players on the team, and he was really depressed about being in the minors. He had played eight seasons with the Canadiens and one with Buffalo, and now here he was in Rochester. It was hard. Scotty got mad at him and sent him down. Yvon worked his ass off in practice; he was respectful. We had a few French Canadian kids on the roster, and they looked up to him. He was a strong presence in the dressing room. But because he was unhappy, he spent a lot of time in the bar. This came to a head one night when we were in Halifax.

On the road I always gave a curfew. I did it to protect the club. If the curfew was 11:30 p.m. and something happened to a player at 1:30 in the morning, the club was protected. I don't know if that would have held up in court, but I did it. When I got to the NHL, I would give the bellman in the hotel a stick or a hat and then tell him to get the players who came in after the curfew to sign it. In the morning I would know who broke curfew.

That night in Halifax, Yvon was out after curfew. I walked into a bar near the hotel and saw him. He says, "Jeezus, Mike, I'm sorry." I ordered a beer and sat down with him. I said, "Yvon, I understand you won the Stanley Cup with Montreal, you won the Calder Cup with Nova Scotia, you played in Buffalo and now you're back in the AHL. I understand why you're so disturbed." He said, "Mike, I appreciate that. You can fine me but the only thing I want you to do is not tell any of my teammates that I broke curfew tonight." I told him it wouldn't be a problem. He said, "You'll never have a problem in the dressing room again." He told those young French kids to "shut up, listen and do what you're told." He became a very important part of our success, a great buffer for me.

To bring the team together, we had to change our style of play, the system we played. It helped that guys like Yvon and Phil bought in. We had a great attacking team based on two forwards—the offence was built on the centre and right wing; they were the only two who would forecheck. The left winger would stay back, unless we were carrying the puck in, of course. It was the left wing lock, which I had seen the Czechs use in the Canada Cup. That year at times I ran out of defencemen, so we adjusted how we played, used the left wing lock and won. I explained to Scotty what we were doing. He employed the same strategy years later in Detroit, although I'm sure he saw the Czechs doing it as well.

Rochester could score, we had good special teams and our goaltending was solid. We were also tough. We had the heavy-weight, middleweight and lightweight fighting champs in the American league—in order, Val James, Chris Langevin and Lou Crawford, brother of Marc Crawford. Those three would walk around before the game in silk boxing robes; they were Pizza's idea. At the old War Memorial, the opposition had to walk in the back door, past our dressing room and go downstairs. It was a brutal set-up. We would turn the heat up and down in their room. It was awful. Val, Chris and Lou would be out in the hall-way cutting their sticks. Pizza would spray them with water, or the boys would do some push-ups. It looked like they were drip-ping in sweat. It was very intimidating.

Val, who played seven games for Buffalo and later four with Toronto, was really tough, maybe the best fighter ever in the AHL. And a good guy. We got along. But there was one time when he was pissed off at me. I said, "We've got to talk in my office." I knew he was mad, and he was intimidating. I said to Pizza, "I'm meeting with Val. It could get heated, and if he gets pissed I'm trapped behind my desk." I said, "Go up in the rafters"—there was a drop ceiling over my office. "If Val comes over the desk you drop through the ceiling and jump on him." And so he did. Pizza dropped down, but not because of anything Val did. Val was great. Pizza said it was just stifling hot up there and he was dripping in sweat.

There was one game we were playing Nova Scotia, and one of their players, who was a tough guy, said a very bad thing to Val—who is Black—as we were lining up for a faceoff. Well, they got into it. When they got to the penalty box, there was just a piece of plywood between the boxes. Val went through the plywood and he got the guy underneath the riser and was pulling him so his face would hit the riser. The box was next to the bench, so I went in and grabbed Val and said, "Stop it, because you're going to kill the guy." He said, "You know what he called me." I said, "It's completely wrong, but you can't kill him." We were in Fredericton one time, and Val got into a fight and hit the guy so hard his eyebrow disappeared. But Val was a great guy, very popular with his teammates and the home fans.

Anyway, after that losing trip and bag skate down east, when we adjusted our playing style and rode Phil in goal, we turned things around big time, going from worst to first by Christmas. Winning builds confidence, and I was very demanding. I would not let them take any shortcuts. There was no wavering from discipline, responsibility—when you realize it as a group, the team takes on a life of its own. Once you get them believing in themselves, trusting each other, the power of the team is a lot greater than its individual parts. Part of my strength as a coach, and I enjoyed it as much as anything, was being able to understand the psychology of an individual player and what that player needed, whether that was more support, more instruction, more clarification or a kick in the ass.

It turned out we had a great season, finishing 46–25–9 for 101 points, first place overall. We were playoff ready, although that might not have been evident in our opener against Binghamton when we blew two, two-goal leads in the third period and lost 6–5. Yvon stepped forward. He told the group about the Canadiens losing badly to New York in the opening game of the 1979 Stanley Cup final, then sweeping the rest of the series. We went on to win the next four.

Next up was New Haven, and that was a hard-fought series. We won the opener but lost the second game in triple overtime. We blew a three-goal lead in the next game, but bounced back to win in double overtime. There was more overtime in the fourth game, which we won in the second extra period to take a 3–1 series lead. But both teams had played more than 100 extra minutes in those three games. There were a couple of days until Game 5, but we didn't play well. I think our young guys got a little cocky, but that's part of the process of learning playoff hockey. We went to a seventh game, and even though we blew a lead, we battled to a 4–2 victory and a trip to the final against the Maine Mariners, farm team of the Philadelphia Flyers.

Sticking to the script, we blew leads in the first two games but managed to win both. We went on to sweep the series, winning 5–1 and 3–1 to give Rochester its fourth AHL championship and my first. It's incredible to win, to enjoy and appreciate all that work you put into it. And I still have a picture of an almost four-year-old Gayla sitting in the Calder Cup. A treasure.

Needless to say, we celebrated after the game and flew home early the next morning with very little rest. There were hundreds of fans waiting for us at the airport, which was very nice. A few days later, we had a parade and rode in convertibles as thousands lined up along the main street in downtown Rochester. At City Hall, we had Nik and the Nice Guys play in a tent. Gary Webb, my old friend and teammate at St. Lawrence, had moved to Rochester. And he kept the band alive, recruiting some new musicians. I got up on stage with the band. When I found myself a little too close to the edge, the crowd bodysurfed me, about 10,000 people. Man, that was fun.

"IF YOU COACH university hockey you'll never coach in professional hockey again."

That's what Scotty Bowman said to me when I told him I was going to accept the head coaching job at the University of Toronto with the Varsity Blues, with whom I had won a national championship ten years earlier under Tom Watt.

I told Scotty I would take my chances.

Rochester had won the 1982–83 Calder Cup, but my contract was set to expire on July 31, and I had heard nothing from Scotty about a renewal. Meanwhile, I was hearing from NHL teams, including Watt and the Winnipeg Jets, about assistant coaching jobs, and U of T was recruiting me, too. Scotty just thought I would sign with Rochester again. He was shocked. But I told him, "Look, in Buffalo I have yourself, Jimmy Roberts and Red Berenson ahead of me." He had twice looked past me when he was hiring assistant coaches. I said, "I appreciate it, but I've learned all I can learn in the American Hockey League; it's time for something else." When he said I would never coach in the pros again, I think he was trying to intimidate me into staying put.

Even my dad, Ted, was disappointed and couldn't understand my decision. He figured any chance of making it to the NHL was gone. But it was the University of Toronto, a very prestigious school. I had played for them, had a great affiliation with them, and Gib Chapman, the athletic director, was going to make me the highest-paid university coach in Canada at $75,000 a year, almost double what I was making in my final year in the minors. I told my father, "I haven't taken my eye off being an NHL coach one day, and if I do get an NHL job offer, I can leave even though I have a two-year contract." I wanted a different experience coaching. I told my father that in my mind this was a lateral move. I'd coached in the pros, senior, junior. I wanted to expand my knowledge of the game with the university.

And if the NHL never worked out, I could at least have long-term security, be the next Tom Watt. And in fairness to my family, this was about as good as a coach's life could get: live in a great city, work for a prestigious university, be well paid, have stability, and not play 40+ games all over the place, out of the house 100 days a year. It was a good job.

Although Rita had made good friends in Rochester, she liked the decision, too. It was back home, even closer to family. And she had a degree from U of T and liked the school. Her family were all very academic. We bought a house just off Avenue Road near

Lawrence Avenue in midtown Toronto. The Lindros family were our neighbors, and a 10-year-old Eric would play ball hockey on our street. It seemed like the right decision at the time. And it was.

I started aggressively recruiting players, knowing I was starting a bit later than the other schools. Watt helped out big time. He helped us land a talented centre from Winnipeg named Darren Boyko. I was able to find a couple of good goalies in John Kemp and Kevin Hamlin. Andre Hidi, who played left wing for me with Peterborough, was back at U of T. Mike Pelino, a hard-nosed defenceman I'd had in junior B Oshawa, was in his fifth year, earning his teaching certificate. He became our most valuable player. There were other good players on the roster already enrolled at the school, including the likes of Don McLaughlin; Jim Byrne, who went on to teach at St. Michael's College School; winger David McCarthy, who is now a prominent lawyer; and Mike Todd, who was already a dentist and my captain. I was fortunate that I had Paul Titanic as an assistant coach. He had attended Bowling Green State University but was coming to U of T to get his teaching certificate, just as I had done. He was excellent and went on to coach the Blues himself. I am still friends with so many of those guys.

The goal for that season was to win the national championship. Nothing else was good enough. We had to bring back the glory—and we did. We finished with a 20–1–3 record, first in Ontario. Our only loss was to the University of Western Ontario, 5–3, and we tied Wilfrid Laurier and Laurentian a couple of times. Beyond those three schools, our toughest challenges came in exhibition games against some NCAA schools and other Canadian teams. For instance, we played Michigan State, which has a very good hockey program and was ranked number one in the United States. We split a two-game series. We ended our regular season on a six-game winning streak, then ran the table in the playoffs 7–0, outscoring our opponents 50–15. Pretty dominating. We beat Western 2–1 and 5–2 in the Ontario University Athletic Association (OUAA) final, giving U of T its second provincial title in three years. Then, in the national championship, we beat Concordia 9–1 in the gold medal game, our seventeenth straight victory, earning the Blues a tenth national title.

Hidi was named an All-Canadian and won the most valuable player award in the OUAA playoffs and the University Cup. Hidi and Pelino were both first-team all-stars; Boyko and McLaughlin were on the second team. Everyone from that team went on to have success in their lives and careers, which is rewarding. I still see a lot of those guys 40-plus years later. Pelino has been my assistant coach at various NHL stops, in the KHL and in Italy.

It was a great season and a fun season, not just because we won but because of the group that won. And then the phone rang, and for one of the few times in his career, Scotty Bowman was wrong.

5

READY FOR THE CHALLENGE: PHILADELPHIA, 1984–85

ARE YOU CRAZY?!

It was a fair question, I suppose. And one my family was asking again.

It's funny how history can follow you. When I was coaching in Rochester, we beat the Maine Mariners four straight to win the Calder Cup. Maine was the farm team of the Philadelphia Flyers. Of course, I left Rochester and went home to coach the Varsity Blues (prompting the first *are-you-crazy?* question), but it turns out the Flyers, who knew me from my three years with the Amerks, had kept an eye on me. Long-time scout Gary Darling was probably most instrumental in the effort. Gary was from the Peterborough area, was a former Pete and played senior hockey in Whitby. He was very familiar with my work. He had been a scout with Boston but moved to the Flyers to become assistant general manager.

I won in Peterborough, won in Rochester, won with the University of Toronto, and so, in the spring of 1984, Gary went to Flyers management and said, "Keenan keeps winning championships; we at least have to interview this kid." The Flyers, despite having had some good regular seasons, had just one playoff win (and nine losses) in three years, so the owner, Ed Snider, decided to replace Bob McCammon as coach. McCammon disagreed with the decision and decided to remove himself as general manager as well.

Around the same time, the Vancouver Canucks were expressing interest in me. I flew out to Vancouver to meet with the Griffiths family, Frank and his son Arthur, owners of the team. But they thought I was too much like Roger Neilson, who they had just gotten rid of. My coaching style was nothing like Roger's, apart from the use of video and statistics. But I was a university guy, a high-school guy, a Peterborough guy. Vancouver ended up hiring Bill LaForge, a hard-nosed coach who had taken Kamloops to the Memorial Cup. He lasted just 20 games before the Canucks fired him. I also interviewed with the New Jersey Devils and GM Max McNab, but that really didn't go anywhere.

Mr. Snider was trying to convince his legendary Flyers captain Bobby Clarke to retire as a player and become the new GM. Clarkie would want more of a disciplinarian as coach, after McCammon, who was easygoing. They had expressed interest in LaForge, who at 32 was a couple years younger than I was. And now the Flyers approached me—and presented me with a 28-item questionnaire, which was prepared by the Wharton School of Business. I decided to provide the answers in essay form. I don't know how many hockey guys could do that, so I felt Philly's search had likely already been narrowed down to two or three candidates. I heard that LaForge, Dave King, who had been coaching the Canadian national team, Ted Sator, who was an assistant with the Flyers, and I were on the shortlist.

I said I needed a week to write my reply, so I flew to Florida with Rita and Gayla and locked myself in the hotel room. They would go to the beach every day while I worked on the paper. It took me all week to write. It ended up being 19 pages long. I let my agent, Rob Campbell, and E.J. McGuire, my part-time assistant and friend in Rochester, read it. At the time, the Flyers were still waiting for Clarkie to decide on the GM job, but when he finally accepted he read the paper, and then interviewed me twice after reading it. Bobby called Scotty Bowman about me, and Scotty said, "I don't know anybody in the game that hates losing more than he does." Bobby told me that, and said he hated to lose, too. That call between a couple of future Hall of Famers was probably a good conversation.

In the essay, I described myself as being "a man with a mission, and that mission is to win. Personally I have experienced a contagious phenomenon whereby the more I win, the more I want to win. Nothing short of this is acceptable. In order to achieve this quality in life, my focus is clear, my energies high, my efforts tireless, my will determined."

I went on: "I am probably impatient at times, certainly direct in approach, but I think also sensitive, energetic, honest, loyal and above all a competitor." I mentioned how my motivational abilities were based on "predictable unpredictability." I talked about coaching philosophies, practices, motivation.

I finished by saying: "I feel I am the man the Flyers need . . . I have learned from my experiences at various levels of the game and have a proven record of success. Ownership and the fans demand and deserve no less . . . My goal and that of the Flyers is the Stanley Cup. I am ready for the challenge."

The Sniders and Bobby were impressed with the paper. Clarkie was looking for discipline, structure, new ideas. I was probably ahead of my time. We were the first team in the NHL to keep track of time on ice and use video as much as we did. Teddy Sator, who stayed on as one of my assistants, logged a summary of each day in a binder—tracking everything we did every single day, from practice drills to coaches' interactions with players, everything. A player would come to us and ask why we weren't working on the power play. We would open the book and, yup, worked on it 10 days ago.

Bobby, who wanted to play another year, formally accepted the GM job on May 15. He said he couldn't say no when Mr. Snider asked him. And he decided to hire me as head coach. He flew to Toronto to negotiate with Rob Campbell. I was in the room, and the discussion wasn't going anywhere. He offered a three-year deal starting at $80,000, and then progressing to $85,000 and $90,000 in years two and three. I told him I needed the three years because I was leaving a plum job at U of T, where I was the highest-paid college coach in any sport in Canada. I had the security of my daughter eventually going to the school for free, tenure, all that stuff. But when Clarkie offered the money, Rob got into an argument with him, telling him he was fucking cheap. I eventually stepped in and told Rob to leave the room. I said to Bobby, "I'm pretty confident in my skills and ability. If that's what you want to offer, I'll take it." I was the lowest-paid coach in the NHL for sure. I was making $75,000 at the university and he was offering me $5,000 more. My father-in-law said to me, "Are you fucking crazy? You're going to give up U of T and all of that for $5,000?" I said I want to give the NHL a shot.

After I had accepted the offer, I met with Mr. Snider. He said to me, "If you make the playoffs with this team"—remember, we had lost Bobby Clarke, Bill Barber and were about to trade Darryl Sittler, all Hall of Famers—"I will kiss your ass at centre ice!" Words to remember.

That summer, I sent a questionnaire to the players asking for our goals as a team and their goals as players. I met with them individually to discuss.

It was a no-brainer to keep Teddy on the staff. I knew him from when we worked summer hockey schools. I was also able to bring in E.J., who Clarkie lowballed, too. Clarkie didn't know him from Adam. I remember the day they announced my hiring. I was wearing a suit and my dark glasses, and someone said, "The Flyers have hired a fucking accountant!" One thing I really liked about the Flyers organization was that Mr. Snider had a football background, as a part-owner of the NFL Philadelphia Eagles. He liked the idea of having a coaching team, which was common practice in football but not much done in hockey. I became the head coach. I had Teddy and E.J. as assistants, Billy Barber as skills coach, the great Bernie Parent as goalie coach, Pat Croce as strength and conditioning coach, and Mike Finocchiaro as video coach. Later on, I added Cal Botterill as the team psychologist. Mr. Snider liked that. The Flyers, remember, were the first NHL team to have a full-time assistant coach, when Fred Shero hired Mike Nykoluk and they won two Stanley Cups.

Clarkie was really good to work for. He respected the coach. As a player, he'd won those two Cups with Freddy, and he'd later had Pat Quinn, who was a players' coach. Clarkie would come to our practices and ask to put the gear on. I said, "I don't mind, you're the boss, but when you're on the ice and have a uniform on, I'm the boss. You have to do what I tell you, otherwise it's not going to work." And he did. He knew where the line was drawn.

We got off to a so-so start to the 1984–85 season with Clarkie and Barber gone. We played 11 exhibition games that fall, probably didn't win one. I would have hard practices in the morning, and then we would have a game that night, and I made the rookies play every game, or close to it. And there was bit of upheaval to start. With Clarkie retired, the plan was to make Sittler the captain. We were going to the season-opening banquet to introduce the team and the new captain and Clarkie says to me, "You can't announce Sit as captain." I said, "Why not?" Turns out he had just traded him to Detroit for Murray Craven, a good young forward, and Joe Paterson. We wanted to make the team younger. Sit was 34. But we didn't say anything at the banquet. I went to Sit's house, just around the corner from mine, and told him. He broke out in tears. Clarkie, who had been Darryl's roommate and close friend, said trading him was the toughest thing he had to do. It was even worse for Darryl because he'd had a tough departure from Toronto and was enjoying playing for the Flyers.

But now we had the youngest team in the league, actually in pro sports, with an average age of 24.5. When I think back to Mr. Snider saying he would kiss my ass if we made the playoffs, it's clear that they thought it was going to be a developmental year, with young players and a young coach who was new to the NHL, and that it would take two or three years for the team to be good. We made centre Dave Poulin the captain. He was a Notre Dame grad, a smart guy, just 25 at the time. He had been in the dressing room with Clarkie, knew how he trained, how hard he worked and led. They were tight. He was a great choice. The oldest of the regular players was defenceman Mark Howe, son of the great Gordie.

Even though our start had been so-so, we got the team organized, got some momentum going—I played the best players the most; Mark Howe and Brad McCrimmon played 32 minutes a game—and got on a 15–2–4 roll, including a 7–5 win over the Edmonton Oilers on November 11 that ended their 12–0–3 unbeaten streak to open the season. We had a lot of first- and second-year players, guys like Craven, Peter Zezel, Rick Tocchet and Derrick Smith. And a bunch of our guys, such as Poulin, Brian Propp and Tim Kerr were in their mid-20s. Some of them became rock stars. Zezel would sign autographs at a mall and a thousand young girls would show up. He'd need security.

During the summer, just after I was hired and when I was interviewing every player, I took Pelle Lindbergh to lunch and told him, "No matter what anyone says, you're my number-one goalie." He said, "Mike, how can that be? I haven't even practised with you yet." I reminded him about coaching in Rochester and how we beat Maine, with him in goal, four straight in the Calder Cup final—and said that he was one of the main reasons they got to the final. I told him he was an unbelievable goalie. And he was. He appeared in 65 games that season and won the Vezina Trophy. He just needed someone to believe in him.

Propp was our most talented forward. Kerr was great on the power play; you couldn't move him from the front of the net and he had wicked, quick hands. Poulin and Proppy killed penalties. Those three were my top line. The kids really developed, too. Zezel was great in faceoffs. Craven could skate like crazy. Ilkka Sinisalo was talented. We had toughness with Tocchet and Lindsay Carson, the Sutter twins, Ron and Rich. Beast (McCrimmon) and Howe were plus-52 and -51 respectively. And our team was in great shape, to my mind the most fit team in the league. Pat Croce, our trainer and fitness guru, was invaluable. It got to a point that when guys got hurt, they couldn't wait to get back in the lineup because he was training them so hard. He would have them in at 7 a.m. Everyone says Iron Mike was a ball-buster—well, so was Pat, and he knew how to train hockey players. He was very demanding, but he made them better athletes.

We had short, hard shifts, and because we were so fit, we could grind teams down and beat them in the third period. It was because of that fitness that I could play guys so many minutes a night. I also tried to control the game flow with the officials. I'd put out five guys, then another five on a change, and by then they'd had a rest. I tried to work the changes with the officials. Mark would come off and go to sit down, I'd put my foot on bench, and he'd sit on it. "Oh fuck, I have to go back out there."

We used a system that was about hard forechecking and not spending a lot of time in our zone. The goalie was first to initiate the attack, to get the puck to the defence, and our next pass had to be out of the zone. I got that philosophy from Bowman. It was very simple: if we keep the puck outside our blue line and they score, it's the goalie's fault. But they can't score if they're not in our end. Move the puck as quickly as possible. Our practices were high tempo, game-like but not long. At the start of the year, I'd go 70 minutes; by the end of the year it was 35 minutes and we worked a lot on skills, executing properly.

I remember one time, we were doing a cross-ice passing drill. Zez was skating through the neutral zone with his stick across his waist. Mark was passing the puck—and hits him right in the chest. Zez said, "Why did you do that?" "Well, that's where your stick is. Put it on the ice and that's where I'll put the puck." Next time, Mark passed the puck so hard he broke Zez's stick. If the kids whined about practices being too much, Mark or Beast would tell them to shut the fuck up and do what they're told. Those two wanted to kill me at times, but they were leaders.

Was wanting to kill the coach a popular idea throughout the year? No doubt. I was firm, I kept them on edge, but I think I was more of a teacher with those young guys—which is not to say I didn't have my moments. I wouldn't let them off the hook. If they didn't do something right, they'd miss a shift or two. But if they did something really well, I might double-shift them. The accountability of my coaching was very transparent. You had to be responsible to yourself and your teammates, and if you let the team down, you were going to hear from me. Everyone bought into it. As Beast said, "He's demanding, but we're winning and he knows what he's doing."

One time they were definitely ready to kill me was just before Christmas. Poulin had asked if the team could skate early on the 24th, and pizza and beer had been ordered for after practice. We had a rough patch in mid-December, with a four-game losing streak, five losses in six. So we practised at 8 a.m. I think they were all expecting an easy practice. I brought out the boom box, had Christmas carols playing, and then I put them through a 45-minute bag skate. I said, "Expect the unexpected, Merry Christmas, see you in Washington" and left the ice. We had beaten the Capitals the night before, 7–4, but then got spanked 6–0 the day after Christmas. Then the message started to sink in. We won six of the next seven. My message to them was simple. We had a young group and were having pretty good success; the guys were becoming very popular in the city. That was all well and good, but I wanted to stress that we had a long way to go here, that there couldn't be any complacency. It's fine to have swagger, but you can't get cocky and cheat on the ice, which we had been doing.

Seeing them pick it up, I tried to make it up to them on New Year's Eve. That Washington game on Boxing Day was the last before a six-game road trip that took us out west. We played in Los Angeles on the 30th and won, and we were playing in Edmonton on January 2nd. I told the guys, "Everybody on the bus on New Year's Eve." They're all on the bus and I walk on smoking a cigar and carrying a beer. I took them to a bar in downtown Edmonton called Goose Loonies that was frequented by a lot of teams over the years. We had some fun.

With our speed and physicality, teams would be saying, "Holy fuck, they're full throttle right from the beginning." We were a force at home at the Spectrum, where the fans were right on top of the action. It was a tight building. Teams would come and say, "Let's get the hell out of here, they're going to run over us." We finished with a 32–4–4 record at home, which included a 14-game winning streak in Philly to close the season. Overall, we won 16 of our final 17 games and finished first overall with a 53–20–7 record.

Which reminded me of what Mr. Snider had said when I was hired. There was a night when we'd had a stinker at home, and he came down the hall pissed off. Every time he did, people would scatter, afraid to catch his wrath. I just stood there waiting for him. He said, "This team's not ready for the playoffs, that's a disgusting effort." I said, "Mr. Snider, can I remind you of something—that you said you'd kiss my ass if this team makes the playoffs?" He said, "You're right," turned around, and added, "I'll never bother you again."

Was I surprised with the success we had, especially with such a young team? To some degree, of course, but our team was well prepared, and they bought into what I was teaching. I set the bar high in terms of expectations. Our job was to win the Stanley Cup, not just make the playoffs. To that end, we had broken the season into 10-game segments. The idea was to win at 600 percent every segment. We gave bonuses for various categories in that segment. When we got the six points, bonuses for things like goals for and against, special teams, would kick in. As we achieved those goals, our expectations continued to rise and we expected to win. It wasn't *if* we win, it was *we are going to win*, there's no other choice. And they bought into it. Once they believed in themselves, we were very difficult to beat.

Having said all that, when we opened the playoffs against the Rangers, our young team seemed really, really nervous. But we found a way. Clarkie and I had to convince them that we were the best team in the regular season and that whatever had happened in previous years against the Rangers was history. We managed to win the opener 5–4 in overtime, and then swept the best-of-five, but the games were close.

Then we had to play the New York Islanders, the four-time Stanley Cup champions—five trips to the final, 19 straight series wins before they'd lost to Edmonton the previous spring. All those future Hall of Famers—Bryan Trottier, Denis Potvin, Mike Bossy—and the great Al Arbour behind the bench. I had to convince our guys we could beat this team that was still very, very good and playoff hardened. Well, we did beat them, in five games, at one point taking a 3–0 lead in the series. It wasn't easy, but it was huge for our confidence. I can remember being embarrassed while shaking hands with Arbour and apologizing. Every time we went into the Nassau Coliseum he would wait in the hallway, call me into his office and we would chat. I was very grateful for that, especially being a young coach. He was an unbelievable coach and person.

Next up was the Quebec Nordiques, another powerful team with a bunch of future Hall of Famers—Peter Stastny, Michel Goulet—and a really good Dale Hunter. It was a difficult series as well. We lost the opener 2–1 in overtime in Quebec, but we bounced back and took a 2–1 series lead. But Quebec played hard. They evened up the series and at one point I sensed our confidence was faltering a bit. And I could also sense perhaps a little of "Okay, we've had a great year, we won two playoff rounds. This is good enough. It's getting really tough to beat this team." I got up in the middle of the room—I jumped up on a table— and I told them, every which way, "There is no fucking way you're going to give up on yourselves now." I could feel it on the bench; they were getting nervous again. But they found a way.

By the time we got to the Stanley Cup final against the defending champion Oilers—with Wayne Gretzky and Mark Messier and Paul Coffey and their own list of future Hall of Famers—we were a beat-up team. We had so many guys banged up: Kerr,

McCrimmon, Poulin, Howe. Howe was playing on one leg. We paid a price, and while they were banged up, the Oilers didn't have any of their stars out. At one point I tried to talk Clarkie into playing in the final, and he almost did it. I told him I knew he could help; he had experience, and we didn't have anyone in the room who had won the Stanley Cup. But he said that in fairness to the players, he didn't want to be a distraction; they had worked so hard to get to that position.

So now we were playing this great team, one of the best ever, and the format in the final was 2–3–2, meaning we had the first two games at home, then three in Edmonton. I hated it. We'd worked hard all year to get home-ice advantage and won the first game 4–1, but the advantage went to the Oilers after they won the second game 3–1. They had all that experience and star power, and they had just won the Cup. We didn't even have anyone with deep playoff experience. The feeling that we could not beat this team had crept in, and it was true. We were in Edmonton for seven days and, of course, lost all three games. They won in five games. If we had been playing the normal format, 2–2–1–1–1, and I had been able to bring the Flyers home after two games in Edmonton, it could have been different. But we lost to a great team, so maybe it wouldn't have been different after all.

It was a great year, a great run. We were the youngest team in the league and the fans went crazy for us. The club even made a promotional video based on the season called *Beyond All Expectations*. Still, losing in the finals was difficult—I cried afterwards—but the kids learned so much about how to win.

Mr. Snider never did kiss my ass, but he did give me a new contract. I was up north of Toronto at our cottage on Georgian

Bay when he called and said he wanted me to fly back to Philly. He presented me with a Mercedes and thanked me for the great season. Then he extended the contract and bumped my salary up to $120,000 and $125,000 for the remaining two years. I also won the Jack Adams Award as coach of the year. I hadn't thought much about winning the award, but I was obviously happy. I had a great staff and I shared my feelings with them. Clarkie was quoted as saying "the best thing we did was to hire Mike Keenan."

It was definitely a good start for my first year in the league.

6

A DEVASTATING LOSS: PHILADELPHIA, 1985–86

ON THE HEELS of a terrific season that ended with the disappointing loss to the Edmonton Oilers in the Stanley Cup final, I wanted to make sure the young group wasn't complacent at the start of the 1985–86 season, that they remembered how hard they had to work to achieve everything. That led to an ill-advised benching of my star defenceman, Mark Howe, on opening night, but the message did get through.

We had only a few lineup changes, the biggest being the addition of talented centre Pelle Eklund, a draft pick from a few seasons earlier. Ted Sator, one of my assistant coaches and still under contract, was pursued to be the head coach of the rival New York Rangers, and we decided to let him leave. We replaced him with former Flyers bruiser Paul Holmgren, who had finished his playing career because of an injury the previous season in Minnesota but had been a Flyer for nine seasons.

After the opening night 6–5 home loss to New Jersey, we won two, lost again, then went on a winning streak of 13 in a row, in pursuit of breaking what was at the time the league record of 15, held by the New York Islanders. Our tenth consecutive victory came on November 9, a 5–3 Saturday night win over the Boston Bruins at the Spectrum, raising our season record to 12–2. Our next game was five days later, November 14, at home against the Oilers. So I gave the team Sunday off, with Monday an optional skate. All was good.

And then, in the wee hours of Sunday, the phone rang.

It was my captain, Dave Poulin. A bunch of the players had gone out after the game to celebrate the wins and the day off, and obviously they enjoyed some drinks. At first, Pelle Lindbergh, our Vezina Trophy–winning goalie, wasn't planning to join them. He told his fiancée, Kerstin Pietzsch, that because he was disappointed he hadn't played against Boston he was staying in. Later, he changed his mind. A bunch of the guys, including Pelle, ended up in an after-hours bar that was in the same complex as our practice rink in Voorhees, New Jersey, close to where most of us lived.

At 5:41 a.m. that Sunday morning, driving 80 miles per hour in his red Porsche 930, and with two passengers in the two-seat car, Pelle wasn't able to handle a turn. He lost control and slammed into a cement wall leading to the steps in front of an elementary school. The injuries were severe, and it took the jaws of life to get him out of the demolished car. According to later reports, Pelle had a blood alcohol level of 0.24. At the time, the legal limit in New Jersey was 0.10. I had warned Pelle about that car and how he drove it. He used to come into the practice arena parking lot driving a hundred miles an hour and doing donuts.

I said to him once, "You're going to kill yourself." That's exactly how I said it.

Dave lived around the corner, so I met up with him and we drove to the hospital in Camden, New Jersey, but by then Pelle and one of his passengers, Kathy McNeal, had been transferred to another hospital, about 20 minutes away. The other passenger, Ed Parvin Jr., stayed at the first hospital and was listed in critical condition with a fractured skull. He survived. Poulie and I drove to John F. Kennedy Hospital to see Pelle. Incredibly, I was allowed to go into the emergency room. He had a broken leg and was really banged up, and he was hooked up to a life-support system. I went into the young lady's room, which was against protocol, and asked her what happened, but she was too groggy to answer. Despite a ruptured spleen and liver and a broken pelvis, she survived.

In the morning, the players started showing up at the hospital. Peter Zezel broke down completely in my arms in the hallway. Rick Tocchet was incredibly shaken because he had almost gotten into the car. We were eventually told by our team doctor, Ed Viner, that Pelle was essentially dead. As you can imagine, the emotions ranged at once from utter shock to anger to overwhelming sadness.

Pelle's mother, Anna Lisa, was visiting from Sweden, staying with him and Kerstin. Pelle was kept alive until his father, Sigge, could arrive to say goodbye to his only son. Pelle officially died on November 11 at the age of 26.

A tragedy of this magnitude is difficult to process at any age. Pelle was very popular, and a lot of these young guys hadn't yet experienced death in their lives. But this was a tight team. On the Monday, I decided to call everyone to the rink and put them back on the ice. There had been all sorts of discussion about when we would play again, or practise, but I made the decision. It probably wasn't one of my usual practices, but I still worked them pretty hard. It was just a chance for everyone to be together, and maybe, for a precious few moments, it could be a distraction, an outlet for their anger, frustration, disappointment and sadness— their grieving. They might have thought of Pelle more because we were on the ice and he wasn't, but I think it was an important release. I remember saying that it was what Pelle would want us to do. Even today I think it was the right thing to do. That first practice we kept his net empty, and his stall remained in the dressing room all season.

I also brought the entire team home to use my house as a grieving centre. Rita and I hosted, and we wanted the guys to be able to express their feelings, to share them with the group. It was okay to cry; it was okay to tell a Pelle story. They were such a young group. They didn't need Iron Mike just then; they needed an empathetic person to help with their grieving. Maybe because of my personal situation—I lost my brother when I was very young, and Rita and I had gone through several late miscarriages—I didn't seek out any professional assistance or advice to handle the situation. I just felt the players needed my support and direction, and I focused on that.

As horrible as we were all feeling on a human level, the decision was made to play the next game against the Oilers. We had debated cancelling the game, and the Oilers had offered to cooperate, but we figured getting back sooner rather than later might be beneficial. So, somehow, we had to focus. I didn't think, *Well, there goes our season because we don't have our Vezina-winning goalie.* I was thinking, *What is the best way to coach them game-to-game? How do I keep them focused?*

I will never forget the Spectrum that night. It was an emotion-filled arena, as you would expect, for the team as well as the fans. Before the game there was a 20-minute memorial service. Some guys were crying on the bench. I think the Oilers were affected as well. A decision had been made to remove the advertising on the boards, and the souvenir stands were closed. That season, our game tickets had a picture of a different player on them for each game. That night, by fate or coincidence, it was Pelle. Our players wore No. 31 shoulder patches. There was a wreath of flowers in the shape of Pelle's 31 at centre ice, and a capacity crowd of 17,000-plus stood in silence. Pelle's parents were there, too, sitting in Mr. Snider's box.

The players weren't as emotional after the memorial ceremony because they'd been grieving all week. But as they lined up for the opening faceoff, I had no idea how they would respond. There was a lot of pressure on them to perform in Pelle's honour, but it wouldn't be easy, especially against the defending champion Oilers, who wore black armbands in tribute.

We went out and we won, 5–3, a team-record eleventh-straight victory and the start of new era—without Pelle. I was very proud of that group, of how they played the game, the intensity they had. It's interesting. Bob Froese was scheduled to start in goal, but during practice he took a puck in a very sensitive area and wasn't able to play. We decided to call up rookie Darren Jensen from Maine, who had one game of NHL experience, a 7–0 loss to the Islanders the previous season. To say the least, he was under a lot of pressure, too. We didn't have a morning skate, but maybe the quick turnaround helped him—although he did admit later that he was so nervous before the game he couldn't eat.

The game started a little slowly, as you would expect, but it heated up. Ed Hospodar started to get things going a few minutes in when he took a roughing penalty. Mark Howe opened the scoring late in the first period and the building exploded with raw emotion. The second period featured a fight—Craig MacTavish and Tocchet—and the Oilers tied the game, with coach Glen Sather given a game misconduct by referee Don Koharski at the start of the third period for arguing a bunch of penalties late in the second and bringing the team out late to start the third. He was replaced for the third period by Bob McCammon, who had coached Pelle in Maine and with the Flyers and who I had replaced in Philly.

We started the third on a two-man power play. Ilkka Sinisalo scored 24 seconds in, then Brian Propp scored on another power play a few minutes later to give us a 3–1 lead. The Oilers cut the lead to one, but Rich Sutter put us ahead 4–2. Mark Messier cut the lead again, but Brad McCrimmon iced it for us with 3:10 left. The Flyers won it for Pelle. The reaction afterwards in the arena was amazing, from cheers to tears.

Jensen did himself proud, stopping 29 shots. I remember Gretzky was minus-2. But for us to beat them—having just played them in the final, and then after Pelle dying—to win under those circumstances impressed the hell out of me. I think the team rallied around the rookie, Jensen. Part of our winning formula had been how tight the team was. We might not have had the most talent, but we had the best or second-best team in the league in terms of the meaning of *team*—accepting our roles, growing as a group. It was a very special group of guys.

I also remember seeing a sign in the seats that night: "Get Pelle's name on the Cup. It's his last chance." That was our goal, of course, but it wasn't going to be easy. Among other reasons, Pelle's death had an impact on us for the rest of our season. To his credit, Mr. Snider, who had been about to sign Pelle to a six-year, $1.7 million extension, honoured the deal. He understood more than I did what a blow his loss was to the team.

We won two more games before the Islanders ended our winning streak at a franchise-record 13. There was a stretch in early December when I thought we might be hitting the wall. The team was exhausted, mentally and emotionally. Physically, we were fit, but I don't think we ever fully recovered from Pelle's loss that season, even though we went on to win 13 of the next 16. I rode Froese pretty hard, in the sense of being up in his grill, sometimes for his play, sometimes for not being disciplined in practice. I never considered him a number-one goalie, but he was a great backup. He might still be upset with me. As coach of the Wales Conference All-Stars, I did add him to my roster, but along with ownership I also pushed Clarkie to trade for 37-year-old Glenn "Chico" Resch. Our goaltending was just okay, but our goaltenders obviously had a very tough act to follow.

I continued to push the group, slammed some doors, kicked some butt. But going to the final against the odds in that first year, and then the tragedy—I think it all caught up to us. We still had 53 wins and 110 points, but it was obviously a different season from the one before, and in some ways, under the circumstances, it was maybe even more impressive. And night after night I was still driven by my win-or-nothing approach. But it couldn't counter the one huge loss—Pelle.

The expectations had changed after that first season. We had been a fun, unknown team, a bunch of young guys who had some great games and success. But we had raised the expectations of ownership, management, fans and the team. Now we were expected to win, and we did. But by the time we got to the playoffs we were spent emotionally.

We met up with the Rangers and my former assistant Ted Sator, who had improved his team by 16 points. But we had also beaten them in 18 of the previous 19 games, including the sweep in the 1984–85 playoffs. In the opener we twice fell behind and ended up losing at home unimpressively, 6–2. With back-to-back games to start the series and four games in five nights, we stayed in a local hotel and tried to regroup with individual video sessions. We did respond and held on for a 2–1 win in the second game, sending the series to Broadway. In Game 3, we led 2–1 eight minutes into the third period and then fell apart with penalties and turnovers. The Rangers scored twice within four minutes, including one on the power play, to take the lead. Fourteen seconds after that they made it a two-goal lead, at which point I had the entire bench get on the ice for a lecture about how poorly they were playing. We lost 5–2, with Game 4 of the five-game series set for the next night.

Facing elimination, and despite falling behind early, we made adjustments and responded in a big way. Froese played well, Zezel scored a hat trick, and we returned home for the final game with a 7–1 victory. But we fell behind in that deciding game, trailing 1–0 after the first, looking a little tight. Sinisalo tied it, but we trailed 3–1 heading into the third. McCrimmon got us to within a goal midway through the third, but the Rangers and goalie John Vanbiesbrouck shut us down after that. We outshot them 36–25, but New York scored two into our empty net: series and season over.

It may have come down to goaltending, because Vanbiesbrouck was excellent. We outplayed them and outshot them, but he stood on his head. Froese wasn't Pelle, and he wasn't as good as John, even though he shared the Jennings Trophy with Jensen for fewest goals against, though some of that was credit to our good team defence. But as I said, the team was emotionally and mentally done. Some of that was them carrying the weight of a tragedy, and some was on the coach. But we'll come back to that.

When it was over, I wasn't thinking, *Thank God it's over*. I was such a poor loser. I had the expectations of winning in my DNA. I always expected us to find a way, even with the loss of Pelle. I never allowed myself to think we couldn't find a way to win.

Rita and I went on vacation to Boca Raton, Florida. I was on the beach one day and I was still so pissed that I got up and went back to the hotel room and—unbeknownst to her—shaved my moustache, which I had begun to grow in university. Rita had never seen me without it. But I was just so angry, I shaved it off. She said, "What are you thinking?" I said, "I'm pissed about losing." It wasn't rational, but I hated to lose, no matter the circumstances. Next time I saw Gayla, she didn't recognize me. It all didn't settle very well for me, especially when the Oilers were knocked out in the first round by Calgary. With the champions out, it felt like a hugely wasted opportunity for us, but it ultimately wasn't meant to be, and our biggest loss hadn't been on the ice.

7

CLOSE, BUT NO CUP: PHILADELPHIA, 1986–87

IF IT'S NOT clear by now, let me say it again: I hate losing. Finding a silver lining for the 1985–86 season was difficult, although the way the team dealt with the Pelle Lindbergh tragedy truly was impressive. Losing in the first round to the New York Rangers? Not so much. But because we were done early, after my getaway to Florida with Rita, I watched our Hershey Bears farm team on their run through the AHL playoffs, losing in six games to Adirondack in the Calder Cup final. I had to give a lot of credit for their success to goaltender Ron Hextall.

I knew about Ron before watching those games. I had seen him play in Hershey and I wanted to call him up when Pelle died, but Clarkie thought he wasn't ready for the NHL, especially under those conditions. It was probably the right decision. That season, Ron appeared in 53 games and won 30 for the Bears, with five shutouts, and was named AHL rookie of the year. In the playoffs, he appeared in 14 games.

With that experience, Ron was ready. I had the same feeling about him that I did with Pelle when I first came to the Flyers, when I told him he was going to be our number-one goaltender. Ron was a big kid, 6 foot 3, 200 pounds. He was very agile, handled the puck exceptionally well, and he had a fire in his belly, hugely competitive. He still had to prove himself in the exhibition games, though, and he didn't prove me wrong. He went 4–0 in the pre-season and I told him he was going to start opening night at home against the Edmonton Oilers. I was hopeful our goaltending troubles were solved. We carried three goalies to start the season: Ron, an unhappy Bob Froese, and Chico Resch, who was re-signed by Clarkie.

We made a few roster changes in the off-season, trading Rich Sutter to Vancouver for defenceman J.J. Daigneault, which split up the twins, leaving us with Ron (who was the better player) and an unhappy mother. When I phoned the Sutter house to tell them about the trade, Mrs. Sutter really gave it to me. Thomas Eriksson, a talented defenceman, left to go home to Sweden. I had been hard on him, and Clarkie said that was the reason he departed, but I'm not so sure he only wanted to get away from me. I think he wanted to go home. We started the season without Brad McCrimmon on the blue line. Beast was in a contract dispute and missed the first nine games.

As for the coach? I realized I probably should have let the team breathe a little the previous season, given all that had gone on. The team had matured. It had been through a lot—from going to the final in 1984–85 to the tragedy in 1985–86. The team had good leadership and should probably have been left to deal with more things themselves. After a talk with my coaching staff, we all agreed I had to back off a bit, at least by Iron Mike's standards. That's not to say I didn't push hard. Just ask winger Scott Mellanby.

Mellanby was a second-round draft pick out of the University of Wisconsin, where he played just two seasons. I didn't think he was ready to play for us and should have been in Hershey, but Clarkie thought otherwise. Scott was the son of Ralph Mellanby, the executive producer of *Hockey Night in Canada*. I was very hard on Mellanby. I thought he wasn't prepared; Clarkie thought he was. One day after practice, I kept him on the ice and roughed him up, trying to show him how to battle hard. Other times I put him through bag skates. I took his dressing room stall away from him once when we had a call-up. Clarkie didn't like what I was doing, but of course that didn't stop me. Mellanby was 20 years old and he hadn't finished university; the other young guys had gone through two years of learning how to win. To his credit, he responded. To this day he says he has no ill feelings, that I helped make him a better player, faster. He wound up playing surprisingly well, finishing with 11 goals and 32 points in 71 games, with 94 penalty minutes. He eventually earned his place.

Back to opening night. Ron lived up to my expectations. He gave up a goal two minutes in but was solid after that, as Ron Sutter and Peter Zezel scored in the third to give us a 2–1 win over Edmonton. I used Ron again two nights later in a 6–1 win over Washington, then gave Froese the start against Vancouver, a 6–2 win. But I rode with Hextall, who showed his feistiness and puck-handling skills. He picked up six assists that season. I remember Mark Howe saying he would add years to his career because he didn't have to skate deep into our zone all the time with Ron firing pucks out to the blue line.

Our crowded goaltending situation came to a head sooner rather than later. Froese asked for a trade. He had asked for one the previous season and went public about it, just before Pelle passed, but Clarkie couldn't find a good trade return for him. Then, obviously, we needed him, and he played a lot, finishing second in Vezina Trophy voting. But I still thought he was just a good backup. His success was in large part because he played behind a strong defensive team. This season, after Froese had played only three games by mid-December, Clarkie traded him to the Rangers for 6-foot-6, 235-pound defenceman Kjell Samuelsson, which I thought was a very good pick up.

I never blamed Froese for being pissed off and wanting to play more, but I didn't like that he went to the media with his trade request. I also didn't like that he sometimes didn't treat Ron well. There was always some drama.

We got off to a strong start to the season, winning our first six games, and we were 25–8–2 by Christmas. But the injuries continued to mount. We had already lost Brian Propp earlier in the month with a fractured knee and then Ilkka Sinisalo broke his arm in Buffalo. Post-Christmas, we travelled west and proceeded to lose to Vancouver, Edmonton and Los Angeles. In the first of those games, on December 27 in Vancouver, we were a sluggish bunch, and I started giving it to the guys, including Mellanby. I said to him, "I sent you home to eat some turkey, not the whole thing. Your face is redder than a baboon's ass!" I gave it to a few others, too, but we still lost. At various times we were also without Mark Howe and Peter Zezel, injuries that really hurt us.

We meandered through the next two months, playing at a 12–13–2 clip heading into March, but there were a few interesting games. We got a glimpse of Hextall's temper in a game in New Jersey in late January. At the end of the game there was a monster brawl. At first there was shoving, and Ron, who hadn't played, grabbed Devils goalie Alain Chevrier and fists were flying. We lost 4–3.

We had no shortage of toughness on our team. One of the tougher guys was defenceman Daryl Stanley, who was a character, to say the least. One day he didn't show for practice. One of the players said he had gone bear hunting. I thought it was a joke. He turned up the next day and I asked where the hell he had been, and he said, "I thought the boys told you, it's hunting season!"

We played better in March, despite losing Tocchet, Zezel and Sinisalo again to injury. I pushed the team hard to try to keep them focused for the playoffs, hopeful our injured players would return. Despite finishing with 46 wins and 100 points, our final game of the season was disappointing. We were in the lead to win the Jennings Trophy, but wound up losing it because of a 9–5 loss to the Islanders. That prompted Clarke to announce to the media: "There are no excuses for that kind of a regular-season effort. The coach has to share some of the blame."

So, we finished first in our division, had 113-, 110- and 100-point seasons, 52-, 53- and 46-win seasons, a trip to the final. Three division titles. And the GM is on my case—even after all the injuries. Obviously, I gave it out, so I couldn't complain about someone taking a shot across my bow. But heading into the playoffs, Clarke's comment certainly left me with the distinct impression that another early exit would not be good for my job security.

The playoffs brought yet another first-round meeting with the Rangers. While still a good team, these Rangers were a different team than the one that had knocked us out the previous spring. Coach Ted Sator had been fired after just 19 games when they got off to a 5–10–4 start to the season. The new GM, Phil Esposito, replaced Ted with Tom Webster. But when Webster took ill, Esposito went behind the bench himself for the final 46 games. Despite not being as formidable defensively as they were the previous season, the Rangers and goalie John Vanbiesbrouck blanked us 3–0 in the series opener at the Spectrum.

Despite the loss, I still felt confident about our bunch, and I wasn't pushing too hard. I believed we would bounce back and we did, winning big, 8–3, to even up the series. We chased Vanbiesbrouck in that game and got three on Froese. We weren't just beating up on the goalies, either. Our enforcer Dave Brown, a big, mean fighter, beat up the much smaller George McPhee, which prompted Esposito to announce to the media that I had sent out Brown to go after McPhee. What can I say? Brownie knew what his role was.

According to reports, Esposito was especially pissed that the fight had been replayed on the scoreboard. When he saw Jay Snider before the third game, he called the owner's son a "no-class fuck." Jay's response was a simple "Fuck you, Phil." We won that night, 3–0, with Ron earning the shutout. Before Game 4, Esposito went after me with the media, with the sending-Brownie-after-McPhee rhetoric. If we were in his head, all the better, although we didn't play well at all that night and lost 6–3. I pulled Ron down 3–0 to try to kick-start the team, then put him back in. He was making saves and taking hacks at the Rangers, which had Esposito chirping him at the end of the game.

The fifth game was tight, but we managed to win 3–1, the final goal into an empty net. Froese played very well, but he shared the net for the next game and we cruised to a 5–0 win. To win that series in six was special; it was revenge, knocking them out in the first round. And being able to come back and win gave our team confidence going into round two.

Next up were the Islanders, who two days earlier (actually, just less than two days) had played the longest Game 7 in Stanley Cup history. Down 3–1 in their series with the Washington Capitals, the Isles battled back to force that seventh game on the road. Down 2–1 late in the third, they got a goal from Bryan Trottier to force an overtime that refused to end. The game became known as the Easter Epic, because it started on Saturday night and ended in the early hours of Easter Sunday, with Pat LaFontaine scoring at 8:47 of the fourth overtime. The two teams played a total of 128:47, more than two full regulation games.

Given how quickly our opener put New York on the ice after that marathon game, it was important we have a good start. And we did, scoring early and taking a 3–0 lead after one period. We were missing some key players. Sutter was out, Poulin again had cracked ribs, and Murray Craven had a broken foot. We called up Al Hill and Don Nachbaur, who both contributed. But the Isles were missing Denis Potvin, Mike Bossy, Brent Sutter and Patrick Flatley, all good-to-great players. We made it 4–0 in the second, with Tim Kerr scoring a hat trick, and won 4–2.

The second game was settled by power-play goals, and I took the blame for one. We outshot them 41–26 on the night, but Kelly Hrudey was brilliant in goal, just as he had been in the epic series finale against the Caps. We finally beat him early in the third period, Doug Crossman scoring on the power play, but two minutes later Potvin, who was back and playing well, tied it with the man advantage. In the final minute of the period, we got caught with too many men on the ice. I had told Zezel to be ready for the change; he jumped on, not realizing Propp had already hit the ice. I was running the bench; I took the blame. Truth is, I was mad at Propp, who needed to play better. Mikko Makela scored on the power play with three seconds left. That stung.

Propp responded to a firm, honest talk we had after that second game and scored what proved to be the winning goal in Game 3 as we built a 3–0 lead, played well defensively and won 4–1. Tim Kerr, playing with a bad shoulder, continued to carry a hot stick in the fourth game, scoring two power-play goals. Propp, who had been quiet in previous playoffs, had a goal and an assist, and we beat the Isles, who had Bossy and Sutter back, 6–4 to take a 3–1 series lead.

Remembering full well how the Isles had come back against the Caps, and knowing they had a lot of their injured back in the lineup, we wanted to finish them off in Game 5 back home. We didn't. The Isles won it on a Randy Wood deflection early in the third.

That loss was hard to take, but we had an even tougher one in Game 6. That bad shoulder Kerr was nursing had become unplayable, although I still dressed him and hoped he might be able to do something on the lip of the crease on the power play. But he was done for the playoffs. A huge loss. The entire night was a huge loss, actually. The Isles led 2–0 after one. We cut the lead in the second, but Hextall was called for an iffy delay of game early in the third. I thought it was a bad call by Andy Van Hellemond— Ron had swatted the puck over the glass while making a save; he wasn't playing it. On the power play Trottier scored. Propp got us back to within one, but the Isles won 4–2 to force Game 7.

Obviously, all the talk after Game 6 and between games was about the never-say-die Islanders: Were they about to pull off another stunning upset comeback? And there were questions about us not closing the deal. But in fairness, we were a banged-up team, missing several key pieces. Between games, Clarkie suggested that we take the team to a comedy club. It was a great idea. The pressure was so immense; they needed the diversion to take their minds away from it all. And it was a bit of set-up—the comedian made fun of me, much to the players' delight. It was a good break for them.

Without Kerr and Craven, we received a huge boost for that seventh game with the return of Poulin. He had been fitted with a flak jacket and took painkillers and somehow played with those damaged ribs. Our team was jacked. Brown opened the scoring early with a tip-in, then we scored two short-handed goals 33 seconds apart—Propp and Brad Marsh—and we led 3–0 after one. We controlled the game after that. Sinisalo scored twice in the third and we won 5–1. I was very proud of the group: battling through the injuries, our farmhands contributing and playing well, Poulin being the consummate leader, and dealing with the pressure of Game 7.

In the third round, we met the defending Stanley Cup–champion Montreal Canadiens, who had taken advantage of our elimination and Edmonton's the previous spring. The Canadiens had swept Boston in their opening round, and now were coming off a hard-fought seven-game series with the Quebec Nordiques. They were a good and big team, and our series would be a good one, but it is remembered more for what happened before a game than during it.

We took a 3–1 series lead, again, but couldn't close the deal at home in the fifth game, losing 5–2 and sending us back to the Forum, where all hell broke loose. Habs winger Claude Lemieux and centre Shayne Corson had a habit at the end of warm-up of waiting until our guys had left the ice and then shooting the puck into our empty net. It was a ritual. In Game 3, big Ed Hospodar had stayed on the ice and intercepted Lemieux's shot and sent it back into their goal. Same thing had happened before Game 4, except this time Chico Resch turned the net around before leaving the ice. Prior to the fifth game, Chico had turned our net around again, but Chris Chelios turned it back around and Lemieux fired the puck into it.

Now it's Game 6. Lemieux and the Canadiens left the warm-up without shooting any pucks. Hospodar and Chico waited for the last of the Habs to leave the ice before leaving it themselves. But our guys lingered in the walkway to the dressing room, keeping an eye out, and wouldn't you know it—Lemieux and Corson came charging back on the ice. Hospodar and Chico went flying back on the ice themselves. Words were briefly exchanged, and next thing, Hospodar is beating the crap out of Lemieux, rag-dolling him. Our equipment guy came back to the dressing room hollering that there was a fight. At first there were only four or five guys from both teams watching Eddy pummel Lemieux. Pretty quickly, though, everyone went charging back out of the dressing room and onto the ice. Some guys were half undressed. Doug Crossman had flip-flops on. Of course, all the Canadiens came out as well. We had a lot of fighters and so did they.

Unlike today, when officials watch the warm-up (as a result of this brawl), they were in their locker room getting dressed. I came out of the coach's area to the bench, and Mr. Snider had made his way down to the hallway. There were a bunch of fights going on. Brown, without a shirt, was fighting Chris Nilan, and it was a long one. Chris Chelios tried to step in, but that's when the melee really started. Nachbaur took on Larry Robinson, and there were a few other scraps, too. Mr. Snider hollered at me to go out and stop the brawl. I said, "No way, I have patent leather shoes on. I'm not going out there." One thing I did do, however, was order one of the trainers to lock the dressing room door with Hextall inside. I didn't need him fighting. He was yelling; he wanted out. I said, "no way." He said he had to fight for his teammates. I said, "You have to play goal for your teammates."

I had dressed extra players for the warm-up that night. I think I had 24 skaters and two goalies, while Montreal had 18 and 2. I don't think I brought so many players out because I sensed something would happen. I just wasn't sure about our lineup, because I had contemplated putting Poulin back in, for instance.

The brawl lasted about 10 minutes. The late John McCauley, who was the league's director of officiating, and stand-by referee Don Koharski watched the brawl from the penalty box. Eventually, referee Andy Van Hellemond and linesmen Bob Hodges and Wayne Bonney emerged to settle things down. All the while, the organist kept playing and the fans were screaming and hanging on the glass. *Hockey Night in Canada* came on the air and the brawl was still going on. The first period started late. Out of all of that and lots of discussion, Hospodar received a game misconduct and was suspended for the rest of the playoffs.

The Canadiens came out strong in the first period, but a pissed off Hexy—he had been damn near in tears in the dressing room—stood on his head and gave us a chance. We were down 2–1 after the first—a banged-up, courageous Poulin had scored short-handed—and 3–1 early in the second, but then we started to assert ourselves. We did not want another Game 7. Tocchet ended up scoring the winner seven minutes into the third period. We won 4–3. When it was over, Canadiens coach Jean Perron wouldn't shake my hand, like I was responsible for the brawl. The media was fixated on the brawl at the post-game press conference, which I partly understood, but we had just beat the defending Cup champions, setting up a rematch from two springs earlier with the mighty Oilers, and there were plenty of storylines to the Flyers' victory, including three wins at the Forum. Needless to say, I expressed my displeasure.

We were a more experienced team than the first time we faced the Oilers in the final. We knew how to play them. But we were banged up. Kerr was out, Poulin was playing with broken ribs, Crossman had a sore groin, Sinisalo a bum knee. Not having Timmy was huge—he was a 58-goal scorer. If he's healthy, maybe we can beat them. They were a great team, and looking for redemption after losing to Calgary the previous spring. The injuries mounted. In the first minute of Game 1, Howe got hit by Messier, suffered a thigh contusion and was never quite the same after that. I know injuries are an excuse, but sometimes they're also a reason.

In my mind, the Oilers were even better than the 1985 team that beat us. They had all the usual future Hall of Fame suspects, led by Gretzky and Messier and Coffey, but they had added depth. In the opener, we were tied 1–1 heading into the third period, but the Oilers flexed their offensive muscle and beat us 4–2. There were two days off between games. I had gotten so frustrated with Zezel's play that I made him sit in a separate dressing room between games for practice, in part to embarrass him and in part to motivate him. Iron was pissed, but upon reflection not proud. We actually led 2–1 heading into the third period in Game 2, but a couple of mistakes and the Oilers won 3–2 in overtime.

Despite the crazy atmosphere in the Spectrum, Game 3 did not start well. We were down 3–0 two minutes into the second period, but the character of the team shone through again. The guys refused to quit. Craven and Zezel scored before the period was over to narrow the lead to a goal. Then, in the third, Mellanby and McCrimmon scored early, 17 seconds apart, to give us the lead, and Propp capped it off with an empty-net goal for a 5–3 win, the first time in 43 years—we were told—that a team had erased a three-goal deficit to win a game in the Stanley Cup final. The excitement was short-lived. Gretzky went to work in the fourth game, a decisive 4–1 Oilers win. It was a few minutes after Mike Krushelnyski had scored the final goal midway through the period that Hextall got slashed by Glenn Anderson, so he gave a vicious two-hander to the first guy who crossed his path, whacking the back of Kent Nilsson's leg, leaving him down and out and us with a five-minute penalty to kill—and uncertain whether Hexy would receive supplemental discipline. He did, but incredibly the eight-game suspension was deferred until the start of the following season. That was a break for us.

To take away some of Hexy's effectiveness, the Oilers would dump the puck into the left corner as often as possible, to make him handle the puck on his backhand. We told him to be a little more selective leaving the net.

Prior to the fifth game, the City of Champions—as Edmonton liked to call itself, for its numerous hockey and football championships—was pretty pumped and ready for a big celebration. I knew the Stanley Cup was in the building just in case, so I asked if we could bring it into our dressing room after the morning skate. I figured it couldn't hurt to give the guys an up-close look and a reminder of what we were playing for, not that they needed it. But when you see the Cup, when you see the names inscribed on it, it can be very inspiring, to say the least. Despite that, we started the game like we wanted to see the Cup presented to Edmonton that night. We gave up a power-play goal three minutes in, and early in the second period we were down 3–1, with the Oilers trying to push Hexy over the brink once again. But he stood tall.

I reunited the Propp-Eklund-Tocchet line, which had been excellent at times against the Canadiens, and they responded with three goals, including Tocchet's third-period goal to give us a 4–3 win and send the series back to Philly, with Hextall outstanding again.

The atmosphere in the Spectrum was electric for Game 6, as you would expect. We had adopted the Starship song "Nothing's Gonna Stop Us Now" as our playoff anthem. That night, when Hexy came flying onto the ice, the music blaring, the building exploded. It was amazing. Unfortunately, for the fourth straight game we gave up a goal early and trailed by two after the first. But our goalie gave us a chance, kept the damage to a minimum, and held on to give us a 3–2 victory and a return trip to Edmonton for Game 7—and a chance to dream.

It would be our league-record 26th game of the spring in 52 days, but no one was complaining. We had a chance. Down 3–1, facing elimination, and now taking it to a Game 7: I was proud of the group. In Edmonton, Glen Sather was an experienced coach. I think Slats kept the Oilers away from the arena; he didn't want them answering for how they twice didn't finish off this beat-up team from Philly.

We had a good feeling. The night before the game, I remember sitting in a bar in the hotel with Clarkie having a beer and saying, "Is this the best time ever?" I was wondering if Hexy had gotten into the Oilers' heads a little bit with his saves. They had been running him, trying to get him unsettled. In fact, just 34 seconds into the game, Messier cross-checked Hextall and we were on the power play. Thirty-nine seconds after that, Coffey was called for holding and we had a two-man advantage. Craven scored to give us the lead and then Crossman had a chance to put us up by two. His shot went through Grant Fuhr's legs and the puck sat on the goal line, but it got cleared away. If only . . .

The Oilers scored an incredible goal to tie it. We had our chances, but it was Hexy who kept us alive, outshot 43–20. Jari Kurri, who had found another gear, put the Oilers ahead in the second and Anderson finished us off in the third. Edmonton won 3–1 and our hearts were broken again. As he should have, Hexy won the Conn Smythe Trophy as most valuable player in the play-offs. At the time, he was just the fourth player from the losing team to win it, and only the third goaltender—Detroit's Roger Crozier had accomplished the feat in 1966 and St. Louis' Glenn Hall in 1968. The only other was Flyers winger Reggie Leach in 1976.

Years later, Hexy was quoted as saying, "The moment I take the most pride in as an individual and as a team was to take that Edmonton team to Game 7. It was a monumental task for us.

Timmy Kerr was out and we had a lot of guys who were beat up.
Poulin had broken ribs. Howe had a bad leg. We were literally
bandaged together and for us to take that team as far as we did,
I take a lot of pride in that. But also—and I don't know if 'regret'
is the right word—but the one thing I would change about my
career would be the outcome of one game. We put so much into
that playoff run. We only played two games below the maximum
number (28) of playoff games, all the travel . . . it was a grind. It
was incredible. It really was."

I couldn't agree more. And as proud as I was, getting that close
only made it hurt more. If we'd only gotten that second goal
early . . . Another time, another team, we might have been the
champions.

I remember sitting down on the plane to come home. I was
totally exhausted. And the tears started rolling down my cheeks.
I was sad for the players because of how much they had given me
and each other, their effort, despite their injuries. As Ron noted,
we played 26 games that spring. We couldn't win quick and it
took a toll. We'd had a lot going on in Philadelphia: the early
success with the youngest team, the death of a Vezina Trophy
winner, three 100-plus-point seasons, 152 wins—the fastest ever
for a rookie coach—but there was shit to come with the Flyers.

8

OH, CANADA: GRETZKY TO LEMIEUX— THE 1987 CANADA CUP

I WAS SITTING on the deck at my cottage one July night, staring out over Georgian Bay, when the idea first came to me. It was five or six weeks after my Philadelphia Flyers had lost the Stanley Cup final in seven games, and the loss was still grinding on me. It was also just a few weeks ahead of my next big assignment, coaching Team Canada in the 1987 Canada Cup. I was still thinking hockey.

The idea was to put the game's two greatest centres and players—Wayne Gretzky and Mario Lemieux—together on the same line at some point in the tournament. I wouldn't do it in the first game, but I wanted to have a trump card to play when we really needed it. I thought, *What is going to be the difference maker? What is going to surprise the opposition and be effective?* I didn't want the Soviets to see that combination practising or playing together before that final series, although I would have used it in the semifinals if we were desperate. I kept that to myself. I didn't even tell my assistant coaches or the managers. And I didn't tell the players, including Wayne and Mario.

Yes, they were together on the power play and I would sometimes double shift them, landing them on the ice at the same time, but I decided that night that I wouldn't play them as a set line until we needed it most. But more about that later.

That 1987 Canada Cup, especially the final three-game series with the Soviets, was the best hockey I had ever been involved in. Gretz said the same when it was over.

The general managers for Team Canada were Glen Sather, who I had just coached against in the Stanley Cup final; Bobby Clarke, my boss with the Flyers; Montreal GM, Serge Savard; and New York Rangers GM, Phil Esposito, the star of the 1972 Summit Series, the forerunner to all these great international series. The Canada Cup was organized by Alan Eagleson, who was also part of the 1972 series and had become my agent when Rob Campbell was busy with other business. He oversaw Team Canada, as well. Eagle first offered the coaching job to Sather, who had led Canada to victory in the 1984 Canada Cup and was the defending Stanley Cup champion, but he said no. Slats suggested they hire me. We had just come off our second Cup final against each other, and he said I was an excellent coach. Eagle reached out and I was honoured to accept. I have to admit, the prospect of coaching that team was a little intimidating. I was a young coach, and I had a team with the likes of Gretzky, Messier, Lemieux, Coffey, Fuhr, guys who had won Stanley Cups. But I welcomed the challenge and the experience.

Slats recommended his co-coach with the Oilers, John Muckler, as one of my assistants. Serge recommended his head coach, Jean Perron, who had coached the NHL All-Stars at

Rendez-vous '87 back in February. So my staff consisted of one guy I had just coached against in an emotional final and a guy who wouldn't shake my hand after a pre-game brawl in Montreal. I asked to also have my old University of Toronto coach Tom Watt, who was coaching the Vancouver Canucks. But we came together as a staff: we had a job to do and couldn't let anything personal get in the way.

The GMs, obviously, ran the selection process for training camp, which started in Montreal on August 3, but I had some input into the invitations. I didn't want too many players showing up, because that meant making more cuts. We settled on 35 players, leaving only a dozen to be trimmed to get down to the 23-man roster. Gretz was actually late in saying he would play; he took some time after his Cup win on May 31—the longest season in NHL history, at the time. Wayne was tired. He had played a lot of hockey, and he had even suggested, earlier, that the tournament be played in 1989. He was also trying to renegotiate his contract with the Oilers. Eagleson pushed hard with the patriotism card. When it was announced I would be the coach, I flew to California to ask Wayne to participate. We knew we had to get him on board to convince the rest to come. He eventually accepted and arrived in great shape.

The 1984 Canada Cup team had taken a while to come together because the Oilers and Islanders didn't like each other. The Oilers and Flyers didn't have that issue. Earlier in the summer, I'd driven an hour or so north of my cottage to see Paul Coffey at his. I asked him a question: "With the Flyers and Oilers having met twice in the final, would me coaching the team be an issue for the Oilers?" He said, "No problem whatsoever. The Oilers are all about winning—let's win." I also asked him if there were any lingering hard feelings from the Cup final and he said, "No, we won!" To make certain the Oilers and Flyers got along, I had them room together. I made the two captains, Gretz and Dave Poulin, roommates, and I put Coffey with Rick Tocchet, who also later roomed with Mess.

As it evolved, I had to cut some future Hall of Famers, a lot of them. When we first gathered, I was thinking about putting together a balanced team, not an all-star team, with people willing to take on different roles. In our first meeting, I asked the players how many minutes were in a game. Larry Murphy said 60. I said no, 720. Each team has six players on the ice at the same time, for a 60-minute game. Barring overtime, that makes 360 minutes per team. Give the goaltender 60 of those 360 minutes and distribute time after that. I was standing at the whiteboard and asked the group, "Do you mind if Gretz, Mess, Coffey and [Raymond] Bourque play 25 minutes each out of the remaining 300?" I also thought of this while I was sitting on the deck at the cottage. I said to Dale Hawerchuk, "You're a 100-plus-point player. You're going to play 15 minutes, not the 25 that Gretz is getting." It was a way to show how I was going to distribute ice time for certain players and roles. I got down to five minutes left and Tocchet, who was playing for me with the Flyers, put up his hand up and said, "Can I have the final five?" I answered, "Only if we stay out of the penalty box." Rick remembers this differently. He has said he didn't have the jam to speak up like that, but someone did, someone made the crack, and we had a good laugh. But the point was made. I thought it was a neat way to explain to superstars that you're getting a certain role and you know what your minutes are going to be, so you can prepare to be the best at your role. Doug Gilmour said, "I don't care how much or where I play, I just want to be on the team."

Our first practice in camp at the Forum started at noon. One of my favourite sayings is *If you're not five minutes early, you're five minutes late*. It was 11:59 a.m. and Gretz wasn't on the ice. He was trying to run the media gauntlet, fulfilling another of his obligations. I will never forget how, when he stepped on the ice, his face lit up. This was where he wanted to be. This was where he was free. I remember thinking, *This is why he's one of the greatest.* Someone asked me later if I was going to discipline Gretz for being late. I said, "I may be crazy, but I'm not that crazy." His father, Walter, used to drive with me to the rink and he always said, "Don't treat Wayne special. He's just one of the players." Humility from father to son. But no, I wasn't going to punish Wayne. He was representing the team with the media. It didn't hurt, either, that when the team was standing at centre ice, together around the faceoff circle, he stood next to me, pushed himself against my shoulder and said, "Guys, we're going to do whatever Mike wants us to do." Great stuff.

We were in Banff for the last part of training camp—in part because Slats had a house there and we were opening the tournament in Calgary—when we made the final cuts. I remember we had a big barbecue at Slats's house, and he was so pissed at me. I kept the team a little longer at practice and we were late arriving. The management team and a bunch of sponsors and guests were all waiting for us. Ann Sather sensed Slats was mad. I had a Flyers jacket on. She grabbed an Oilers jacket and we switched. Ann was from Philly. She introduced me as the newest Oiler; she was the newest Flyer. Everyone had a laugh. But showing up late was an Iron Mike move. Practice came first. I did that with Mr. Snider in Philly, too, making the coaches late for a gathering at his house while we did our season-ending summaries, which could have waited. Just another example of me sometimes being too focused to read the political and social landscape.

Anyway, making the cuts was not easy. Even if I wanted a balanced team, it would still be an all-star team, because everyone competing for a spot was just that good. Virtually none of these guys—throughout their careers, growing up, in junior hockey, even in the pros—had ever been cut. They had always been an important part of their teams. On defence, Kevin Lowe, Doug Wilson and Paul Reinhart were injured. I didn't have to worry about cutting Larry Robinson. He was committed to a polo tournament. Larry was big into polo.

We decided to keep Doug Crossman, who had gone to the final twice with me in Philly, and James Patrick. We cut Scott Stevens, who became a Hall of Famer, and he was not happy with that decision. He wasn't interested in being a seventh defenceman. But I wanted a mix on the blue line. We had Coffey, Bourque and Murphy, so plenty of offence. Crossman was a bit of both, good with the puck, solid defensively. Normand Rochefort from the Quebec Nordiques was a surprise. Serge recommended him. Normand was a steady, stay-at-home, dependable defenceman. He played exactly as Serge assured me he would. We also had Craig Hartsburg on the blue line, who was rock solid. We built a balanced defence.

I told the goalie group that Grant Fuhr was going to be our number one unless he stumbled. Patrick Roy denies it to this day, but he said if he wasn't number one he wasn't going to stay.

Serge believed otherwise, that Patrick would back up. Exhibiting my characteristic political savvy, I cut him while we were in Montreal. That got the local media fired up, and Serge wasn't happy with me and the management group, either. If we based the selection process on what the players actually did in camp, Kelly Hrudey was the best goalie. I said to him, "You've been the best, but Grant just won the Cup. I want to give him a chance to step up his game when it gets to the real games." Kelly and Ron Hextall, who had just won the Conn Smythe Trophy, didn't have an issue with that.

Some of the earlier cuts were future Hall of Famers Steve Yzerman, Al MacInnis, Dino Ciccarelli and Cam Neely, who might have had a bad hip or knee. We also cut Kirk Muller, Doug Lidster, Tony Tanti and Wendel Clark, who had a good camp. But again, we were fitting together pieces and moved guys around. Gilmour and Hawerchuk, for instance, moved from centre to the wing. We had so many centres. Sylvain Turgeon broke a bone in his arm courtesy of a Hexy slash, which my goalie insists to this day was unintentional.

Stevens and Poulin were the last cuts and the toughest. Poulie was tough because he was my captain with the Flyers, a heart-and-soul guy, but he was still hurting from the Cup final, in which he'd played with broken ribs. And we were deep at centre. Poulie understood. I told him, "If there is some solace, at least you lasted longer than some future Hall of Famers." We had to make hard decisions, but that's what running a hockey team is about.

Those who survived the cuts were all willing to accept any role, to play any position. We had a lot of winning experience and character. We may have cut six future Hall of Famers, but we kept 12. And of the final 23, five were Oilers and four were Flyers, the two Cup finalist teams.

It still took a while in camp for the team to come together. I was trying to find the proper mix and balance. Who plays well together? How do you make a checking line out of these guys? We got spanked 9–4 in an exhibition game against the Soviet Union, but I wasn't much concerned. My practices were demanding, as always, but short and hard at game tempo. It's what the players liked. They didn't want to stand around and be told what to do. Fifty, 60 minutes was enough. And during camp I had the players on the ice at noon or later so they could have some fun at night and still get their rest.

The fun, of course, stopped after our opening game of the tournament at Calgary's Saddledome on August 28, a disappointing 4–4 tie with Czechoslovakia, although I later heard some of the players weren't happy with me and my methods from the first day of training camp. We outshot the Czechs 40–36, and a young Dominik Hašek was terrific in goal, but we allowed three leads to slip away and I wasn't happy. And soon enough the players weren't happy with me. Or they were unhappier. Their wives, girlfriends and families had all arrived when we were in Banff. After the game, I was so mad that I took the players back to the hotel for the post-game meal and kept them away from their families. That did not go over very well. But I wanted the group to focus, to understand what we were up against. And if being pissed off at me would help to bring them together faster, so be it. It wasn't the first time I had used that method to pull a team together, and it wouldn't be the last.

The next day, the players met on the ice following the morning skate. Later, the leadership group of Gretz, Mess and Bourque called Eagleson to voice their complaints about me. Eagle says, "Okay, I'm not going to fire him, let's work this out." He encouraged them to meet with me. It was later, when we were in Montreal and there were more complaints, that we met. They wanted me to back off. Mess talked to me about it. The guys complained that I was pushing too hard. They said, "We're giving up our summer. You're working us so bloody hard, our families are here and we don't see them." They said some guys had refused to give up their summer to be here, but they were here. Gretz made the point that the Oilers and Flyers had played so deep into the spring; they were tired.

I took it all in. I listened. And then I said to them, "Does Canada want us to win the tournament?" They said yes. I said, "In training camp, did you ever have curfew?" No. "Did I ever check?" No. I said, "Do you want me to tell the Canadian public that you guys don't want to work? I have practices at noon so you can sleep in. Do you want me to tell the public you're enjoying the night life?" Wayne says, "Mike, there will never a problem again, see you tomorrow." I knew that in the final we would likely play the Soviets, who train for 11 months of the year. They were an unbelievable team. In the end, our players needed those short, vigorous practices to help with their conditioning.

Years later, Mess said I might have miscalculated the players' commitment, that I pushed the players in a way I didn't need to. But it did galvanize the team. It was a short tournament and we simply couldn't lose. When you're coaching a group of superstars, you have to convince and mould them into certain roles, pull them together. To their credit, no one complained about ice time. The egos never surfaced. I am glad the leadership group—Wayne, Mess, and Bourque, in particular—handled matters the way they did.

I listened to them, too, and I did back off, because I knew my message had been received, and I knew the group we had would respond,
especially with those guys in charge of the room. And they did.

Of course, none of that meant I was done pissing them off.
I was big into proper nutrition and inflicted my dietary restrictions on the group. I didn't believe in steaks for the pre-game meal.
I was more into chicken, fish and pasta, and definitely no ice
cream for dessert. Well, apparently Gretz grew up eating steak and
potatoes before every game—his father's orders. And he had
vanilla ice cream for dessert. Before one of the games, he announced
to the group that if he didn't get his steak, potatoes and ice cream,
he wasn't playing. The waiter ran out of the room and returned
with his order. Everyone laughed. Mess was adamant about getting
his ice cream, too. I gave in on that one. The next game, I made
sure there were steaks and ice cream on the table.

In our second game, two nights later in Copps Coliseum in
Hamilton, we took an early lead, played better and beat Finland,
4–1. We followed that up with a 3–2 win over the United States,
which was really the Mario and Wayne Show. We trailed by a goal
after the first period, but then Mario tied it early in the second,
and he gave us the lead on the power play, set up by Gretz, with
three seconds left in the period. He completed the hat trick, again
on the power play and set up by Gretz, six minutes into the third,
and we held on to win.

Next up was Sweden at the Forum in Montreal. The Swedes
are always a test, and they pushed us on this night. Gretz on the
power play gave us the lead two minutes in, but we trailed by a
goal after one. Mario and Mike Gartner put us up in the second,
but we were tied early in the third. Mario, with his fifth, again

from Gretz, gave us the lead, and Michel Goulet sealed a 5–3 victory. An even bigger test was ahead against the Soviets to close out the round-robin portion of the tournament.

It was a dandy of a game, too, between two incredibly skilled teams. The Soviets had the famed Green Unit. This consisted of the KLM Line, which was at its peak, of Igor Larionov between Sergei Makarov and Vladimir Krutov, with Slava Fetisov and Alexei Kasatonov on defence. Knowing we would most likely be meeting in the final, I needed to create a line that could shut down their big five. I used a number of combinations, but I knew Mess at centre could handle Larionov. Those games were vicious, and I knew Mess would punish Larionov. Mess didn't have an ego; he embraced being on the checking line. I put Mike Gartner and Glenn Anderson on the wings, both exceptional skaters.

It was a terrific game. We led 1–0 after the first period, with Anderson scoring from Mario. The best was yet to come in the tournament for Mario, of course, but this was his coming-out party. Wayne was an incredible example, mentor and leader. He talked a lot with Mario and taught him everything he knew in a crash course for two reasons: one, to make the team better, of course, and two, because Wayne needed to be pushed in the NHL and this young guy coming along could do that. Wayne was so unselfish. He would talk to all his teammates, but particularly this young player, who grew up as a player overnight, or so it seemed to me. Mario had been in the league for three seasons and was living up to his advance billing in terms of goals and points, but taking his play to the next level was new to him; he had never won.

We didn't have a strong second period and trailed 3–1, but Bourque on the power play and Gretz late earned us a 3–3 tie. It would not be our last great comeback against the Soviets. We finished the round robin in first place with a 3–0–2 record and a semifinal date with the Czechs. The Soviets finished 3–1–1 and would play the Swedes in their semi.

The Czechs gave us a mighty scare again. Hašek was outstanding, and they led 2–0 halfway through the game. To say there was some tension in the Forum was an understatement, but we were still confident on the bench. We generated a lot of quality chances, but couldn't get anything by Hašek. I felt that if we kept pushing, we could break through. We just had to make sure the next goal was scored by us. As is my way, I put the lines in a blender and used upwards of 20 different combinations. It was new to some of the players, but I liked to keep them on edge and keep the opposition guessing, especially in a short tournament.

Finally, Hawerchuk got one past Hašek, and that ignited the team. Just 42 seconds after that, Mario tied it, and 43 seconds after that he scored again, his seventh goal of the tournament. We were ahead, and Michel Goulet gave us a much-needed two-goal lead. It survived until late in the third, when David Volek scored, but Brian Propp sealed the victory with 2:04 left.

The Soviets, meanwhile, had a relatively easy go of it with Sweden, who had beaten them 5–3 in the round robin and had nine NHL players on their roster. But on this night, the Soviets took a commanding 3–0 lead midway through the second period and went on to a 4–2 victory, setting the stage for the best-of-three final everyone had expected and wanted—Canada versus the Soviet Union. What was to follow was arguably the greatest hockey series ever played.

No doubt, the 1972 Summit Series was magnificent for many reasons, not least because it was the first time our best professional players took to the ice against theirs. That series was about more than establishing international hockey supremacy—it was political as well. It was the West versus the East, capitalism versus communism, our way of life versus theirs. Talk to the players from that '72 team and it's clear that in their minds it was a war of sorts—a hockey Cold War that I'd experienced as a student at U of T. I watched the final game standing on Yonge Street, following the action on TVs in a department store window because I didn't have a TV. I remember the immense feeling of pride when Canada won.

The political tensions might not have been as intense this time around, with Soviet communism on the verge of collapse, but it was still us versus them, the last hurrah for good versus evil, as Murphy put it. I did feel the pressure and expectation of winning for our country. For a bunch of young guys, that was a lot of pressure. And, of course, hockey supremacy was at stake, with a fresh dose of bad blood in the mix. Remember, a few months earlier, back in January in Czechoslovakia, our juniors were involved in the famous Punch-up in Piestany in the final game of the World Junior Championship, also against the Soviets. A bench-clearing brawl stretched on for 20 minutes, so long that the officials actually turned the lights out in the rink to try to stop the fighting. Both teams were disqualified from the tournament, which probably cost Canada gold.

In February, Quebec City had hosted the two-game Rendez-vous '87 series, which replaced the traditional NHL All-Star Game. The Soviets played a team of NHL all-stars that was made up of mostly Canadians, but included a few Swedes, Finns and Americans, too. Each team won a game, and the hockey was terrific.

The Soviets may have surprised the nation when they'd beat Canada in a few early games in '72 and proved their toughness in Piestany, but we weren't taking anything for granted this time around. We all remembered the 8–1 loss in the 1981 Canada Cup. We knew how good the Soviets were, and we knew how prepared we had to be to beat them. And there was no love lost.

Gretz later said he felt this was the best Soviet team he had played against. Coach Viktor Tikhonov rode four lines, and that ended up being part of the reason we beat them in the series. The plan was to use Mess up against Larionov, with Gartner on the right wing and Anderson, normally a right winger, on the left side. It started well for us in that first game at the Forum, with Gartner scoring 1:49 in, but then the Soviets scored three times in 8:10 to take a 3–1 lead after one, and they added another early in the second. They were clearly in control. I never seriously thought about pulling Fuhr—not at this stage of the tournament—because his trademark was to bend but not break.

We stopped the bleeding when Bourque scored on the power play to make it 4–2, and that gave us a lift heading into the intermission. Fuhr did what he does best and made a huge save early in the third. Shortly after that Gilmour scored at 1:35 and it was game on. I was again juggling my lines. I used 21 different combinations in that game. But we needed to kick-start the offence, and I wanted to keep Tikhonov wondering what was coming next. I got no pushback from the players; it didn't faze them. A lot of them wouldn't have been used to that much line juggling. With five minutes left in a thrilling period, Anderson tied it, and a couple of minutes after that Gretz gave us the lead. But just 32 seconds later, the Soviets tied it, and after Mario had a near miss, we were headed to overtime. What an amazing comeback. Just 5:33 into the extra period, Alexander Semak snapped a shot off the crossbar past Fuhr, and we lost, 6–5.

The flight from Montreal to Hamilton—the series was moving to a sold-out Copps Coliseum for Games 2 and 3—was very quiet, especially after mounting such a comeback only to lose. The great confidence of a team as talented as ours was now balanced by a measure of concern. The margin of difference between our talent and theirs was unbelievably slim. We could be great and still lose.

I remembered then something the Soviets said after the 1972 series. After they had taken a 3–1–1 lead in the series and put the Canadian team in a position where it needed to win all three remaining games, they underestimated the resolve of the Canadians. No matter the odds, that team refused to quit, in a game or a series. Years later, someone said, "You can't teach Canadian." It's true—at least, you couldn't teach one that they were beaten. And that resolve became my greatest asset as Team Canada's coach. I never had to deal with confidence in that group; I knew they would be more than ready to play the next game. Many were young, but they were experienced at winning. They took on the responsibility of representing our country and they were very proud to wear that sweater.

As it turned out, Game 2 was an absolute classic, considered by many as one of the greatest games ever played. The tempo, the flow, the back and forth, the incredible action, the drama.

Fuhr made a huge save in the early going, then Normand Rochefort—who was on the team for his defence—gave us the lead 43 seconds into the game. But the back and forth began, and the Soviets tied it 44 seconds later. We had to be better, be ready for their quick pushback. Gilmour scored a couple of minutes after that, and midway through the period, after the Soviets had a goal disallowed, Coffey gave us a 3–1 lead. Special teams got the Soviets back to even with us. But before the second period was over, Mario had us ahead again, 4–3, with the set-up from Gretz.

Remember when I said that back in July, sitting on the deck at my cottage, I had thought about playing Wayne and Mario together, but not until I needed it most? Now was the time. Yes, they had been together intermittently and on power plays, but now it was time to roll them out together shift after shift. I was playing my trump card. I looked over at the Soviet bench; coach Tikhonov was staring at me, totally surprised by what I had done, creating a power line.

Tikhonov may have been surprised but he was hardly deterred. There was no more quit in this Soviet team than there was in ours, and the score was even again five minutes into the third. Then Mario and Wayne combined again to restore the lead on a power play. The action was riveting. As the coach, your level of concentration has to be extremely high—you can't get caught up in the moment or the excitement; you can't lose your focus. With just 1:04 remaining in regulation time, Valeri Kamensky, a very talented winger who would win a Cup with Colorado several years later, made a great end-to-end rush and sent the game to overtime. And the action just kept getting better. Both Fuhr and Soviet goaltender Evgeni Belosheikin, who had replaced Sergei Mylnikov after Game 1, were stopping everything thrown at them by what might be the two finest offences ever assembled in hockey. Krutov had an amazing chance in close on Fuhr in the first overtime, and then the rebound, but Grant stood tall and it was off to a second overtime. One thing we knew was that with Grant we had an edge in goal, and he would make the big save when we needed it most.

Midway through the period, Coffey rushed the puck from behind our goal towards the Soviet blue line, where Gretz was waiting on the right boards. Gretz carried the puck in and fed Mario in the slot, but he shot wide. Propp got on the puck quick and backhanded it in front. It went to the point to Murphy, who fed Gretz down low on the right side of the crease. He fired a shot, was stopped, but managed to slide the puck across the crease to Mario, who had a wide-open goal at 10:07, the 90th minute of the game, to give us a 6–5 victory.

Utter elation. Gretz finished the night with five assists, and Mario a natural hat trick. I can't say I had that extraordinary result in mind back in July on my cottage deck. But thank goodness those two great superstars meshed, because it isn't always easy for a star player to play with another star. And it wasn't easy finding another winger; there weren't too many who could feed off Wayne the way Mario did. We used a variety of players on the other side. Anyway, another great moment in Canadian hockey history with another yet to come. What a ride.

I remember after that second game, which ended in the early hours of the morning, getting back to the hotel and not being able to sleep. I ended up going for a walk to clear my head. Naturally, I was thinking ahead to the third game. I feared that a few of our guys—Gretz, Mario, Mess, Coffey, Bourque and a few others who played a lot in Game 2—might be physically and mentally drained.

Years later, Wayne said our Canada Cup team in 1991 was better than the '87 team, but I would say the Russian team in '91 was not as good as the Soviet team in '87. They were all over us at the opening of Game 3. To say we had a bad start would be an understatement. Just 26 seconds in, we turned over the puck and Makarov scored. On the second goal, seven minutes later, we got caught pressuring, and Alexei Gusarov finished off a two-on-one rush. A minute after that, Fetisov scored.

Eight minutes into the final game, we were trailing 3–0. Fans were still getting to their seats. Copps Coliseum had gone very quiet, the crowd very nervous. I'm sure a lot of fans had visions of the 1981 Canada Cup final, when the Soviets spanked Scotty Bowman and the Canadians 8–1. Now, here I was, a young coach. I'm standing behind the bench. I look up at the scoreboard, and I'm thinking if I don't do something really quickly, I might as well get in my car, drive to the cottage at Port McNicoll, go to the island and stay there and never be heard from again. This was Canada versus the Soviets, capitalism versus communism, us versus them. Losing was not an option, and certainly not a blow-out loss.

I'm sure a lot of people were wondering—down 3–0 that early, the team flat—if I would pull Fuhr. I didn't even consider it. Grant was spectacular for us. He had been in plenty of big games and we could rely on him to give us a chance to fight back. He would come up big. In his career, Grant always shut the opposition down at the right time. I knew he wouldn't be rattled, so there was no point rattling the team. Knowing those guys and how they would react, no way I pull him. I might have done it in the middle of an NHL season, to give a team a jolt.

But in a critical game like this one, 99 percent of the time you don't make that change, and the players are just as likely to appreciate your faith in their teammate and step up.

I remember Wayne telling me he was spent and needed a break, he was so exhausted. So I gave him a few shifts off. He and Mess and Mario had played so much hockey in the first two games. I caught Tikhonov looking at me again, with another confused expression. He was probably thinking *That crazy bastard Keenan has benched the best hockey player in the world.*

I started to rework the lines and used our grinders more, the likes of Tocchet, Brent Sutter, Propp, Gilmour—yes, on a team like that, those guys were our grinders. Less than two minutes later, Tocchet scored on a power play to put some life back in the building. The bench felt it too. Propp scored five minutes after that. We were back. Unfortunately, a Bourque turnover with 28 seconds left in the period led to a goal and a 4–2 deficit. Despite the score, the players had their heads back in the game. We had come back against these guys before, and we felt we could do it again. There was no panic in the room between periods.

In the second period, we came out playing very well. Gretz, Mess and Mario had found their legs again. But it was Murphy who scored on the power play midway through. Then Sutter and Hawerchuk scored, making it three goals in roughly six minutes. We were ahead 5–4. Once we got back in the game, I played Gretz and Mario every second shift. The lead held up until there were just under eight minutes left in the third period, when Semak tied it. Again, no panic, and we believed Grant would not crack. He was our advantage in goal.

With 1:36 remaining in regulation time, there was a faceoff in our zone to the left of Grant. I'm sure everyone was surprised I didn't put Mess out to take the draw, including Mess himself, who was prepared to jump on the ice. But I knew we would see Larionov and the KLM line one more time before regulation was over. I had to save Mess. I already had Gretz and Mario on the ice, and rather than put out a winger, I selected Dale Hawerchuk. He was winning a lot of faceoffs, and I had coached him in junior. I just had a feeling he could win that faceoff. That line had never played together. On defence I had Murph and Coffey, two offensive defencemen in the defensive zone. I ran the bench, both the forwards and defence. Putting out all that offensive talent in the defensive zone isn't something a lot of coaches would do, but I was coaching to win, not survive that shift and make it into overtime. Tikhonov rode four lines and they had their fourth line out.

The guys get out there and Gretz says, "I'm not taking the faceoff." Mario says, "It's the wrong side for me." Dale says, "I guess I'm taking it." At best, he wanted to win the faceoff, at worst, just tie it up, make sure they didn't win it clean, which he did. Mario jumped into the circle and pushed the puck past pinching defenceman Igor Kravchuk, who was inexperienced. Mario jumped around him and pushed it up the left wing to Gretz, who carried it into the Soviet zone. We effectively had a three-on-one. Behind the play, Hawerchuk had hooked Vyacheslav Bykov, who went down, but at that point in the game the officials were not making that call, and it did feel like a dive.

Gretz had Murph on his right side and open. Mario was the trailer. The lone Soviet defender was Igor Stelnov, and he went down trying to block a pass across to Murph, but there was no way Gretz was giving it to him, not when he had the big guy coming. Murph made a great play by going hard to net and that opened the lane for Mario, who put it top shelf, glove side—just as our scouting report had suggested—on Sergei Mylnikov, and the roof blows off Copps Coliseum. Gretzky to Lemieux! And on the other bench, Iron Tikhonov was blasting Kravchuk, who had pinched when he shouldn't have.

But we still had 1:26 remaining. The Soviets had scored in the final minute before and erased leads seconds after our goals. I remember Harry Sinden, who coached Team Canada in 1972, saying that after Henderson scored the big goal in the final game, he looked up at the clock and said, "Oh my gawd, there are still 34 seconds to go." I was having that same feeling. And I was right about holding Mess back; Larionov did come out the next shift. Facing Mess between Anderson and Gartner, and Rochefort and Bourque on defence, the Soviets never got a scoring chance in those final 86 seconds. In fact, we had a great scoring chance off the faceoff, Anderson and Gartner on a two-on-one.

In the end, we won on guts and desire. We tied the game with the muckers and grinders, and we won it with the super-skilled players. And Grant was the better goalie. One of the nicest compliments I received came from Gretz, who told everyone that Keenan outcoached Tikhonov.

I remember we had a jukebox in the hallway outside the dressing room at Copps. One day, Mike Finocchiaro, who was my video coach in Philly and with Team Canada, our public relations guy Bill Tuele, and massage therapist Juergen Merz pushed the jukebox into the dressing room. There were a few songs that we were always playing: "Bad to the Bone" by George Thorogood and the Destroyers, "Catch My Fall" by Billy Idol, Whitney Houston's "Greatest Love of All." Our theme song was "The Boys Are Back in Town" by Thin Lizzy. After we won, Dougie Gilmour was standing on the jukebox singing. And the celebration ensued. There was a big party in the banquet room at the rink, with all the families and friends. And the next morning, everyone was gone, headed back to their club teams.

I can say without a doubt that that was the greatest game I have ever been involved in, and the Game 2 was a close runner-up. Looking back, winning the Stanley Cup in New York years later, Game 7, that was incredible too. But when it's country against country, especially at that time, the context is different. The political aspect was huge. But the speed, intensity, physicality—that series had everything you could ever dream of as a player and a spectator. Guys like Gretz and Mess said they were absolutely the best games, the best hockey they ever played. The pressure on the Canadian players to win was incredibly intense. Just playing great wasn't going to fly; we had to win. Everyone could feel it, but they thrived on it.

As I mentioned earlier that tournament was a coming-out party for Mario. He ended the tournament with 11 goals in nine games, including the winners in the second and third games of the final. Gretz led the tournament with 21 points, 18 of them assists, including setting up both game winners in the final. He was named tournament MVP. Together, Gretz and Mario combined on 29 percent of our goals in the tournament. Mario learned so much from Wayne. I knew Gretz was great, but he took his game to a level I had never seen before. The leadership on that team was profound. Mess was amazing. Guys like him,

Gretz, Raymond, they made everyone feel important. They were a team—it wasn't just Wayne or Mario. They understood that to have success everyone had to buy in. And it's always nice to have a nonchalant goalie. Let one in and it's "Oh well, I'll shut the door now." That was Grant. His calm demeanour was contagious. He never got rattled.

As I mentioned earlier, one thing I learned from Gretz and Mess and a few of the Oilers in that series is that it's one thing to hate to lose, and that's fine, but you also have to celebrate the wins, find and embrace the joyful moments of winning. It took me a long time to learn that.

In the end, maybe the series wasn't 1972 but it was close, with three 6–5 games, the same score as the final game in Moscow 15 years earlier. And it ended with a where-were-you-when? moment when Mario scored, the "Henderson-has-scored-for-Canada!" moment for the next generation. It was the next-biggest goal in Canadian hockey history and an iconic moment in Canadian sports history. People in Copps Coliseum or watching on TV probably saw the best hockey of their lives that night, and we might not see hockey played to that level again.

Gretzky to Lemieux . . . the stuff you dream of while sitting on the deck at the cottage.

9

A SENSE OF FAILURE: FIRED, 1988

I TOLD BOBBY Clarke I needed a break.

It had been pretty much non-stop for me, with the Flyers playing until May 31 in the Stanley Cup final, the Team Canada training camp starting in early August, and then the incredible and intense tournament, which ended in mid-September. I needed some time to breathe. It was the same for Rick Tocchet, Brian Propp, Doug Crossman and Ron Hextall, who played for me in the Canada Cup. We all needed a break and got one. I let my two assistants, Paul Holmgren and E.J. McGuire, run the Flyers training camp and pre-season games. With a dozen days off, Rita and I went to Bermuda, which was a nice getaway until we got stuck there because of a hurricane, and I missed the end of training camp. That was quite the experience. Needless to say, there was damage to the island, the power was out for a long while, and the airport was damaged. Maybe it was a hint of the storms to follow.

My Flyers didn't get off to a good start that season. Maybe my missing training camp was a reason. It might also have had something to do with what happened on the flight home from Edmonton after we'd lost in the Stanley Cup final to the Oilers. Years later, I was told that several players had a few beers on the plane and were urging Clarke to fire me. Hearing about that, even at a distance, hurt a lot. We had just lost in Game 7 of the Stanley Cup final and all they could think about was getting the coach fired? So maybe the players weren't fully invested, maybe they had tuned me out, and maybe Clarke was having second thoughts himself.

It didn't help, either, that Hextall, the Conn Smythe winner, was suspended for the first eight games of the season because of the wild slash on Kent Nilsson during the final. We also didn't have Tim Kerr—our leading scorer and a four-time 50-plus goal scorer—because of his ongoing shoulder issues. The earliest he was going to play was two months into the season, if then. Another contract dispute—a $25,000-a-year gap—led to Brad McCrimmon, who was playing 30-plus minutes a night alongside Mark Howe, being traded to Calgary for a first- and a third-round draft pick. Tocchet had sprained his knee in the Canada Cup final and he wasn't ready to go, either. Clarke decided not to re-sign Chico Resch, so he retired, leaving us with Mark Laforest as our backup goaltender, although he started the first four games. On top of that, there was the same hangover any team experiences after losing in the final and making do with a short summer.

Whatever, excuses. After we had a decent home opener, a 2–2 tie with Montreal (and no pre-game shenanigans), we won two nights later, 5–4, in Minnesota, but then started to struggle. I pulled Laforest after two periods in a 6–0 home loss against the

New York Islanders. Wendell Young replaced him and started the next three. We were 3–4–1 when Hextall returned and helped us to a 2–2 tie against the Rangers in New York. Late in that game, Dave Brown was called for high-sticking and intent to injure Tomas Sandström, who had speared Howe. Brown levelled the hated Sandström with a cross-check to the neck and was ultimately given a 15-game suspension. Of course, there were people who blamed me for that incident.

We went 5–12–3 in our first 20 games, and I made a concerted effort to back off during that time, although I had a few moments when my temper got the better of me. I remember Clarkie and Mr. Snider getting anxious, very antsy, but I told them explicitly that the team was spent—that they were emotionally, mentally and physically drained from the previous spring, but they would come around, they would respond. And they eventually did. But I couldn't push them too soon, so I really backed off for the first 20 games. And, as I mentioned, we lost Timmy, Beast was traded, all the other stuff. It was a tough start. There was a lot of noise in the media about whether a coaching change was coming, and I'm sure the players were talking about it too. I think Mr. Snider thought maybe they were quitting on me and wanted me to be more positive. I was told years later that Clarkie didn't think they had quit.

One thing that was perhaps underestimated at the time was the loss of McCrimmon. He played those big minutes with Howe, and I believe Clarkie sent a bad message to the group by trading one of our best players over a contract difference of $25,000. Beast was also good for me in the dressing room. He may have hated me as much as the others did, but he delivered the message that we were winning, so shut up and play.

One "crisis" we had during that stretch of losing came on November 10 in St. Louis when I benched Tocchet, who afterwards told the media that I'd sat him because he ignored my orders to start a brawl. I don't remember ordering him to start a fight, but I did say after the game that the players were putting their needs ahead of the team's. Hextall, who was ornery himself after signing an eight-year extension, put an exclamation point on my point, saying, "We're a disgrace to the uniform." The next day, I resisted the temptation of putting the team through a bag skate and confronting them in the room. Instead, I had the team meet amongst themselves to discuss their struggles. The losing was putting pressure on all of us.

As much as some of the players and management would have been fine with a few more losses to prompt Clarke to fire the coach, we got some momentum in mid-November. Late in the month, I took the team to Lake Placid for a getaway. We practised in the morning, then had intra-squad games in the afternoon, which included me suiting up and taking my punishment, much to the players' delight. I might infuriate them in hopes of motivating them, but I wanted them to know I wasn't going to hide from their anger. At night, it was off to the bar, on me. From that 20-game mark, we went on a 13–1–2 run (including a 12–0–2 stretch) through December 26. Merry Christmas! In the middle of that, Hextall made hockey history. On December 8 at the Spectrum, the great puck-handler became the first NHL goalie to shoot at the goal and score, in a 5–2 win over the Boston Bruins. With their net empty, the Bruins dumped the puck into our zone and Hexy fired it right back to seal the victory.

The retreat proved a success, but I had also brought a new face to the team, Cal Botterill, a sports psychologist. I had met Cal at a coaching seminar in the summer and was impressed with him. He was a smart guy. He'd played for Canada's national team for a few years, earned a PhD at the University of Alberta and was a professor at the University of Winnipeg. His son, Jason, was a first-round pick of Dallas and has been an NHL GM. His daughter, Jennifer, is a Harvard grad and one of the top Canadian players ever.

Cal's arrival wasn't expected. In fact, we might have been one of the first teams with a sports psychologist. A coach could be afraid that bringing one in made them look unsure of themselves. I didn't see it that way. Cal's arrival was a big help. He had a different perspective, a fresh view. We did psych and personality profiles. We discussed the needs of each individual. Cal gave everybody a different perspective of where we were at as a group, helped the players build confidence. And it didn't hurt them to hear a different voice than mine.

Later in the season, I brought in yet another voice, one I respected greatly. I asked Tom Watt to watch a couple of our games and practices and give his assessment. I also brought in Scotty Bowman's old assistant from Buffalo, Red Berenson, for a few days as a consultant. Red was now the head coach at the University of Michigan. Just as Mr. Snider had supported my hiring a full coaching staff, he paid for these guys to come with some fresh ideas. I appreciated the support.

We had a ton of injuries over the second half of the season. Tim Kerr needed more work on his shoulder. Brian Propp hurt his knee. Brad Marsh got banged up. Kerry Huffman, our first pick the previous season, suffered a charley horse. On it went, leaving us to battle for a playoff spot despite spending a long stretch of the season with the best record in the league. Then Mark Howe's back started acting up again. More injuries followed, but in early March we caught a break and got Kerr and Howe back, though Timmy still needed more time. Then Hexy separated his shoulder after a collision with Mario Lemieux. Poulin also missed a long stretch. Tocchet hurt his shoulder.

We limped into the playoffs, going 4–11–2 down the stretch. We ended up third in the Patrick Division with 85 points thanks to a blown lead in the final game and a 2–2 tie against Washington and my old friend Bryan Murray, who earned second place and would be our first-round opponent. The Islanders finished first with 88 points, then Washington and us with 85—identical records but they won the tie breaker. The division had flattened out.

Despite our late-season struggles, we managed to win the series opener in Washington, 4–2—although we had another blown lead and Hexy was a bit spotty—and we went up 3–1 in the series. I pulled him in the fourth game after we trailed 4–1, but we managed to come back and win in overtime, 5–4, with Laforest between the pipes. It should have been series over already, even though we hadn't been great. We were healthy, and the Caps had a history of underachieving in the playoffs. But I give them credit; they didn't quit. The likes of Rod Langway and Scott Stevens showed their resolve. Hexy struggled again in the fifth game, and we lost 5–2. Back home for Game 6, I asked the coaching staff and Clarkie who we should start in goal. Everyone, including Clarkie, said Laforest. I went with Hexy, figuring he could get things turned around. He was our guy. We lost 7–2.

I had made my bed at that point and stuck with Hexy for the seventh game. We pumped his tires with a highlight reel from the previous spring, and we started well, leading 3–0 a few minutes into the second period. I was playing the crap out of my best players, guys like Howe and Samuelsson on the blue line. But by the end of the second, it was tied. And it was tied by the end of the third, 4–4. The Caps dominated the overtime with several great chances, and Dale Hunter scored to end the series. And my time in Philly.

Few teams could have beaten us with that kind of lead. Hexy was really struggling, but he had battled through injuries. Maybe at times he was over-competitive, which is what a lot of people said about me. But the violence became a distraction. Teams picked up on it. Guys like Hunter would talk it up, be a prick and try to distract him. Ron got sidetracked. He was a highly effective puck stopper but not technically great. And for whatever reason, he didn't like working with Bernie Parent, our goalie coach.

Nobody said anything to me right away, but I sensed it might be over for me in Philadelphia, and after the game I shared that sentiment with my coaching staff over drinks. Holmgren and E.J. and others didn't think so, or at least that's what they said. With a record of 190–102–28, and with all the injuries and Pelle's death working against us, they figured it would be status quo. Jay Snider said during the series that he was going to give me a contract extension. Maybe he was planning on it, but his father wasn't. He hadn't forgotten the brawl in Montreal when I told him there was no fucking way I was going on the ice to break it up. He was pissed, too, about the coaching staff showing up late for that party at his house after the '87 playoffs. And he thought the players had quit on me a few times through the season.

After a few weeks of silence, Alan Eagleson called Clarke to ask what was going on. The media had been speculating that I was going to get fired, rumours some people believed had come from me. There were suggestions that the players were sick of me, sick of being pushed so hard. Finally, 25 days after the season ended, Clarke called me and asked to meet the next day at the practice facility in Voorhees. I walked into my office, and he was sitting in my chair, behind my desk. He said, "Mike, I've got to fire you." I started to cry. *Fuck*. As much as I knew it could happen, I wasn't ready for it. But it was suddenly real. We'd had a tough season, but we had also gone to two Stanley Cup finals, won three division titles, finished first overall once and dealt with Pelle's death. He was pretty stoic; it was just kind of matter-of-fact. That was it. Years later, he told Jay Greenberg that it was Mr. Snider's decision. Clarkie had wanted to give me another year. He said to Mr. Snider, "He's done too much for us," but Snider said, "No, fire him." He would come to regret his decision.

Mr. Snider didn't say a word to me. But he did tell Eagleson that he wanted back the Mercedes he had given me after I took the team to the final in my first season. Eagleson said, "Are you kidding me? Do you realize how bad you're going to look when I tell the media you're taking the car back?" Turns out he had leased the car.

I guess I was naive. It blindsided me. I believed I still had the team, otherwise I wouldn't have been so emotional. I think the media was shocked as well; I'd had four very good years. A few reporters came to my home in Voorhees, waiting for me on my front yard. I had never heard Rita swear like this before, but she opened the door and said, "All of you, fuck right off!"

I know Clarke was quoted as saying the team wasn't happy and wasn't playing with emotion or enthusiasm and he thought we were going downhill. Maybe he really did feel that way. I never asked why. Maybe he did support Snider, who had the final word. He was an active owner. But at the time, I could only think the firing was unfair.

Once it had settled in, I really didn't feel sorry for myself. It was just a sense of failure. I was a perfectionist, and I didn't take losing well. I was so driven. Even my routine at home was set— we'd have a pre-game skate, then lunch, and then I would have a sleep and get up at four o'clock. Rita would give me a bowl of soup and a sandwich, or something like that. But I wouldn't talk to anybody but the coaching staff or the team from four until the game started. I was a social misfit. I didn't want to have a conversation with anybody unless we were talking about our team and what we were doing that night. I wouldn't even talk to Rita.

It felt strange not to need my mid-season routine. It was far more involved than I've let on so far. In those hours after my nap, I'd start mentally rehearsing the night's line changes and match-ups. I could tell you at the end of the game, within a minute or 30 seconds, what everybody's ice time was—on both teams. I had a computer-like mind that way. It felt like I could elevate myself and see the play from above. Now, you're going to say, *This guy is fucked up*. But it was like an out-of-body experience, although I kept that comparison to myself. People would think I was boasting or crazy, but that's what it felt like to me. I would rehearse in my mind the entire game, every situation, who would be on the power play for them, who would penalty kill for us. I'd memorize everything that was going to be done by the opposing coach and myself, our bench management skills to adapt to injuries and penalties, all the scenarios. Once the game was underway, I didn't easily get distracted. The roof would be blowing off the Spectrum and I couldn't hear the noise because I was so deep in concentration. Credit the super-focus routine I had developed back in Peterborough.

I go back to a comment Wayne Gretzky made once when someone asked him about watching video. He said, "What video, I don't watch the video, and I only know one other person who doesn't have to watch the video and that's Mike Keenan. He memorizes every play, every shift." I was able to do that. After a game, it would be very difficult to get myself out of that trance and walk into a press conference 10 minutes later.

I had an intuitive feel on the bench. We're all human beings— you can't be spot-on all the time—but on any given night, when the puck dropped at seven, I could identify who was on and off. The saying was, "With Keenan don't have a bad warm-up or a bad first shift." If Mark Howe wasn't going, I would double shift him and get him focused. If it was Derrick Smith and he had a bad shift, he might sit the rest of the period. I controlled the entire bench, forwards and defence. I built a rhythm, and I could time shifts in my head. I'd give the command: I'd put my hand up and that meant get off the ice, make a change. I'd rehearse what I could expect from the different officials. I knew who I had a rapport with and who I didn't. I knew the different linesmen, how I could mess around with the line changes to manipulate the matchups. I knew which coaches were good at it, or not, and who didn't care. Scotty always cared. You had to work really hard to get control of that part of the game, coaching against him. I had learned the game within the game, even when I played. It's art and mathematics, both. And you either learn it yourself or you don't.

Anyway, when I was let go they promoted Paul Holmgren to head coach. His wife, Doreen, was friendly with Rita. She felt guilty and flew out to say Paul hadn't undermined me and had no intentions of taking my job. I didn't think he had. Though I was kind of surprised they hired him. Maybe I shouldn't have been. He and Clarkie were best friends.

After four years, I didn't have to defend my accomplishments, just, at times, my methods. But for all my demands, there were also times when I told the players how much they meant to me, how proud I was of them. In the fall of 2023, I was watching when Ken Hitchcock, another demanding coach, was inducted into the Hockey Hall of Fame. He mentioned how much he cared about the players, even though it didn't always show. That's exactly how I feel.

Now it was time to feel it somewhere else.

10

MY KIND OF TOWN: CHICAGO, 1988–89

AFTER I WAS fired by the Flyers, I was supremely hurt, pissed off and angry. Iron Mike might not have been beloved by all, but we won and twice got close to taking the big prize. Alan Eagleson, arguably the most powerful man in hockey, was representing me. He was the head of the NHL Players' Association (NHLPA), the biggest player agent in the game, and he also represented coaches and, likely, managers. I knew Eagle from the Canada Cup, of course, and after I called him he came to my house, talked to me, and said, "You're moving to Chicago."

I was surprised. The Blackhawks had just signed Bob Murdoch to coach them the previous season. Eagle said it didn't matter. He was very tight with Blackhawks owner Bill Wirtz, who was also chairman of the NHL board of governors. As it turned out, there were other teams interested in me—the St. Louis Blues, for one,

and the Minnesota North Stars wanted me as their general manager. But I still wanted to coach.

I went to Princeton, New Jersey, to meet with North Stars
owner Gordon Gund, who owned the team along with his
brother George. Gordon was a very nice man. I walked into his
office and everything was completely in order; he was meticu-
lously dressed, very articulate. George was a little bit more like
the television detective Columbo, more dishevelled. I told
Gordon that I wanted to coach and eventually add GM to my
portfolio. Then I went to St. Louis and met with club president
Jack Quinn and new owner Mike Shanahan, who had just fired
my old St. Lawrence University teammate Jacques Martin as
their coach. I told them the same thing and then waited to hear
back from both teams. But it was feeling like the Blackhawks job
was a done deal, in large part, looking back, because of Eagleson's
relationship with Wirtz and GM Bob Pulford, a former client
who was part of the early days of the birth of the NHLPA.

I went to Toronto to meet with Pulford at Eagleson's house.
Because I was being pursued by multiple teams, I told Pully that
part of the deal was I wanted at some point to be the GM as well.
I felt I shouldn't have been fired in Philly, and if I was GM as well
as coach, I could control my own destiny. Eagleson talked to
Pulford and they made a proposal that would see Pulford step
down as GM after two seasons. That would give me time to get
acclimated with the organization and the players. I agreed to that.
Eagle and I were on a plane to Chicago to meet with Mr. Wirtz,
sitting in business class, and Al wrote out the contract in long-
hand. When we got to Chicago, in negotiations with Wirtz—
who had the nickname Dollar Bill because he could be cheap—we

worked out a five-year, $1 million deal. And we both signed it, a handwritten contract.

Although the Blues had made a similar offer, with the same promise of becoming GM after two years, Chicago was a better fit from the standpoint that Rita (with Gayla, who was now nine), could drive home to Toronto in one day to see Rita's family. They couldn't do that from St. Louis or Minnesota.

And so, 25 days after I was fired in Philly, I had a job with Chicago, and I had gone to the top in terms of salary. Eagleson had also managed to get me that leased Mercedes that Ed Snider wanted back.

I was able to hire my two assistants as well, which was a bonus. E.J. McGuire had decided to leave Philly after I got fired. He could have stayed, but he was a very loyal guy. I hired Jacques Martin, free now of his commitments to the Blues. Jacques had experience, but he also knew the Norris Division well, having worked in it the previous three years.

The first time I arrived in the old Chicago Stadium, I was shocked by what I saw. I knew the visitors' dressing room and facilities were rustic, but I didn't expect the home team to be roughing it as well. There were partitions between each dressing room stall, so you couldn't see the teammate sitting next to you. And between each stall was a stand-up ashtray. I said to Mr. Wirtz, "First, all the ashtrays are going out of here, there's no more smoking. And the room has to be revamped. I want all those partitions ripped out. You have to be able to look at your teammates." Half the players couldn't see the other half. That doesn't work. And I didn't have an office; I had to share one with my assistants. We didn't have a video room or a strength and conditioning room, either. We built out an adjacent storage room and turned it into the strength and conditioning space, and then turned another change room into the video room. We restructured the dressing room.

It's funny to think back on it. The Chicago Bulls and Michael Jordan were next door to us. Phil Jackson was the coach. They didn't have a medical room. If they needed medical assistance, they had to come to our room. There was no comparing these facilities to what I'd had in Philly. They were so archaic, behind the times. It's a wonder Chicago ever won anything.

The next thing that had to change was the culture. Two days after I was hired, we headed to Montreal for the annual entry draft. I was in a restaurant the night before, which is something I would always do with the staff and scouts. I went to have a leak and was standing at the urinal when I got a tap on the shoulder. I was still pissing. I looked around and there was a young guy standing there. "You better draft me tomorrow," he said. I said, "Who are you?" "I'm Jeremy Roenick." Soon enough I learned that was a typical Jeremy move. We chatted for a few minutes in the bathroom and I asked him why I should draft him. He said, "If you want someone to go through a wall for you, I'm the guy." Then we went out and, holy crap, at the table beside us a lady's dress had caught on fire. There was a big scene, and they rolled her up in the tablecloth to extinguish the fire. What a night. What a kid.

The next day we took our places on the draft floor at the Forum. Going into the draft, we thought if Roenick was available at eight, he was the guy we wanted. We didn't have quality depth at centre. We only had Denis Savard. We knew the kid was spunky. He could have waited outside the bathroom or stood back until I was finished! I remember laughing, saying "let me finish my business and I'll talk to you." He had great speed, he was a terrific skater. He was so skilled.

As it evolved, Mike Modano went first overall to Minnesota, Trevor Linden next to Vancouver, Curtis Leschyshyn to Quebec, Darrin Shannon to Pittsburgh, Daniel Doré to Quebec, Scott Pearson to Toronto, Martin Gélinas to Los Angeles, and . . .

History would show we made a really good pick. Rod Brind'Amour went ninth to St. Louis, then Teemu Selänne to Winnipeg, both great players, but we were very happy with Jeremy and thought he could become a star in Chicago, maybe even a number-one centre to eventually replace the aging Savard.

We knew he had a lot to learn about the game. He hadn't really played that much. He came out of Thayer Academy, a prep school in Braintree, Massachusetts, not far outside Boston, so he was drafted out of high school. He was very competitive and he wanted to be a hockey player. He got a scholarship to Boston College, went for two weeks and said *fuck this, I want to be a hockey player, not a student.*

He started during my first season with Chicago, 1988–89, played three games and scored in his first, but it was clear he wasn't ready. We sent him to play with the Hull Olympiques of the Quebec junior league. Wayne Gretzky owned the team, and he had previously met with Jeremy and talked him into playing. He had a pretty good year there, with 70 points in 28 games and another 19 points in nine playoff games. He played in the World Juniors for the United States and had a terrific tournament. The Blackhawks were running into injuries, so we called him up. He played in the final 17 games of the season and playoffs for us and never went back. That season he had in junior was a quick acceleration on the development curve. He was ready.

The Blackhawks, however, were not ready. Like I said, we needed a culture change that first season, and we needed to move some players to help make it happen. If we hadn't been in the weak Norris Division, we wouldn't have made the playoffs. As it was, we barely did. We went to overtime in the final game of the regular season against the Toronto Maple Leafs. There was a giveaway in front of the Leafs net, Troy Murray scored and we won 4–3 to get in.

There were moves I was pushing for that weren't happening quickly. Pully was a procrastinator. If you were a Blackhawk, he wanted you to stay a Blackhawk. He was very loyal to his players, to a fault. I said, "Pully, we need change here, a transition to develop a new team." He was so methodical in his decision-making, especially regarding trades. He couldn't pull the trigger on some of the players.

We weren't very good in many areas. In goal we had Darren Pang, who had been the number one the previous season. Ed Belfour was a rookie and wasn't ready. We had Jimmy Waite, who was just out of junior and not ready. His nickname was Jimmy Late; he was never on time for anything. We got shelled a few times early and were giving up a lot of goals, and I know Pang wasn't happy with me and was public about it. I was pushing Pully to get us a top goaltender. Buffalo was shopping Tom Barrasso early that season, but Pully couldn't pull the trigger and he was moved to Pittsburgh. We ended up bringing in Alain Chevrier from Winnipeg and he played lights out.

But our goalies weren't the only problem. We had to work on fitness. We still had guys smoking, only they had moved out of the dressing room and into the hallway. During one game, we were getting bombed by Boston, and I told Troy Murray and Steve Larmer to take their uniforms off after two periods, they were done. I loved both players, but I had to send messages to get this team to understand the work and fitness commitment. We had two wins in our first 10 games and lost nine straight in late November. It was a struggle. We had some good talent; we just had to get guys to buy into the program.

Savard always seemed to be a hot-button topic, certainly with the media and probably with Denis himself and his teammates. He was a good guy and a great talent; I liked him. When a young guy would get called up, Denis made him feel comfortable. I pushed him quite a bit, but I certainly wasn't ready to push to move him out. We didn't have anyone to replace him. Roenick was waiting in the wings, but we weren't certain when he would be ready to be our top centre. Denis missed three weeks in mid-January with an ankle injury and I made Dirk Graham the captain. When Denis returned, I kept Graham as captain. Pully really liked Dirk, who had a strong presence in the dressing room. He was a shy guy but very competitive, underestimated in terms of his ability, a strong personality in how he played, hard-nosed, and how he fought.

I'm sure Denis thought I hated him. That's not the case, although I was very tough on him. He was an individual on the ice, an artist. But the way we wanted to structure the team, the way we wanted to play, wasn't how he wanted to play. I believed it was okay to dump a puck occasionally and start a strong fore-check. He didn't have to do an end-to-end spin-o-rama every shift. If he had a bad shift, he would come to the bench, take his gloves off and say, "I'm not fucking playing anymore." He was moody. Larmer, who was good friends with him, would tell Denis, "Get your gloves back on and get ready for the next shift." It happened many times. It was bizarre. I said, "What the fuck is that?" There was no way Denis could be the captain behaving like that on the bench.

One day I had a real tough bag skate. We were losing a lot, and I didn't like the efforts of some. I skated them hard for almost an hour. Denis decided he'd had enough and was going to leave the ice, but the players, led by Keith Brown, wouldn't let him. They said, "You're staying with the rest of us." That was a huge event. To his credit, the next day Denis apologized to me and the team. "I totally lost my mind," he was later quoted as saying. "I never had any real problem with Mike. We're both emotional and intense and we both want to win, and he's made me learn how." Another time I had a bag skate and young defenceman Trent Yawney was the one to lose his cool, but he didn't quit. I was sitting on a chair at centre ice, skating them hard, and eventually a pissed-off Trent skated by and knocked me off the chair. I said, "Okay, practice is over." I had been waiting for someone to react, and I told Trent, "It's about time you hit someone." At least there was some emotion. I later heard Denis said that if he knew that's all they had to do to get off the ice, he would have hit me the first shift.

These players had to learn and understand the expectations. I told them on the first day that they had no idea what hard work was. I pushed players to be better, no question. One thing I couldn't accept was a player not playing to their potential or trying to push themselves beyond it. If you're a fourth-line player, that's fine. Not everyone has the skill level of a first-line player. But give it your all.

And it drove me crazy if a top player just cruised. I once had a player on my fourth line who came in and asked why he wasn't getting more ice time and why he was on the fourth line. I said, "Do you really want me to tell you?" He said yes. I said, "Because we don't have a fifth line. Get out." Sometimes players overestimated their abilities or didn't understand their role.

Over time, Pully made some desperately needed changes. We moved Rick Vaive, who I didn't think was quick enough anymore, to Buffalo for centre Adam Creighton. One night in Calgary, the local TV crew asked for Ricky to be interviewed between periods. I saw the TV runner grabbing him to take him to the studio. I said, "Why don't you interview someone who can play the fucking game?" Rick remembers that to this day. Pully also moved Gary Nylund and Marc Bergevin to the Islanders for Bob Bassen and Steve Konroyd. I liked the moves. Another great pickup we got was winger Greg Gilbert from the Islanders for a draft pick. I remember one of the guys telling one of the new players, as I've mentioned before, "Don't have a bad practice, don't have a bad warm-up and don't have a bad first shift, or you will see what Iron is all about." I was stern, some thought I was a prick—but a good prick, because most often over my career we won. Players such as Gretzky, Chris Chelios, Chris Pronger, Mark Howe and Messier, who I had at various times, liked that I demanded a lot of the lesser players, because the team would get stronger and we would win. Winning matters.

In the case of that first season with the Blackhawks, winning was slow to arrive. When we got Chevrier, he gave us some better goaltending, although he got hurt. We had several injuries, with Wilson and Savard banged up, and we struggled, blowing leads and teetering on the brink of missing the playoffs, going 5–10–5 down the stretch. It came down to that final game of the season at home against the Leafs. For most of that game I was standing on the bench, not behind it, pushing them in a confident way. That was a huge, huge victory for us.

We finished the season with a 27–41–12 record, good for an opening-round matchup with the first-place Detroit Red Wings, who finished 14 points ahead of us. But the Wings finished first with only a .500 record, so we weren't exactly facing the 1977 Montreal Canadiens (hint: only eight losses, 132 points). In other words, play better and we have a chance.

We lost the series opener, 3–2, but then won three straight. A key, obviously, is that after we'd blown yet another two-goal lead—I think it was the eighth of the season—Duane Sutter scored in overtime in Game 2 to give us a 5–4 win. We'd acquired Duane from the Islanders, of course. He and Gilbert were the only guys in our room who had won a Stanley Cup, and they were an important influence in changing the culture of that dressing room. I remember one day, after we'd lost, Duane went up and punched the glass covering the framed picture of the Stanley Cup I'd hung at the front of the dressing room beside the whiteboard, a reminder of what we were playing for. He obliterated it. There was glass everywhere. He said, in essence, "This is the only reason we're playing." He had a big influence in the dressing room; he really impacted the team. The morning of that overtime game, I did a drill in the morning skate called diagonal dump-ins, in which the puck comes off the boards to an attacking winger. Well, we had a diagonal dump-in in overtime, and Duane one-timed it and we won the game. If we'd lost that one, we would have been done. Winning that game accelerated our level of play in the playoffs. We won the next two at home and finished off the Wings in six games.

The team was starting to grasp the game plan, which was to be relentless on the forecheck, to play fast with quick exits from our zone, and to be physical. We played the Blues in the next round. They had owned us in the regular season, but that didn't matter. Roenick was with us after his junior season ended, and Stevie Thomas was back from injury. We would have swept the Blues had we not lost 5–4 in double overtime in the second game. All of a sudden we had won eight of our last 11 playoff games and three in a row, and we were meeting the Calgary Flames in the conference final. The Flames, of course, were a different beast. They had finished first overall in the league with 117 points, just 51 points ahead of us!

We got to the rink in Calgary the day before the first game and discovered we had one dressing room, that's it. Cliff Fletcher was the Flames GM, a nice man, a very smart hockey guy. I asked him, "Where is the change room for the coaches?" He said they didn't have any rooms available. I said, "Okay, we've got one room for the players and the training staff are in there. The coaches will just sit on the bench and change." I stripped naked in the hallway in front of the media. I said, "Sorry, but Cliff says there isn't a room available for the coaching staff." The next day there was a room for the coaches and the trainers.

Anyway, we won that battle but were overwhelmed in the first game, outshot 39–19, losing 3–0. I benched Savard in that game for a lazy giveaway. Despite everyone writing us off, including the Flames, it seemed, we bounced back in the next game and took a three-goal lead in the first six minutes before Calgary even had a shot. We held on for a 4–2 win, heading home. The Flames had a history of underachieving in the playoffs, so on the surface an element of doubt had entered the series. But they were a good, deep, physical team with a lot of firepower. They beat us 5–2 in the next game, but again we battled back. We took Game 4 to overtime, tied 1–1, but Al MacInnis beat us with one of his patented slapshots. I remember looking over at the Flames bench and coach Terry Crisp was so excited and relieved he had climbed over the glass behind the bench into the stands where the Flames wives and executives were sitting. He planted a big smooch on a lady he thought was his wife but turned out to be the wife of Al MacNeil, the Flames assistant GM. The Flames, with their history, did not want to return home with the series tied. They beat us 3–1 in the next game and went on to beat Montreal and win the Stanley Cup.

It was disappointing to lose, but to make the playoffs was a huge success considering the work we had to accomplish that season, with the culture change. These guys had been allowed to smoke in the dressing room; there were chain-smokers on a professional hockey team! We weren't fit, didn't have proper fitness training. The demands I had brought over from Philly were all brand new to the players. By the time we got to the playoffs, we'd been playing desperation hockey for so long, just trying to get in—and I pushed them very, very hard—that they were mentally toughened.

They were ready.

11

COMING TOGETHER: CHICAGO, 1989–91

WHEN HE APPROACHED me in the washroom of a Montreal restaurant and told me it would be a mistake if the Blackhawks didn't draft him, Jeremy Roenick was right. He was proving himself to be the real deal—and in the 1989–90 season, he started to emerge, as did the team. Losing to Calgary, even though I knew we were playing a better team, had been tough. There were tears after the final game and it wasn't just me doing the crying this time. It was the players, too. They had come a long way, and they felt the sting of the loss. But our playoff success, limited as it had been, was huge. We had started to change the culture. They cared. And now it was time to push them to the next level while also teaching them to believe in themselves, to believe that the Chicago Blackhawks were a team to beat.

With his speed and skill and competitiveness, Roenick was a key part of our change on the ice. His speed was perfect for the heavy forechecking style I liked to play, especially in the tiny Chicago Stadium, and he was willing, with some prodding, to become a more physical player. Jeremy has told the story that I grabbed him on the bench during an exhibition game and said he would never play again if he continued to swing by his checks. He got the message. Yes, he had a lot to learn, and he had to push himself to be better. As his season progressed, it was becoming clear that he would be our next number-one centre, which would allow us to make a very big move. That season, his first full season with the NHL club, he finished with 26 goals and 66 points and 54 penalty minutes. He also finished third in Calder Trophy voting as rookie of the year, behind winner Sergei Makarov of the Flames and Mike Modano of the North Stars. Makarov, who had 86 points, was 31 years old; Jeremy and Modano were 19. The league changed the rules after that, allowing only players under 26 to be eligible.

That second season, we got off to a bit of a slow start through the first couple of weeks, but we got moving and were 14–6–1 by mid-November. We then had a bit of a slump, winless in seven, but our maturity as a team helped us to bounce back.

We'd made only one off-season move, bringing back hard-nosed winger Al Secord, who was a huge fan favourite and a favourite of mine. Now, we had an issue in net, and I was again pushing Pully to make some moves. Darren Pang got hurt in training camp and didn't look like he'd be back this season. We still had Alain Chevrier, who was very good in my first year, especially the play-offs, but he was just okay in camp. We traded for Jacques Cloutier from Buffalo, my Calder Cup championship back-up goalie in Rochester. At age 24, Ed Belfour still wasn't ready, so we loaned him to the Canadian national team, where he would get more ice and attention, while Jimmy Waite was assigned to the minors. No wonder I got the well-earned nickname Captain Hook.

We acquired Greg Millen from Quebec at the March trade deadline, and he took over and was our starter for the playoffs. I mentioned earlier that I'd been invited to the tryouts for the 1980 Canadian Olympic team. It was the summer of 1978, and the tryouts were at Upper Canada College in Toronto. My roommate was this kid named Greg Millen. One night, I'm in a deep sleep and he comes in and throws a bucket of fucking ice water on me. I jumped up and said, "You could have killed me! I could have had a heart attack!" I chased him down the hall in my underwear. I didn't catch him then, but I had him now.

On his first day in Chicago, when he came into my office, I said, "Millsy, payback is a bitch. Now you're mine." I reminded him of that incident. I said, "If you fucking stray one inch either way, your ass is going to be grass. And not only that, you're overweight. You're going to get on the bike and start getting in shape." He did play pretty well for us and was our starter deep into the second round. But he wasn't great. As part of that trade for Millen, in which we gave up a couple of prospects who didn't pan out, we also received talented winger Michel Goulet, who was just 29. Quebec was in a free fall, dumping salary, and some would say they were continuing to bottom out to improve their draft position. Goulet would give us another scoring threat and power-play option.

What we didn't know when we got Goulet was that he had a heart condition that required a procedure; the Nordiques just didn't tell us. (At the time, teams didn't disclose injuries.) Once that was done, though, he continued on to have a Hall of Fame career.

There was lots more noise on the Savard front, a large part of it my doing, of course. Our rink was tight. Unlike today, the arenas then weren't required to have the same dimensions. The "Madhouse on Madison" was almost 15 feet shorter than the 200-foot length of a traditional rink. As a result, the neutral zone was shorter. This is why I wanted my team to be fast, to dump, chase and bump. That wasn't Denis's game. As I said earlier, he was an artist, and he wasn't prepared to change. So we butted heads. In December, word leaked out that we'd had conversations with Winnipeg Jets GM Mike Smith about a potential Savard-for-Hawerchuk trade. I had Dale, of course, in junior B in Oshawa and in the Canada Cup. We had a great relationship. The trade talk ended when Denis broke his finger in January, although his absence accelerated Roenick's development.

We hit the skids in late February, going on a 1–8–2 slide. Even with injuries, we shouldn't have fallen that badly. We managed to recover down the stretch and finish first with 41 wins and 88 points, which was an improvement of 14 wins and 22 points over the previous season. We had gone from barely making the playoffs the year before—only squeaking in because the Norris Division was weak—to first place. Progress. Steve Larmer led us in scoring with 31 goals and 90 points. Denis had 80 points in 60 games. Doug Wilson had 73 points—man, he could pound the puck from the blue line. Jeremy had 26 goals, Stevie Thomas 40, Adam Creighton 34. My centres were Savard, Creighton, Roenick and Troy Murray, all guys who could score. We were deep at centre.

In the first round, we drew Minnesota, which was a pretty good team with Modano. For whatever reasons, in both Philly and Chicago my teams didn't finish business quickly. We went seven games with the North Stars, but won the seventh game, 5–2. We fell behind to St. Louis 2–1 in the next round, which is when I made the switch to Eddie Belfour in goal. He won three of four to win the series. His save percentage was .915. Putting him in was a bold move. After sending him from training camp to the Canadian national program, I had kept tabs on him. I knew Millen and Cloutier weren't going to win this for us. Calling up Eddie turned out to be the right move.

During the Blues series I had another incident with Savard. We stayed in a hotel the night before home games during the playoffs. He and I got into an argument. I read later that he was pissed I hadn't included him in a meeting with a group of players and he wasn't happy with his ice time. I called him to my room to talk. It didn't go well. I got very upset; so did he. It was a heated, loud conversation, and I sent him packing. The next day, I asked the team to vote on whether to allow him to return. Wilson said the players wouldn't vote, and that was no doubt the start of our relationship getting nasty. Or nastier. I know a lot of the players were confused, wondering why I was even considering the move, but I had to make a point to Denis and the team. The team was unified and we won the series in seven games.

Next up in the conference final were the Edmonton Oilers, who had beaten me twice in Philly in the Stanley Cup final. Only this time, they were without Wayne Gretzky, who had been traded to Los Angeles in August 1988. We were up two games to one—we had split in Edmonton and won back home—but then the great Mark Messier, already established as one of the greatest leaders in the game, inflicted his will on the series. I remember Mark sitting in the stands watching the morning skate. I could see him; there was fire in his eyes. That night, he made a statement to the Blackhawks on the first shift. He went after Denis, who I benched after two shifts, and broke his stick over Wilson. And that was the series right there. We lost 4–2, and we were done. Messier scored twice and assisted on the other two. What a performance. He broke our spirit.

As per my contract, in the summer of 1990 I took over as general manager, while retaining my coaching duties. Under Pulford, I had a lot of say, and we got along pretty well. But I'd negotiated to be GM and coach for a reason, after my unfair dismissal in Philly. I wanted control of my destiny, or as much control as anyone ever really has.

And my first order of business was to make a franchise-building trade. On June 5, not long after I took over as GM and Pulford had moved into the role of senior vice-president, we were in Vancouver for the draft. I had the owners, the management group and the coaches together in a room. I had posted the roster on the whiteboard, and I said, "Here's the plan." We had Roenick, who was close to being a top centre; we needed a top defenceman in order for us to take the next big step. I said I wanted to trade Savard—there was no sense having both him and Roenick. Mr. Wirtz listened. He was a pretty stubborn guy and he loved Denis, but he also loved that we were winning and the seats were full. And, as you'd gather from his nickname, Dollar Bill was aware of finances. He was afraid there would be a backlash from the fans if we traded Denis. When I first arrived in Chicago, season ticket sales were at an all-time low, with about 8,000 fans in the building most nights. By the end of my first year, the Blackhawks were back to a full house every night. We had gone to the final four twice and were an entertaining, competitive, physical team.

I tried to convince him that Roenick was ready and that we needed to capitalize on Denis as an asset. We didn't need two number-one centres, and the fans would love Jeremy. Denis and I obviously didn't see eye to eye over how he and the team should play. He was a solid citizen; he just didn't like to be told what to do. I convinced Wirtz that any attendance backlash wouldn't be severe. We would be getting a good player back, and they would love Roenick even more. After a while, Wirtz said okay, but he told me I could make the trade only if I could get one of Raymond Bourque, Paul Coffey or Chris Chelios. That's big-game hunting.

I targeted Chelios, who was playing for Montreal and had won the Norris Trophy in 1989. I knew there was no way I was getting Bourque out of Boston and, at the time, no way of getting Coffey out of Pittsburgh. Chelios was 28, a former second-round pick in the 1981 draft who had played seven seasons with the Habs. For a few reasons, I thought there was a chance of making that deal happen. First, Montreal had bypassed Denis in the 1980 draft to take Doug Wickenheiser first overall. That was a mistake. They'd bypassed a very popular French Canadian player, who was still very good—so here was a second chance at getting him. Second, at the time, Quebec nationalism was growing, and there was a feeling within the province that they didn't have enough French Canadian athletes, artists, businesses and such. I did my homework on the politics and figured Montreal would consider a big trade to acquire Denis. Third, there was some feedback from the Molson family, owners of the Habs, that they were concerned about Chelios, who was a bit of a free spirit. I thought I had a chance. What I didn't know was that the Habs also had concerns about Chelly's knee.

After the draft, I put myself in a hotel in Montreal for five days. Every morning I walked to the Forum and knocked on Serge Savard's door, and we discussed various scenarios. Serge was going on vacation with his family, so I returned to Chicago without a trade. But I was pretty relentless. I called him at 8 a.m. his time, 7 a.m. my time, every day. Serge is a good guy. I knew him from the '87 Canada Cup. One day I called and he said, "I can't even have a vacation." I said, "Make the trade and have all the time you want." He came back to Montreal and I continued to pursue.

We went back and forth until we got down to a one-for-one trade—Savard for Chelios. The night before we consummated the deal, Chelios and Gary Suter, who were grads from the University of Wisconsin, had gone back to the school and gotten into some kind of trouble with the cops. Word got back to the Canadiens and they agreed to make the trade the next day. Serge and I talked the next morning, then I had to go to Wirtz. He had already said if I get one of those three players he would agree to the trade, but now he says we have to get their number-one pick as well. I said, "Mr. Wirtz, I've been talking to this guy for a month. My credibility goes down the drain if I go back because you want the number-one pick, that's completely unfair."

I hung up the phone with Wirtz, called Serge and said, "I've been dealing with you honestly and now my owner wants a first pick." Serge was mad. I understood. I said, "Can we make the deal with your second-round pick and I'll make sure I get the pick back to you, a soft trade?" He said okay. I call Wirtz and tell him I can't get the first but I can get a second—can I make the trade? He says yes. We made the deal on June 29. I called Denis but he was golfing, so I called his agent to let him know, and then I called Denis later at the golf course. He was pretty rattled, but he'd obviously thought it might happen because we had a contentious relationship. Chelly was shocked, too. Both had trepidations, but both also had reason to be excited. Chelly was coming home to Illinois; Denis was going home to Quebec. After a few years, it worked out very well for both of them. Denis won a Stanley Cup in Montreal and then came back to play with Chelly and end his career in Chicago, while Chelly eventually moved on and won two Cups in Detroit.

At his first meeting with "Iron Mike," Chelly seemed nervous, given the context of what had just happened, but he was happy to come home to Chicago, where he still had family and friends. But in that conversation, I started to establish a relationship with him; he knew he could trust me and I could trust him. That was very important.

Roenick had gone through a difficult time himself off the ice. I helped him through it, got him connected with people who could help. It built a trust between us. I was empathetic, understanding and helpful, reaching out to give these guys some support and guidance and show them that I truly cared about them, probably when the players least expected it. I remember, years later, Jeremy saying that I didn't inspire him, I scared him.

Anyway, I was thrilled to make my first trade—one that would change the franchise. I wasn't worried about Chelly's knee because I didn't know anything about it. Remember: at that time, we didn't have to disclose medical information. Oftentimes, traded players weren't healthy. The off-ice behaviour didn't bother me; I knew he would learn from it. I liked that I could build a trust, a bond with him. And I liked it to a certain extent because you knew the guy had some juice in him. We just had to redirect that focus. Chelly changed the tone in the dressing room and the competitive level of the team. Look at everything he achieved in his career. He was a physical specimen, a fierce competitor. The impact he had really surfaced in Chicago. Serge later told me he made the trade because his medical team didn't think the knee would hold up for a few more years. They were wrong, obviously. Chelly was 48 when he officially retired in 2010.

I felt pretty well entrenched after that deal. I was able to deal away a very popular player, the biggest departure since Bobby Hull, to further change the culture of the team. We made a couple of other significant changes that off-season, as well. Jacques Martin left to take an associate coaching position with Quebec, so Darryl Sutter was elevated from our farm team in Indianapolis, where he had just won a championship. He was a very good, loyal assistant. We shared the same expectations from players. E.J. would clean up a mess, be the good cop; Darryl would go in and tell the player he got what he deserved. He wasn't a fixer. My other assistant, Rich Preston, wasn't an apple-polisher either, but he was a bit more flexible. We all contributed to a great coaching team. My biggest skill was preparing the team mentally. Practices were as good as any in the league, short and hard, specific to game conditions in terms of execution. Creative but demanding.

I also hired the legendary Soviet goaltender Vladislav Tretiak as our goaltending coach, advisor and scout. That was huge. In Philly we'd had Bernie Parent. Chicago had nobody. So I hired Tretiak, primarily because he was Belfour's hero and the reason why Eddie wore No. 20. And Eddie was clear that Eddie was going to become our number one. Also, we had Dominik Hašek in the system. Dominik left his native Czechoslovakia to join us, played 33 games in the minors and five games with us. Dominik loved Tretiak, too.

Tretiak had been a star in the historic 1972 Summit Series. He'd retired from the Soviet league and international play in 1984, and we somehow got word he was interested in coming to the NHL. He was a great goaltender. Pulford and I had a discussion. It's embarrassing to say, but we paid him only $25,000 plus travel, and he could bring his wife, his agent and a translator. He dropped in at various times throughout the season. He loved coming to Chicago. We'd take him and his entourage to the best restaurants. We thought it was a great idea just to have his presence. It was quite a coup.

In practice, Tretiak would put on the full gear and go on the ice. Sometimes he would keep the goalies out for an hour after practice and he would be doing all the drills himself. Besides the puck-stopping, Tretiak really improved their puck-handling skills. I remember one day calling the team to centre ice and saying, "I have good news and bad news." I said, "The good news is we have Mr. Tretiak with us. The bad news is he's better than our goalies, so he's starting the next game." Everyone laughed. He was a very engaged coach. He improved our goalies, especially Eddie. That season, Eddie won the Calder, Vezina and Jennings Trophies and finished third in Hart voting.

Another key member of our staff was our sports psychologist, Dr. Cal Botterill, who had been with me in Philadelphia. Cal had a great relationship with the players, and when they were pissed at me he could help them understand what it was we were trying to achieve. He was excellent in helping them to build their confidence.

Looking back, I'm in awe of the talent that was on that team. Chelios, Goulet, Wilson and Belfour are all Hall of Famers. If you look at what Steve Larmer accomplished, I don't understand why he's not in. He had 101 points one year—1,012 points in 1,006 games. He won the Calder Trophy and a Stanley Cup with me in New York; he was an NHL "iron man," playing 884 consecutive regular-season games; and he played for me in the Canada Cup. He was one of only two guys I could find to play with Gretzky in the Canada Cup, who could read off him. Mario Lemieux was the other. He should be in.

On a personal note, the season did not begin well. A couple of nights before our opening game, I had been at a team function with Rita. Throughout the evening I probably had six beers. I then drove home. We had an elderly lady babysitting Gayla. She lived no more than 10 minutes away, and I drove her home as well. On the way back, I got pulled over by a police officer near our home in Wilmette, Illinois. He said I was drifting over the centre line, and he wanted to give me a breathalyzer. I said no. I failed the field test and was taken to the station and was charged with driving under the influence of alcohol and improper lane usage.

The story was on the front page of the papers. At practice the next day, I apologized to the team and management. I had made a mistake and was embarrassed by it. I am thankful nothing worse happened. I was eventually fined $550 and placed under a year of court supervision. Lesson learned.

One highlight of that season happened when I was sitting in the stands. The 1991 All-Star Game was played in Chicago. The Gulf War—between Iraq and a coalition of forces led by the United States—had been going on for almost six months. It was a very emotional time in the country. The start of that game was an amazing scene. The start of any game in Chicago was an amazing scene, with the organ playing and Wayne Messmer singing the national anthem, and the crowd roaring louder and louder as the anthem went on. That day, though, with all the emotion stirred up by the war, was especially incredible. It was a feeling no sports fan would have had previously. Most nights, the glass would shake during the anthem. That night, the building was shaking.

We had a great year, ended up in first place overall with 106 points, a huge increase over the previous year. In three seasons we had gone from 27 to 41 to 49 wins. We improved our goals-against dramatically. Eddie was great in goal, appearing in 74 games. Just an aside about Eddie: People always accused me of being hard on goalies, and sometimes I was, no question. I didn't suffer bad goals well. But there was also method to my madness. There's the famous video of me pulling Eddie from a game that season— it was December 9 at home. I pulled Eddie, who threw up his hands in disgust and then sat on the bench ignoring me. Here's the deal. When I came into the league, most coaches were playing their goalies 50/50, splitting the games. To me, that didn't make any sense. If one goalie is better than the other, why wouldn't you play your better goalie more? Just like when one defenceman is better than the other and plays more. Before the season, I would go to Eddie and say, "Do you want to play 80 percent of the games, or 50 percent?" He said, "80 percent, of course." I told him there would be nights when the team would need a jump-start, or I would need to terrorize the officials, or he wouldn't be spot-on, so I might make a change in net. But, I told him, "You're going to start 80 percent of the games." Well, that night he wasn't happy. When he was ignoring me on the bench, I grabbed him by the scruff of the neck and I said, "Eddie, do you remember our deal?" I put him back in a minute later, figuring a pissed-off Eddie might shut the door. We lost.

The great year did not lead to a great playoff. In the first round we faced Minnesota, who finished 38 points behind us, and were knocked out in six games, even though we had led the series 2–1. I didn't like how we were playing, and I practised the team hard before Game 4, which we lost 3–1. We got smoked in Game 5, 6–0 (five power-play goals), and I knew it was over. We were out-scored 12–2 in the final three games. In that series, we had twice as many penalties to kill as Minnesota. I know at times we were undisciplined, but we were a physical team and I felt there was a bias in terms of the penalties that were called in that series. They had a good team, but sometimes biased officiating is all the margin of difference it takes. They ended up advancing to the Stanley Cup final, where they lost to Pittsburgh.

In the end, I pushed that team too hard, and we lost. There was a story by the late, great Red Fisher in the *Montreal Gazette*, reporting that the Blackhawks gathered in a bar-restaurant after the series to drown their sorrows. I walked in and Chelly asked me to leave. I told him it was a public place, that I could stay. He said, "You're right, but we don't want you to stay."

That was okay. They were coming together as a team.

12

TEAM CANADA, ROUND TWO: THE 1991 CANADA CUP

FOUR YEARS AFTER Gretzky-to-Lemieux, I was back at the helm of Team Canada, but with added responsibilities for the 1991 Canada Cup. Alan Eagleson, who was still my agent, hired me as head coach and insisted I serve as general manager too. In the 1987 tournament, Canada had had a whole group of managers, which included Glen Sather, Bobby Clarke, Serge Savard and Phil Esposito.

This time, Sather, Clarke and Savard served as advisors, helping with the training camp invitation list. I had the final say on the roster, and I leaned on my coaching staff. My assistant coaches were Pat Burns, Brian Sutter, Tom Watt and Tom Webster. Selecting a roster for that tournament was never an easy task, and our decisions that year were made even more complicated when Mario Lemieux, Cam Neely and Raymond Bourque turned down invitations for health reasons. But it didn't matter which players weren't available—we still had to win.

As usual, we made some controversial decisions. We kept an 18-year-old Eric Lindros, who was refusing to play for the Quebec Nordiques, the team that had drafted him a few months earlier. But there would be no Steve Yzerman, Joe Sakic or Michel Goulet—all cut. Sakic and Yzerman would evolve and win two and three Stanley Cups, respectively, and they would win Olympic gold together in 2002. All three are now in the Hockey Hall of Fame. But they didn't fit with this group.

Joe wasn't in the best condition when he came to camp that summer. He wasn't the dominant Joe Sakic he would later become. We already had Gretzky and Hawerchuk at centre, plus Brent Sutter as the ideal checking-line centre. I didn't like Yzerman on the wing, whereas Lindros easily moved from centre to wing. Hawerchuk could also play the wing if needed. We were missing Messier, though. He had hurt his knee the previous season and was taking the summer to rehab and wasn't going to play, but near the end of training camp Wayne approached me and said, "Mike, we have to get Mess here on this team."

So, the two of us got on the phone. Wayne did all the talking. He said, "Mess, you have to get here. We need you." Messier was not happy with the Edmonton Oilers for letting Adam Graves leave that summer, and was thinking of leaving himself. After some convincing, he replied, "Okay, I'm on my way." Mess showed up two days before we played our first game against Finland. He would make a public trade demand during the tournament and got traded in early October to the Rangers. But we had him for the Canada Cup, and with him in place we had the best group of centres in the tournament.

We were down to the last few cuts at training camp at Maple Leaf Gardens when Mess skated up to me and said, referring to Lindros, "That prick is a player." I said, "I know." Mark wasn't the only one impressed with Lindros; my coaching staff was too. We got into some debates about players, but keeping Lindros and cutting Yzerman weren't among the most contentious.

The most difficult decision was whether to keep Michel Goulet or Luc Robitaille on left wing. Michel played well for me in the 1987 Canada Cup. He was also now one of my significant players with the Blackhawks. But Pat Burns was adamant about keeping Robitaille. Pat coached him in junior in Hull and won the 1985–86 Quebec Major Junior Hockey League championship. Robitaille scored an incredible 93 goals and 190 points in a combined 83 regular-season, playoff and Memorial Cup tournament games. We took a vote, and I was outvoted. The group wanted Luc. Michel often teases me about that decision. He took it in good humour because we were friends and remain great friends, but he'd have loved to have been on that team.

The next difficult step was at centre. With Gretz, Mess, Eric, Dale Hawerchuk, and Brent Sutter down the middle, we had to cut Yzerman. But as the head coach and GM, I had to tell Stevie he had been cut for a second time. I'd cut him back in '87, too. He became very belligerent. He told me and the other coaches we were fools. His words were harsh. Brian Sutter got up and confronted Stevie. He said, "I'm going to beat the shit out of you," in the way only a Sutter can. I had to ask Brian to relax. But cutting Stevie was controversial. Many believed that taking Lindros, who had never played in the NHL, over Yzerman was not wise. But there's always controversy when trying to assemble a team of stars.

We wanted to build an NHL-type team rather than an all-star team, just like in 1987. That's why I tried to make a team that included players such as Brent Sutter, Dirk Graham and Steve Larmer. I addressed the team in training camp and asked them how many minutes were in a game—the same question I'd asked the '87 team. It was a great way to illustrate to players who are used to playing big minutes with their club teams that ice time wouldn't be as bountiful when playing for Team Canada.

We tied our first game, against Finland, 2–2. Finland's goalie, Markus Ketterer, made a remarkable 42 saves. But Luc Robitaille scored. Burnsy wiped his forehead.

After wins against the United States, Sweden and then Czechoslovakia, we concluded the round robin with a 3–3 tie against the Soviet Union. They didn't have their best team because of defection concerns, but that game was a big test for us because it was in Quebec City.

Our players may have been preoccupied with the drama surrounding their youngest teammate. Eric was jeered early and often in that game. Still, he scored. Bill Ranford was terrific in goal, Larmer tied the game at 2–2, and Sutter made sure we left with a 3–3 tie. We efficiently handled a young Mats Sundin and Sweden, 4–0, in the semifinal in Toronto, setting up a best-of-three championship series against two of my Chicago stars, Chris Chelios and Jeremy Roenick, and the United States.

We won the series opener in Montreal, but Gretzky was injured on a questionable hit from Gary Suter. It was borderline, but I don't think it was dirty. I remember our trainer, Jim Pizzutelli, was on the ice attending to Wayne and Paul Coffey said to me, "With the big guy down, you better double-shift me," Coffey said. I did, and we prevailed, 4–1.

In the second game, in Hamilton, and without Gretzky, we jumped out to a 2–0 lead. But the US tied the game by the time we retired to the dressing room for the second intermission. I gave the guys a little bit of shit, but then Dirk Graham, who played for me in Chicago and was one of the controversial roster selections, stood up and gave a passionate speech to the group, including me. He said he believed in the team, that we were experienced and talented, and that we had to finish the job. Larmer scored a short-handed goal to give us a lift, and Dirk added an empty-netter for a 4–2 win.

I will always remember the way the team responded after Wayne got hurt. They played so well without him for the final 91 minutes. Losing any top player, let alone Wayne Gretzky, is a huge load to take on, but the guys persevered. Wayne once said, "As spectacular as the way 1987 ended, we had a better team in 1991." We just had the depth to get the job done.

Something about winning the Canada Cup followed me home to Chicago when I flew back a day later. I had to face Chelios and Roenick, who'd lost to my Canadians. But they were both very professional about it, though I endured no end of wisecracks about Team USA getting screwed by the officiating.

Anytime you have a winning experience, it gives you confidence. Eddie Belfour was backup with Team Canada, but in Chicago he had really emerged as our starter. It's pretty remarkable to look back at our goaltending at that point, when you consider the career Eddie was really just beginning, as well as the person who had established himself as Eddie's backup: Dominik Hašek.

13

FIRED (AGAIN): CHICAGO, 1992

IT IS PROBABLY an understatement to say my popularity level in Chicago was waning as we headed into the 1991–92 season. My overhaul of the Blackhawks roster continued in the summer of 1991, and that meant moving out some more fan favourites, who were no fans of mine. But the reasons were simple. For starters, we had collapsed against the North Stars in the opening round. Yes, I'd pushed too hard, but there were still flaws on the roster. It was obvious that some players were never going to buy in. The old core group needed to be changed, particularly on the blue line.

In late July, I traded Troy Murray and Warren Rychel to Winnipeg for hard-nosed defenceman Bryan Marchment—an important physical player, a low-hitting, dangerous player—and Chris Norton, who never played for us. He was a minor league player. That was an unpopular trade. Murray was a very popular player, but for me losing Rychel was tougher because he had a competitive edge, which you need in playoff hockey.

An even more unpopular trade happened in early September, while I was away coaching at the Canada Cup. This time, I moved defenceman Doug Wilson, who had been with the Hawks for 14 seasons. And this story is complicated.

Wilson is a Hall of Famer. He was a very good defenceman, a former Norris Trophy winner, a smooth skater who had a big slapshot. He was the kind of player I called a politician: he would buy into some changes, knowing they had to be made, but he wasn't coming all the way to where I needed him. Ultimately, Wilson wasn't a fit for me and I told him so, several times. He was never happy with me after I traded his pal, Denis Savard, and I rode Dougie hard.

But the story goes deeper than that. In the spring of 1991, after our series against Minnesota was over, Mr. Wirtz came to me and said, "Doug Wilson will never play for the Blackhawks again," which was something I'd told Doug often when I was giving him shit. But something else had happened. To this day I do not know exactly what it was. Mr. Wirtz said Doug Wilson embarrassed the Blackhawks. Wilson had lacerated his jaw in Game 5, spent a night in hospital, and still wanted to play, but he didn't dress for the sixth and final game. Dougie wasn't on the trip when the team departed for Minneapolis; he made his own way there. But he didn't dress for the game. Wirtz got pissed. Wilson has been quoted as saying I wouldn't let him play, but my philosophy has always been simple: if you're injured you can't play; if you're hurt you can play. In other words, everyone has bumps and bruises and strains. If I told him he couldn't play, it was because of the doctor. There's no way I would have sat him out for stitches.

After the series, Wirtz was adamant that I trade Wilson. He said, "I don't care if you get a box of chocolates for him." Seems everyone was in agreement, because Wilson also requested a trade. He was no doubt frustrated and pissed off with me, but there was something going on with Wirtz, too. Wilson has said that Wirtz and Pulford made him a contract offer that summer, which he turned down. I made the trade happen on September 6, trading him to the expansion San Jose Sharks, which is where he'd asked to go (they made him their captain) for Kerry Toporowski, a big defenceman who never got past the minors, and a 1992 second-round pick, who turned out to be defenceman Boris Mironov, but he wouldn't arrive in Chicago until years later. It wasn't much of a return, but Dougie was 34, and even if I could have shopped him there weren't going to be any better offers. The Rangers, Flyers and Red Wings had expressed interest, but he wanted to go to San Jose. He played two seasons before retiring and later became the long-time Sharks GM. But Wirtz's order to trade Wilson is an example of the dynamic of ownership, management, coaches and players that is always at play. As a GM, you need to be able to manage up and down. After the deal, Wirtz was quoted as saying that Dougie, who'd said he wasn't having fun playing for the Blackhawks, would love it in San Jose—he could play golf year-round and have fun. At his farewell press conference, Dougie said he was "probably the happiest player in Chicago right now . . . I wanted to thank everybody, well, not everybody." We did not have a good relationship.

We started that season without Eddie Belfour, who sat out the first three weeks with a contract dispute. I wasn't negotiating the contracts yet; that was still Wirtz and Pulford. I made the trades, but we had agreed that contracts would be too much when I was also coaching. I did join some of the meetings on big contracts, though, including the one we signed when we got Chelly, as his contract from Montreal was expiring. Mr. Wirtz, his sons, his brother Michael, Pully and I met with Chelly's agent, Don Meehan. Donny told Bill they wanted a five-year contract for $5 million, one million a year. Well, Wirtz exploded and said he hadn't agreed to a million-dollar contract with Bobby Hull, so why should he do it now. Holy fuck, I thought the roof was going to cave in. But Chelly got his money.

Eddie signed as a free agent in 1987 after starring at North Dakota. But he was a work in progress, and it had taken a few seasons for him to truly emerge. He was a feisty competitor and I liked that. As during my time in Philly, with Pelle Lindbergh and Ron Hextall, I wasn't afraid of riding an unproven goaltender. In his absence, we played Jimmy Waite a lot and Dominik Hašek got some work, too. Eddy finally returned on November 2, a 4–3 loss to Minnesota.

I wasn't finished with my roster overhaul. After I'd sat out Trent Yawney the first three games, he demanded a trade, but there was nothing out there. He finally got his wish, but not until mid-December when I moved him to Calgary for winger Stéphane Matteau. That was a huge pick-up for us, although Steph was injured. He had a huge contusion on his femur that calcified and he couldn't play for a couple of months. He played only 20 games heading into the playoffs, but he was a great addition. I moved out Wayne Presley and Greg Millen, and then made another big deal on October 2, trading defenceman Dave Manson and a third-round pick, who turned out to be Kirk Maltby, for defenceman

Steve Smith, who I had coached in the Canada Cup. Manson was hard-nosed and competitive, but Smith was better. He had won and gone through a tough time with Edmonton, and he played well with Chelly. They logged close to 30 minutes a game. It was like Mark Howe and Brad McCrimmon when I was in Philly. We knew we were getting Igor Kravchuk, our first Russian, after the Olympics, so the defence would continue to get better. Igor would be paired with Keith Brown.

In late October I made another unpopular trade, sending Adam Creighton and Steve Thomas to the Islanders for Brent Sutter and Brad Lauer. That trade happened at three in the morning. Isles GM Bill Torrey sent a fax over and it was all convoluted; he got the trade wrong. I had to call him in the middle of the night and ask him to fix it. We gave up a bunch of goals, losing those two in that deal, and I hated losing Stevie, but he apparently had had enough of me. Sutter fit in perfectly, giving us depth at centre behind Jeremy Roenick.

I kept tinkering throughout the season, adding defenceman Steve Bancroft, more depth, for a pick. I moved defenceman Steve Konroyd for scoring winger Rob Brown, who on the surface was an atypical Keenan player—dishevelled, long hair—but he provided offence. We also added wingers Tony Hrkac (for a pick) and Tony Horacek and defenceman Rod Buskas. I think from the core group I inherited, we only kept Keith Brown, who was hard-core into fitness, and Steve Larmer, who was overweight and a smoker but an exceptional player who was willing to change and did. He lost the weight and stopped smoking and became a much better player. Like I've said, he should be in the Hockey Hall of Fame.

There was one more trade, but it was nullified by the league. It happened at the trade deadline. We were at home, playing San Jose and Doug Wilson that night. I made a deal to pick up veteran Sharks centre Kelly Kisio for some picks. The trade deadline was 2 p.m. Chicago time, and I made the trade several minutes before it. We notified Kelly, whose equipment was in San Jose's dressing room. He walked down to the other end of the building with his gear and we set him up in our dressing room. Meanwhile, upstairs, we were trying to notify the league. At the time, when you made a trade you sent the details to the league office by fax machine, but their machine was so fucking backed up with last-minute trades that ours wasn't received until four minutes after the deadline, even though the deal was made and the fax sent well before. The league said no to the trade. I argued and said, "If you ask the player, he had already gone from the Sharks dressing room to our dressing room, got fitted with Blackhawks gear and was sitting in our room. Your fax machine is not our fault." The league said they would review it in a few days, and Kelly actually flew back to San Jose to start packing. When the league got back to us, they said no deal. It was fucked up. It was embarrassing for the league, the players and the team. The good news is we won the game, 5–1.

I always liked to have a getaway with the team during a break in the schedule. I gave them freedom when it was time for freedom, and I asked them to work when it was time to work. And not just work—we were here to win. I'd done it in Philly, when I took the team to Lake Placid and put the gear on myself, and I did it with the Blackhawks one season, too. We had a good group. We played on an outdoor rink in Ontario, California, and I put the gear on again, let the boys have some fun and take some runs at me. I remember Larmer saying it was a bloodbath, that I was a hatchet man, but I let them take their shots. I also gave shots. We also went to Banff once. I had found out there was a band playing in a local bar, so we went as a team. I knew when it was time for the coach to leave, so on my way out I said to Michel Goulet, "Here's my credit card. Pay for the guys' drinks and give me the bill." The next day he comes to return my card and give me the bill. I looked at it and said, "How much did you guys drink?" He said, "Not that much." Turns out I had bought the entire bar drinks!

During the 1991–92 season, I took them on a retreat to La Quinta, California, to a golf course with a spa. I told the guys, "Put your golf charges, the green fees, rentals, on my room account." Well, I go to check out and the bill was over $10,000. Some of them had bought golf clubs, shoes, shirts. I go to Mr. Wirtz—Dollar Bill—and told him the guys went overboard and put it all on my room. I said to him, "I'll make you a deal. Let's hold off until the playoffs. If we go to the final, you pay. If we don't, I pay. He said, "It's a deal." I told the players, "We're going to the final—otherwise I have to pay that crazy golf bill."

There was a night when we were in Vancouver that I was at the Yale Hotel to listen to some live music. I wound up meeting a guy who knew his music, and who was in town doing a film. It was Glenn Frey from the band the Eagles. He was a hockey fan and recognized me. He had a beard and long hair at the time, so no one recognized him. I was asked by the local band to go up on stage. I said, "Only if I can bring my friend." He put on a concert for an hour or so.

That season, Roenick played really well and led us in scoring with 53 goals and 103 points. Larms had 74 points, Goulet 63.

We were a well-balanced team. Marchment became an impact player. Our defence was better overall. Eddie played the bulk of the games in goal, starting—not always finishing—52, while Hašek appeared in 20 and Jimmy Waite 17. But during the regular season, I told myself that it wasn't worth pushing them too hard, that nobody cares about finishing first overall and winning the Presidents' Trophy. To push them again like I did the previous season only to lose in the first round? It wouldn't have been worth it. The important part was to make sure we were in the playoffs, and then do well. We finished with 36 wins, 13 fewer than the previous season, and 87 points, 19 fewer. But that was okay. I liked the team and I thought we were playoff ready.

We met St. Louis in the first round. That was a physical series, two tough teams. There's a reason why they called our division the "Chuck" Norris Division. We won the opener but fell behind 2–1 after a double-overtime loss. We won the next three, and then somehow swept Detroit and Edmonton to advance to the Stanley Cup final, my third trip but my first with the Blackhawks after twice stalling in the third round. We had won a playoff record 11 games in a row. Our best players were absolutely our best players, the likes of Roenick, Chelios, Larmer, Goulet, Smith, Belfour—everyone was contributing. And Mr. Wirtz never said a word about the $10,000 golf bill!

It was an exciting spring in Chicago. We were in the final and so were the Chicago Bulls, who were playing the Portland Trail Blazers. I had a good relationship with the Bulls. Michael Jordan would often come by my office and ask if he could use the medical room. I remember Michael and Scottie Pippen sitting in our stainless-steel hot tub, the two of them squeezed in, knees up to their eyes. It was hilarious. Every year, Michael would give me a game-worn jersey for charity. He was a good guy that way. I did a couple of television commercials for a car company with Bulls coach Phil Jackson. It was a good time to be a sports fan in Chicago.

So, in the final we met the Pittsburgh Penguins. They had won the Stanley Cup the previous spring after Scotty Bowman took over for Bob Johnson, who had become seriously ill. I was pumped to be coaching in the final against Scotty, the guy who had given me my professional start in Rochester so many years ago. I knew it was going to be a tough series. The Penguins had Mario Lemieux, Jaromír Jágr, Ron Francis, Kevin Stevens, Larry Murphy, Bryan Trottier, Tom Barrasso, Rick Tocchet . . . and Scotty.

In the series opener, in Pittsburgh, we came out flying. We'd taken a 3–0 lead 14 minutes into the first period and were up 4–1 midway through the second. But I recall two critical incidents. Jágr grabbed Kravchuk's stick and pulled it out of his hands. No call. And they scored on that play. Then Mario took a horrendous dive in the neutral zone, and they end up winning the game, 5–4, on the power play with 13 seconds left, with Mario scoring. Steve Smith was given a fucking penalty with 18 seconds left. I was furious. I felt that referee Andy Van Hellemond was very biased. I know they were a stacked team, with Mario in his prime, but the way that game unfolded, Andy made a huge difference in the series.

I would criticize myself as well. Our players had played hard and well, but I was so upset after the game, I gave the team shit. We went to dinner afterwards and I scolded them, and I wish I hadn't. I told them I wanted more from them—but they'd given me everything they had. The Mario dive was fucking embarrassing. And the play with Jágr, grabbing Kravchuk's stick, and they scored? What was I thinking? We had just won a record 11 playoff games in a row. It wasn't the time to be forceful; I should have been more compassionate. And they were a great group. I was so incensed with the officiating that it poured over to my address to the team. I had harsh words for Belfour and Roenick. That was a mistake. Giving that team shit is one of my biggest regrets to this day.

Next game, we gave up a short-handed goal midway through the first period and tied it in the second. Then Mario went to work, scoring twice, once on the power play. We could manage only four shots in the third period and lost, 3–1. We had five penalties, Pittsburgh three. Just saying. It was 6–4 penalties in the first game. I sat Roenick for a large part of that second game, but there was a reason. After the game, I brought Jeremy with me to the press conference with a cast on his right hand. He had been slashed by Kevin Stevens and had injured his thumb and the top of his hand. I said to the media, "There was an incident that should have been a call, but there was no call." I raised the roof. I said, "How does a kid end up with a cast on his hand and there's no call on the slash?" After the series was over, Jeremy's agent, Neil Abbott, ripped me for doing it—he thought I had put a target on him by exposing the injury—but I was trying to win a series and get an edge back with the officials. And I was fucking mad.

In the third game, back in Chicago, we couldn't get anything past Barrasso. Jeremy was playing hurt and the offence dried up. It would have been like Mario going down for them. We lost

1–0, with Stevens scoring a fucking fluke goal. There was a shot dumped in from the point; it hit a player and went in. In the fourth game, Eddie started in goal and let in a couple of soft goals on four shots in the first six and half minutes. He'd had such a great playoff run. I pulled him to try to jolt the team, but the confidence was waning, down 3–0 in the series. We did battle hard. Dirk Graham had a hat trick in the first period, and we were tied 3–3. It was 4–4 after two, but the Penguins went on to win 6–5.

It was my third trip to the final, and my third loss. I was very disappointed. Dirk said to me after, "Mike, I didn't understand how prepared you had to be before the series starts; we tried to get prepared during the series." Pittsburgh had already won the Stanley Cup, and we had only a handful of guys who had won. He said, "I'll probably never get another chance." That's how tough it is to win.

I was exhausted. I had coached in the Canada Cup in the summer, been coach and GM all season, and led the team through another long playoff run. When I think back on everything I was doing—dating back to Philly and those two long runs and a Canada Cup, and then everything with the Blackhawks—it was insanity. I had just gone through 11 months of coaching and managing. Within two weeks of losing the final, Mr. Wirtz asked me to make a decision about coaching going forward, because they didn't want to hold up Darryl Sutter, my associate coach, who was getting head coaching offers. Winnipeg and Vancouver had talked to him at some point, Los Angeles as well. If I wasn't going to coach long term, they wanted to make sure they had Darryl, who was still under contract.

I said, "Bill, I just coached and managed two teams without a day off for 11 months. We just lost the final and you're asking me to make a career decision in 10 fucking days." I was exhausted. I said, "Fuck you." Maybe that was the start of it. I respected Darryl. I said to let Darryl be the coach and I'd be the manager only. As the summer went on, though, I resented having to make that decision so soon after the season, and deep down I knew I still had the coaching bug.

Even as GM only, I was busy that summer, trading Hašek to the Buffalo Sabres for goaltender Stéphane Beauregard and a fourth-round pick, who turned out to be Éric Dazé. I then flipped Beauregard to Winnipeg for winger Christian Ruuttu. I traded Hašek because there was another expansion draft on the horizon, and we could protect only one goalie. Belfour was going to play the bulk of the games and we had Jimmy Waite. We elected to keep Eddie. It's funny, but during the season, John Muckler and the Sabres put Dominik on waivers, and I was the only one to claim him. The NHL said I couldn't because I had traded him. Dom was left unprotected in the 1993 expansion draft; six other goalies were selected, but not him. Dom, of course, went on to become a Hall of Famer.

The other business I was involved in was the draft in Montreal. Quebec had finally accepted that Eric Lindros, their first pick in the 1991 draft, wasn't going to play for them, in large part because of owner Marcel Aubut. Lindros and his parents did not like Aubut and thought the Nordiques, on his orders, had tanked to get the first overall pick. The Nordiques had his rights for only two years, so they wanted to trade him before the 1992 draft to get some picks and players and move on. I was knee deep in trade talks with Nordiques GM Pierre Pagé, a really good guy. At one point, there were 14 teams in trade discussions for the rights to Lindros, and the trade offers were incredible. Know this: Lindros was a superstar in waiting and everybody knew it. He was six foot four, 230 pounds; he had great skill and was a physical monster. He was billed as the next Gretzky or Lemieux, or, as Pagé later said, the next Gordie Howe. Because I had invited Eric to training camp for the 1991 Canada Cup, despite him never having played a day in the NHL, he now had Chicago on the shortlist of teams with which he would sign. We were his first choice, Toronto second, New York Rangers third.

On the morning of the draft, I met with Pagé to try to hammer out a deal. There were a bunch of players and draft picks involved. We had pretty much agreed on a multi-player deal, but then Aubut said he wanted $5 million included in the package. Well, Dollar Bill just about lost his mind. No deal. As it turned out, Aubut ended up getting $15 million and a pretty sweet package out of Philly. Too bad. Lindros and Roenick and Chelios would have been an incredible core group.

The season started and I was antsy. It was a hard adjustment, going from coaching to sitting upstairs watching games. I missed the day-to-day, the challenges behind the bench during games. I had been negotiating a new contract with the Blackhawks as GM and I was wondering if I should wait, ride out the final year of my existing contract, and decide whether I was really done with coaching. I still had Pulford looking over my shoulder, too. I told Wirtz that Pully could be an advisor, but I had to make the trades and do contracts and not report to him, just to Mr. Wirtz. That's not what they wanted.

In November, I thought I had a new contract to be GM. I thought we had agreed on a $400,000-a-year deal for five years, a total of $2 million. At the time, coaches were making that much money. I thought I should be making at least what the coaches were making. On November 6, I went in to sign my new contract. I walked into the room and there was Gene Gozdecki, the Blackhawks' counsel, and Peter Wirtz, the youngest son. They didn't hesitate. Gene said, "You're fired." I said, "Fuck." The first thing that came to my mind was *There goes my fucking marriage*, because I knew Rita didn't want to move again. There was no reason given. I had agreed to terms; I thought I was going in to sign the contract. Fuck. And it was my mother's birthday.

Bill Wirtz had agreed to the deal, but maybe he'd had second thoughts about the money. I was going to make twice what I had been making doing both jobs, but it was fair market value. Maybe he didn't want Pully just being a consultant. He was loyal to his management people. Loyal to a fault. Wirtz and the organization had long been dysfunctional. Wirtz had said I wanted too much power; I just wanted to do the GM job. I actually thought Pully was kind of relieved with the new role, but his wife, Roslyn, despised me. She wanted to walk around Chicago Stadium with her husband as GM. She was tight with Mrs. Wirtz. The rumour was that Bob would do the GM's job for $200,000, so Wirtz didn't need Keenan. And they had Darryl as coach. I still couldn't believe it: four years, 60 playoff games, go to the final four three times, the Stanley Cup final once. We had taken over a franchise that was rock bottom. Again, I was asking myself: Why did I get fired?

I got in my car and called Rita from the car phone. She asked, "How did it go?" I said, "It didn't go well. I got fired." She said, "What?" That was the fucking end of it. Why did I know it was the end? I was exhausted when I gave the job to Darryl. I was burnt out. I'd discussed it with Rita when they asked about the coaching job, and she said, "Mike, I really don't want to move again." She had just graduated with her masters of social work (MSW) and now had a job offer. She wondered if I might just go back to teaching, coaching high school and some TV work.

I said, "Rita, I want to coach."

A two-year-old me sitting in my grandmother Helen's rocking chair, with a banged-up left hand.

My elementary school yearbook picture.

My dad, Ted, offering a few tips to his 12-year-old son with the Whitby Pee-Wee All-Stars.

My senior season, 1971–72, with the St. Lawrence University Saints.

University life: my pal
Tim Pelyk and a bunch of
dirty dishes at our place on
5 West in Canton, NY,
St. Lawrence University.

Fighting for position as a
Roanoke Rebel in 1974.

Sitting in the pope's chair in
Krakow, Poland, while travelling
with the University of Toronto
Varsity Blues in 1973.

coach mike keenan
"live and laugh!"

The Forest Hill Collegiate yearbook, 1975.
"Live and laugh!" Words to live by.

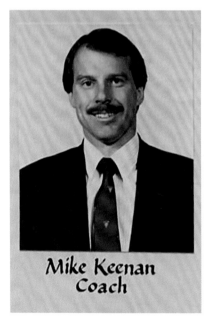

Head coach of the University of
Toronto Varsity Blues, 1983–84.

My first season behind the
Flyers bench, 1984–85.

Jack Adams Award winner as coach of the year in the NHL in 1985, my first season with the Philadelphia Flyers.

A Rochester Americans game program.

The Rochester Americans Hockey Magazine • October 1980

25th Anniversary

Mike Keenan's Rapid Rise to Rochester P. 18

$1

Me and the Great One,
Wayne Gretzky, at the
1991 Canada Cup.

Training camp with Team Canada for the 1991 Canada Cup.

Champions! 1991 Team Canada, the Canada Cup winners.

Two treasures: Gayla and the Stanley Cup.

Celebrating the Stanley Cup win at Gracie Mansion in New York with (left to right) Gayla; my mom, Thelma; sisters, Marie and Cathy; and my dad, Ted.

My father, Ted, after we won the Stanley Cup in 1994.

Celebrating my 500th
career win, 1998.

The champion Rangers
reunion with (left to
right) Adam Graves,
Jeff Beukeboom, Brian
Leetch, Sergei Zubov
and Mark Messier, 2019.

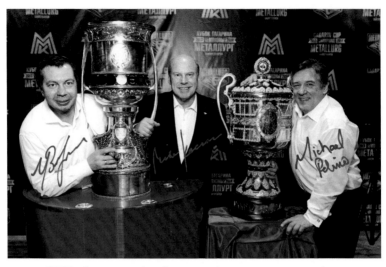

KHL champions hardware, with my assistant coaches,
Ilya Vorobiev (left) and Mike Pelino. In 2014, we won the Gagarin
Cup in the KHL with Magnitogorsk Metallurg, and I became the
first coach to win both the Gagarin and Stanley Cups.

Meeting the media in Beijing
after taking over the Kunlun
Red Star team.

My latest coaching job is with the Italian national
team, along with my assistant coaches and long-time
friends, Mike Pelino (left) and Dave Jamieson.

The legend: Tom Watt in 2022
when he was inducted into the
Ontario Sports Hall of Fame.
He should be in the Hockey
Hall of Fame.

Visiting my former university
teammate Mike Barnett (left),
who went on to become Wayne
Gretzky's agent, and the great
Glen Sather, who was my GM
with Team Canada in 1987.

I had the honour to coach Mark
Messier several times, and here
we're together to celebrate the 25th
anniversary of the 1994 Stanley
Cup win with the Rangers.

At Mark Wahlberg's Children's
Miracle Celebrity Invitational
golf tournament in support
of the children's hospital in
Detroit, with Jeremy Roenick,
Gabrielle and former Ranger
Ron Duguay, 2022.

With Gayla in the pool in Florida.

With Rita and Gayla at the cottage on Georgian Bay, 1987.

Together with family for Craig and Gayla's (left) wedding weekend with my wife, Nola, and her sons, Reed and Grant, 2005.

Having fun teaching grandson, Connor, how to skate, 2014.

With my partner, Gabrielle, at Madison Square Garden for a game in the fall of 2023. It has been great to be welcomed back by the Rangers.

Me and Connor at the cottage.

I am blessed to have a wonderful family. Left to right: my sisters, Cathy and Marie; Marie's daughter Kim and Marie's husband, Peter; their other daughter Kate; Gayla; brother-in-law Dan; John, who is married to Kate; son-in-law, Craig; and granddaughter, Maelle.

My beautiful granddaughter, Maelle.

Visiting with daughter, Gayla and grandkids, Connor and Maelle, in Virginia, 2023.

Vocal

Let You Know Tomorrow

Words and Music by
Mike Keenan and Ken Gardner

arr. Ken Gardner

I wrote this song watching the Super Bowl in 2018 with a few of my pals, including Gary Webb from Nik and the Nice Guys.

The view from the cottage on Georgian Bay, Ontario. My favourite place.

REMEMBER

If I could remember all the changes in my life,
I would remember the moments of tenderness and joy with my wife,
For love and life are the best when most fulfilled and complete,
If I could remember the moments of your grace, the smile of your
    face, the intrigue of that place,

If I could remember the fantasy of it all, the once desired purpose
    carried by a child,
If I could remember the state of well-being,
The place in my heart that always ran supreme,
The measure of your soul so kind,

If I could remember the thrill of it all,
The bittersweet success to stand tall,
Would only bring memories for life is what you live,
It could only bring feeling for life is what you give,

If I could remember to say it just once,
The depth of your being is all that we have,
To share the experience, for knowledge is for you to continue to grow,
To feel life's breath and failures is to live complete,

If I could remember that life can be sweet, so caring, so joyful, so
    wonderful to explore,
As we live each chapter without hesitation or delay,
The art of it all will stay with you, in your soul,
In your mind forever to remember.

Written by: Michael E. Keenan
In Key West, December 2003

14

HIRED: NEW YORK, 1993

EVEN THOUGH I was unemployed for the second time in my NHL coaching career, I was confident I would land another job. The questions were when and where. It had taken me only 25 days to get the Chicago job after I was let go by the Philadelphia Flyers, but because this time I was fired a month or so into the season I knew it would take considerably longer, or so I thought. The other question, of course, was whether Rita and Gayla would be coming with me, wherever I was going. Turns out, things started to heat up sooner than I expected, on all fronts.

When I first left the Blackhawks, I spent some time in Aspen, Colorado, where I had a place, and did some skiing and worked out in the gym. Back home in Chicago, I went to the gym every day. I wanted to get into really good physical condition. I was a big runner back then, and my fitness level became very good. I also did a little television work with TSN and my old friend

Gary Green and his broadcast partner, Jim Hughson. We did four games together doing colour commentary in the booth.

About a month after I was fired I received a call from the expansion Mighty Ducks of Anaheim, who were owned by Disney. I flew to Anaheim to meet with Disney chairman Michael Eisner, and I was eventually offered the coach and GM jobs with a five-year contract at $400,000 per year, twice what I was earning in Chicago and the amount I thought I was going to get from the Blackhawks when they reneged on my new deal. I also met with Wayne Huizenga, owner of the expansion Florida Panthers. But I really didn't want to coach an expansion team. I believe I could have done a good job building one, but I wasn't keen on the time it would take to turn them into a contender from the ground up. I had been to the Stanley Cup final three times and wanted back, in a hurry.

I had an offer in mid-December from Lugano, in the Swiss league, to take over their team for $150,000, but I turned that down. I wasn't leaving home at that point to coach anywhere but the NHL. There had been rumblings about that time that the Flyers were thinking about bringing me back to replace Bill Dineen as coach, but I didn't hear from anyone in the organization. There were also whispers about Buffalo wanting me to coach, but nothing materialized.

It was in January that Mike Ilitch called me. He owned the Detroit Red Wings, and he wanted to meet me and my agent, Rob Campbell (who had replaced Eagleson when Eagleson was having his legal issues), at his suburban home. The previous season, the Wings had 43 wins and 98 points under GM/coach Bryan Murray, but had been swept in the division final by my

Blackhawks. They were having another good season under Murray, but Mr. Ilitch wanted to talk. To avoid being seen in the Detroit airport, Rob and I drove to Detroit from Toronto. It was just me and Rob, and Mr. and Mrs. (Marian) Ilitch sitting around the kitchen table. Marian had made tuna sandwiches. It was nice conversation, a nice lunch. Finally, Mr. Ilitch asked Rob what it would take to get me to Detroit. Rob had told me not to open my mouth. I had no idea what Rob was going to say, but he replied that it would take a $500,000 signing bonus to start. Mr. Ilitch got up, poured himself a glass of water and asked, "Why?" Rob said, "Because if you don't pay it, someone else will."

Mr. Ilitch ended up giving me $150,000 to hold my place, so I wouldn't go to another team. Basically, he had right of first refusal. So there I was, sitting on the sideline. I have a contract to possibly be coach and GM in Detroit the next season, but nobody knows. For now. Word did get out within the organization, and the team president, Jim Lites, who was married to Mr. Ilitch's daughter Denise, was not happy. Neither he nor executive vice-president Jimmy Devellano, their former GM, were interested in working with me, and they let Mr. Ilitch know it.

Mr. Ilitch called me up and said he had a problem: the family was upset, his executives were upset and didn't want me. I said, "Mr. Ilitch, no problem, we'll move on, and I will send the money back." I've been told that Murray also found out about the plan and understandably wasn't pleased. Despite another successful regular season, finishing with 47 wins and 103 points, the Wings were upset in the first round of the 1993 playoffs in seven games by the Leafs. Murray kept his GM job, and Scotty Bowman was hired as coach. Lites left the Wings after the season, moving to the Dallas Stars. Jimmy D., who was tight with Mr. Ilitch, remained. I've heard that Jimmy D. told Mr. Ilitch that if he passed on Mike Keenan, he would get him either Al Arbour or Scotty Bowman. Funny how Scotty knew just how much money Mr. Ilitch was willing to pay.

So I was a free agent again, in more ways than one. In March, Rita and I finally split up. I told her it was time. Years later, she said she would have moved, but at the time I was thinking about how she had gotten her MSW at Loyola, had a job opportunity, and didn't want to move Gayla, who was 14, to another city and school. I think I realized she was burned out in terms of the hockey business. She'd married a schoolteacher, not a hockey coach, and we had moved a lot, from Rochester to Toronto to Philly to Chicago. She was very close to her family. It just got complicated, and it was a very sad, very difficult time for everyone.

On the job front, the next to try to recruit me was Ed Snider, of all people, and the Flyers, who had fired me five years earlier. His Flyers had missed the playoffs for the past four seasons, including 1992–93. In fairness, they had gutted their roster to acquire Eric Lindros, who was becoming a great player. Snider asked me to meet over breakfast at his house. He said, "I made a mistake and shouldn't have fired you." He reached into his sports jacket pocket and pulled out a five-year, $5 million contract to be the coach, but also to be in charge of player personnel. My concern with the offer was twofold: How would it work with me making player personnel decisions and Russ Farwell remaining as GM? And why wasn't Farwell at the meeting? That didn't feel right. It was a big admission by Snider to extend the offer and say he made a mistake. I said I needed time to think.

Meantime, I had other irons in the fire. In March, I had been named head coach and GM for Team Canada at the World Championships in Munich, which were beginning April 18. I recruited Roger Neilson, who had been fired by the New York Rangers in early January, to be my associate coach, and I had Tom Renney and Dany Dubé, who were co-coaches of the national team, as my assistants. With Roger and me both otherwise unemployed, we were able to fly around recruiting players from teams that weren't going to make the playoffs. Lindros was one of the first named, along with Rod Brind'Amour, Dave Manson, Shayne Corson, Adam Graves, Mike Gartner, Mark Recchi and some other pretty good talent.

With the Worlds approaching and the Flyers offer in hand, Rob Campbell had quietly let the Rangers know I was interested in becoming their head coach. Roger had been fired in part because he and Mark Messier and some of the other star players weren't on the same page. The previous season, the Rangers had finished with 105 points but lost in the second round of the playoffs. This season, they struggled under Roger, who was replaced by farm team coach Ron Smith on an interim basis. They wound up missing the playoffs. Before their season ended they contacted me, I'm sure at the urging of Messier, who had played for me in the two Canada Cup tournaments. I also knew Rangers colour commentator John Davidson, who had the ear of management, had passed along word of my interest and his endorsement to Madison Square Garden president Bob Gutkowski.

It's also my understanding that Stanley Jaffe, who was president of Paramount Communications, owner of the team, wanted a powerful coach. A couple years earlier, the basketball Knicks had hired Pat Riley, who had won multiple championships with the Los Angeles Lakers. Under the orders of Jaffe, Gutkowski and Rangers GM Neil Smith flew to Toronto to meet with me and Rob Campbell at Rob's downtown office, near the University of Toronto, on April 16. The Rangers would finish their season a day later, losing their seventh game in a row and tenth out of their final 11. Time was of the essence, because I was leaving the next day for Munich.

Although Neil said at various times that he wanted me as coach, I believe he was pushed to do it, that he didn't want me— and I believed it even more after the way my brief tenure with the Rangers evolved. Jaffe had given orders to get Keenan, and Gutkowski, who was resisting pushes to fire Smith, was smart enough to do what Jaffe wanted. Gutkowski was a sharp guy who knew the lay of the land politically. But I knew Neil really didn't want me; he just had no choice.

One of the things Smith and Gutkowski asked me about was whether I would be satisfied being just coach and not GM. I assured them that with everything I had been through in recent years—being coach and GM in Chicago, coach and GM with the Canada Cup, not to mention the dissolution of my marriage—I would be fine being just the coach. And I meant it.

It actually didn't take long to hammer out a very nice deal, five years and more than $5 million, if I achieved bonuses. First, I received a $660,875 signing bonus. My annual salaries were $750,000, $850,000, $900,000, $950,000 and $1 million. There was a $50,000 bonus for finishing first overall, and $25,000 for finishing second overall. The playoff bonuses included $50,000 for winning the first round, $25,000 for every round after that, and $100,000 for winning the Stanley Cup. There was a $50,000 a year annuity from age 55 until death (which I never received), money for life insurance, a car, and a $975,000 personal loan to purchase a home. They got Jaffe involved when it got to the short strokes, but he signed off. I flew on their private jet for the announcement the next day. I can't recall whether I called Ed Snider to tell him I was going to the Rangers, but he never spoke to me again, and I wasn't invited to another Flyers function until he passed in 2016. I didn't reject Philly's offer because I resented Snider for firing me. I signed with New York because I thought I needed a new start somewhere else.

The press conference went well and was certainly well attended. It was New York, after all. I assured the media I was fine with being just the coach of the Rangers and that Neil and I would work together. Neil also mentioned to the media that he would get me the type of players I wanted, though I soon found out that was going to require some pushing on my part. I did a bunch of interviews with various television stations, the last one with ESPN. I was running late and had to get to the airport for my flight to Munich, so I didn't stop to wash the TV makeup off my face.

Halfway through the flight, my neck started to itch and swell. I went to the washroom and washed off the makeup. By the time I got to the hotel in Germany my neck was very sore and badly infected. Our doctor was Simon McGrail, who was the Maple Leafs' team physician. He took me to the hospital. I was put on morphine for the literal pain in my neck, which they wrapped, almost like a cast. I asked Roger to coach the team, but he refused. I don't know why, other than he said I was the coach. I said, "Roger, I can't even think. I can't stand behind the bench for an entire game. Please take over the coaching job." I added emphatically, "I'm coming *out of hospital* to coach." He still said he wouldn't do it, I was the coach.

I might have been uncomfortable, but the team had a good start, winning five in a row in the preliminary round. We beat Finland 5–1 in the quarterfinals, but then we played Russia and they kicked our butts, 7–4, in the semifinals. We lost to the Czechs 5–1 in the bronze-medal game. Lindros had been a dominant presence in the dressing room. After we got beat, he came to me and said, "Mike, you screwed this up." He said, "You didn't give us a curfew the entire tournament and we won every game, but the night before the Russia game you gave us an 11:30 curfew and we got beat." We laughed.

When I got back after the Worlds, I became part of the MSG radio crew for the playoffs, doing colour commentary with play-by-play guy Howie Rose. We covered the Stanley Cup final, with Montreal beating Gretzky and the Los Angeles Kings. Watching the Cup being presented after that final game, I was more determined than ever it was going to be Stanley Cup or bust in the upcoming season with my new team.

I bought a house in Greenwich, Connecticut, which was a short drive to our practice facility in suburban Rye, New York. It was five bedrooms, a great big place, lots of room for Gayla and anyone else to visit, which many did. There was also a 4 percent difference in taxes from New York State, so it was a significant savings. One of the bonuses in my contract, as I mentioned, was a $975,000 personal loan to help me purchase a home, payable within five years at 5 percent interest. When the first draft of the contract arrived there was a large omission. Rob called me and said, "Do you want to buy the Empire State Building?" I said, "What?" He said they had messed up and hadn't put in an amount for the loan, so I could borrow as much money as I wanted. The lawyer was a guy named Ken Munoz, and he just about had a heart attack when Rob pointed out the error. We fixed the contract, much to Ken's relief.

When I left Chicago, I gave Rita the house in Wilmette. It was a very nice neighbourhood and had great schools. I got a rental truck, put my clothes, hockey notes and a few boxes in the van and made the drive from Chicago to New York by myself. I pretty much cried the whole way. When I told Gayla I was leaving, I was sitting in the kitchen, and she jumped on my lap and started to cry. I still remember Rita standing at the door as I drove away; I could see her in the rear-view mirror.

Holy fuck. That was it.

15

ON A MISSION: NEW YORK, 1993–94

I'D JUST HAD one relationship end badly, and I was embarking on another I was pretty sure wasn't going to be great, either—working with GM Neil Smith. I was thrilled to be the coach of the New York Rangers, and the contract I signed made me feel like I'd won the lottery. There is something about the energy in New York City that I absolutely thrive off, and I loved the challenge of winning the Stanley Cup as quickly as possible. But I knew Neil would be a challenge, no matter how many times he said I was the coach he wanted. I knew deep down that I wasn't. Hell, a few days after he hired me, he asked my agent if he had made a mistake.

The NHL entry draft was set to take place in Quebec City in late June, but the expansion draft to stock the new Anaheim and Florida teams was being held a few days ahead of that. We had to decide which goaltender we were going to protect, knowing we would be losing one in the draft. We agreed that we would keep Mike Richter because he was a few years younger than John Vanbiesbrouck. Credit to Neil, he made the best of the situation, trading Vanbiesbrouck to Vancouver; they didn't protect him, and he was picked up by Florida. In exchange, we got defence-man Doug Lidster, who was a handy player for us.

But, we had to find a backup goaltender. Neil suggested Ron Tugnutt, who had played several years with the Quebec Nordiques and had just finished a season with the Edmonton Oilers. But I was thinking Glenn Healy, who had played four seasons with the New York Islanders and that spring had been outstanding in leading the Isles to a huge second-round upset of Mario Lemieux and the Pittsburgh Penguins, the two-time defending Stanley Cup champions. I said Healy would be a better fit—that he was a better goalie than Tugnutt and would push Richter, and if there was an injury he had proven he could carry the load. And I liked to have options in goal.

Neil said, "But Healy wants $1 million." I said, "What do you care? We're the New York Rangers, we can afford it. We have to win the Stanley Cup this year. Let's get the best guy available." As it turned out, the Islanders protected my old Flyers goaltender Ron Hextall in the expansion draft and exposed Healy, who was taken by Anaheim. But there was a second phase to the draft, with Ottawa, Tampa Bay and San Jose, who had joined over the previous two seasons, allowed to select players from Anaheim and Florida. The teams could keep only one goaltender, so Anaheim chose Guy Hebert ahead of Healy, who was selected by Tampa. Neil was able to get Healy from the Lightning for a third-round pick, and I was glad he did.

Richter played well for us, but Healy was a very good addi-tion. He was 31, four years older than Richter, but they got along and were a good tandem, although there was a time during the season when I was pushing Neil to try to trade Richter to the Blackhawks for Eddie Belfour. That somehow got leaked to the media, and not by me. Heals could be a pain in the ass some-times. He had a quick wit and a sharp tongue, but he delivered in goal. And he admitted later that I was the right coach for the team. I remember one time I asked him what the difference was between me and Isles coach Al Arbour. He said, "Seven Stanley Cups." We laughed. There was one night when I pulled him and he threw his mask into the bench and was hollering at me. I finally said, "Who made you Mr. Hockey?"

Neil also delivered for me when he signed free-agent winger Greg Gilbert, who'd played well for me in Chicago and who I liked a lot, and traded for defenceman Alexander Karpovtsev.

I filled out my coaching staff, keeping Colin Campbell, who had been an assistant under Roger Neilson. When Roger was fired, Collie was sent down to coach Binghamton. I didn't know Collie that well, though we had spent some time together at the training camp of the WHA Vancouver Blazers years earlier. He also played in Peterborough a few years before I went there to coach. I also hired Dick Todd, who had been my trainer/assistant coach in Peterborough and went on to coach the Petes for 13 seasons after I left, winning two championships. I hired as video coach Arne Pappin, the son of former player Jim Pappin, a fine man who was a scout with Chicago when I was there and beyond. I also hired Dr. Cal Botterill as team psychologist—he'd been with me in Philly and Chicago—and renowned high-performance fitness coach

Howie Wenger. I tried to have staff around me who were familiar with the program so there was no learning curve involved; also, I could trust them and know they were very loyal.

Neil called our first staff meeting in July, at our practice facility in Rye, New York. Collie, Dick and I were there, along with Barry Watkins, who was in charge of public relations, and Matt Loughran, who ran team services. Rob Campbell was there, too. He represented me and Collie and was friends with Dick. I said to Neil, "What do you think of the team?" He said, "It's a great team—we could win the Stanley Cup." I said, "There's no way this team can win the Stanley Cup. It couldn't make the playoffs with Roger, a great coach. I get it, there were injuries, but they quit down the stretch, winning one of their final 11 games." Even though Neil had made some nice additions—Mark Messier, Adam Graves, Kevin Lowe, Esa Tikkanen, former Oilers who had won—we were still not big enough, tough enough or experienced enough to win it all. I said, "I've been to the final three times, I know what it takes." I wasn't meaning to be disrespectful or contentious, but how was a team that didn't make the playoffs last year going to win the Stanley Cup this year? That started us off on the wrong foot. But I wasn't wrong, and that wouldn't be our last debate on whether that roster was good enough.

When the team assembled for training camp in Rye, we met in a nearby hotel. I asked MSG Network producer Joe Whalen to put together a video with clips from various New York championship parades. Well, there was no footage of a Rangers parade because, as everyone knew, they hadn't won the Stanley Cup since 1940. I said to Joe, "Get the baseball parades, the Yankees and the Miracle Mets, all those parades down the Canyon of Heroes in Lower Manhattan, and put it to the song by the band Starship—'Nothing's Gonna Stop Us Now.'" It was the song we had made our playoff anthem in Philly in 1987 and I loved it. I can still see Ron Hextall flying out on the ice with the song blasting in the Spectrum.

The chorus had the lyrics about building dreams together and standing strong, and, as the title said, how "nothing's gonna stop us now." Mess, who is an emotional guy, sat in the front row, about 15 feet from me, and I could see tears rolling down his cheeks. He had won five Stanley Cups with the Oilers, but he still had a burning desire to win, and he knew I did, too. He told me I was the first person with the Rangers who had talked about winning the Cup *now*. That struck a chord with him. His beef with Roger Neilson was the style of play: it wasn't Stanley Cup or bust. Mess knew from the Canada Cups that it was winning or nothing with me. When I saw the look on Mess's face and the tears in his eyes, I said to myself, *We have a chance to win the Cup. This guy is invested. We've got a chance and one day it could be us in a parade down the Canyon of Heroes.*

Before that meeting was over, I went around the room and had a message for every player. I told Mess and a few others they would win the Cup again. I told Brian Leetch he would win the Norris, and Richter that he would win the Vezina. When I got to the bottom of the roster, Ed Olczyk has since reminded me, I said, "I don't know what you're going to do. You're probably not going to play a lot, but you'll be a good teammate." He was a great teammate. Eddie had been a 30-plus goal scorer in the league; now he was on the fifth line. But there were no assholes on this team. Eddie would lead the stretching after every practice, and that's where the heave-ho chant started. The players would stand in a circle at centre ice and they'd stretch their arms out and do a rowing motion, like they were rowing a boat. Heave-ho. It was symbolism of our group pulling together. Eddie really kept a professional attitude. We had a lot of depth, and all those guys who didn't play a lot—Mike Hartman, Nick Kypreos, Mike Hudson, Eddie O—there was no complaining. No one was disruptive. It speaks to the leadership in the room, starting with Mess, Lowe, Graves. Tikkanen was the ice breaker. I used to say he spoke his own language, a cross between Finnish and English—Tikkanese. If I got wound up, he'd say, "Mike, take it easy, take it easy" in his broken English. Everyone would laugh.

We started our pre-season with a couple of games in London, England, against the Maple Leafs. We were playing for the prestigious French's Mustard Cup! The previous fall, my Blackhawks played the Montreal Canadiens in London at Wembley Arena for the Cup, which we won. The Blackhawks went on to the Stanley Cup final, so maybe it was an omen. Looking back, the trip was probably a good thing for the Rangers, because we took just 25 players and it helped the group to bond, to come together quickly and early. The players got a quick message about the way I handled the bench, which was probably quite different from how Roger and Ron Smith had done it. They could feel right away: *Okay, it's only the French's Mustard Cup, but we'd still better win it.* And we did. We beat the Leafs, who had gone to the final four the year before, 5–3 and 3–1. I think they actually forgot to bring a Cup and scrambled last-minute to find something to present to us. But the players got an early sense that we were going to be very, very competitive, and we had one goal in mind. I know Mess loved that atmosphere.

Heals had told his wife after our first practice that he felt this team could win the Cup. He could see a noticeable difference in the skill level, the speed of our group. As he later said, "Mike wasn't in for the long term, he was going to come in, crash and burn, and try to get the most out of the players. It was all about winning now." And Heals was probably right that it was all or nothing that year. As it turns out, I pissed off Neil, again, when the team departed London. I wasn't on the plane. Everyone was allowed one guest on the trip, and I brought Rob Campbell. I would have brought Gayla, but she was in school, so I flew to Chicago to see her before returning to New York to finish up camp. I didn't tell Neil about my side trip, and he didn't like it when he found out.

Life on my own was certainly an adjustment. It wasn't easy being without Rita and Gayla, even though during the season I could be quite distant. But that departure kind of worked out for me in a mysterious way. I bought that big house in the country in Greenwich. I had looked at a few places. I looked at some condos downtown, even one that was owned by Jim Henson, the creator of the Muppets. But being on my own really drove me to focus on my job, even more than I usually did, which is saying something. Arne Pappin and I would stay up late watching the West Coast games and do our homework and game prep. I hardly went out. I would go over video, go over practice plans, sleep on the sofa in my office at the practice rink. I was totally consumed and committed to my work. I think it was a good thing.

At the house, I left a key in the lamp post. If anyone wanted to come visit, even if I was on the road, they knew where to find the key. Many of my old university friends came for visits and would stay for however long they wanted. The one rule was: keep the house clean and the key in the lamp post. All sorts of people used it when we were travelling and would tell me later they had been there. I had a dear friend named Tommy Greenaway, who was a state trooper in New Jersey when I was in Philly and then a secret service agent in New York. He was living in his office in Albany, sleeping on the couch. I said, "That's crazy, come take one of the bedrooms and you can come and go as you want." At one point, Tommy was on President Ronald Reagan's security detail, but he wasn't on duty the day he was shot. Anyway, Tommy was around a lot, which was good. It was nice to have some company. And on occasion Nola McLennan, who I had met in Florida when I was on a golfing trip with Roger, would visit as our relationship started to grow.

The Rangers had a somewhat slow start to the season, .500 through the first 10 games, and I still wasn't shy about telling the media that we needed to make some changes and had to get tougher and more experienced, which no doubt didn't make Neil happy. But I had the same conversations with him. Steve Larmer, who had starred for me in Chicago, had decided it was time to move on. He felt the organization had taken a step back after I'd left and we had gotten to the final a year earlier. Here's an example of his character. He had an iron-man streak of 884 games, third-longest in NHL history, but he sat out to get the Blackhawks to trade him. He was committed to moving to a contender and wanted to win a Stanley Cup.

Stanley Jaffe, who was the president of Paramount, owners of the team, would occasionally come to the practice rink on a Saturday morning with his son. We would sit and talk in my office and he would ask, "What do we need?" That upset Neil, of course, but it didn't stop me from answering Stan's question. I said, "Larmer is available, and we have to get this player. I pushed Neil to make a trade for him, but he was reluctant." Well, Stan called a meeting in his office with Neil and Bob Gutkowski, the president of MSG. I'm sure that must have aggravated Neil. Stan said, "What do we need to make the team better?" I said, "Get Larmer." He turned to Neil and said, "Get Larmer for Mike." That went over like a lead balloon.

To his credit, Neil got it done, and he had to involve a third team to make it happen. The Blackhawks weren't keen on sending Larms to the Rangers and Keenan, and they had been asking for a much younger, 23-year-old Tony Amonte, but Neil refused. It made sense—Amonte was a good young player—except we needed Larmer and it was about winning now.

On November 2, Neil traded defenceman James Patrick and forward Darren Turcotte to the Hartford Whalers. I had already asked Neil to trade Patrick, who was scratched in five of our first 11 games. He was an offensive defenceman, but Neil liked him. I didn't think we needed him. We already had Brian Leetch and Sergei Zubov. We also had Jay Wells, who was physical; Kevin Lowe, who was competitive and physical; Jeff Beukeboom, who was physical; Lidster and Karpovtsev. Anyway, Chicago sent Larms and Bryan Marchment to Hartford (whose GM was my old Philly assistant Paul Holmgren) for Patrick Poulin and Eric Weinrich. The Whalers then sent us Larms, along with Nick Kypreos, Barry Richter and a sixth-round pick, for Patrick and Turcotte.

After Larms arrived and started playing well for us, Neil admitted to me that he didn't realize Larmer was that good. I said, "Neil, you have to trust me, I coached him, I know him inside and out." There was obviously discord between us. Neil was upset with being told what to do by Jaffe. I understand any GM would be upset. But I was there for one reason and one reason only. And to accomplish that we needed the player. He was a great player, and there needed to be change on that team.

It was early that season, before the trade, when I really challenged a few players in a vintage Iron Mike way. After a 4–2 loss to Anaheim, I let Leetch know what I thought of his game. It was later reported that I said he was "no fucking Chelios," which I don't remember saying but probably did. Leetch was an exceptional skater and could take charge of the offence. I tried to get him to understand that he had the green light to join the attack, but to just make sure we had support for him before he committed. Sometimes, he would take off and be out in front of the offence. A defenceman can't be in front of the puck. I explained that to him on the bench, but he did it again. I said, "Sit here and let me know when you're ready to play the way I want." He sat the rest of the game. Next game, Mess stepped up. They were best friends. Mess said, "Let's do it, play the way Mike wants." Brian turned around and said, "I'm ready to play." I never had to say anything more.

In that Anaheim game, I wasn't just pissed with Leetch—I was pissed at just about everyone. In the third period I stopped coaching and let them change the lines themselves. The next day, I was so mad at practice that I broke my stick over the crossbar and sent them to the dressing room, then proceeded to call a bunch of them losers. I sent them back on the ice and gave them a wicked bag skate. Lowe said it was the toughest skate he had been through. We lost the next game because we didn't have any legs, but they got the message. I pushed them after that, but I didn't have to push too much. It was a motivated group with strong leadership. As Mess put it years later, the players weren't afraid of me, but they were afraid of being caught unprepared.

Another guy I had to deal with was Zubov, who smoked and was overweight but was a terrific talent. I told Neil to send him to our farm team in Binghamton at the start of the season for a couple of games. His first game back, he had a lousy first period. I brought him in my office and said, "Zubby, if you're going to play like that, you will never play again in New York." I never had to talk to him again. He lost the weight and played unbelievably well. He led our team in scoring with 89 points.

And then there was Alexei Kovalev, a super-talented 20-year-old centre. He would always stay on the ice too long. One night in late February, we were playing Boston and losing 3–1. He was on the ice for 65 seconds and I decided I would send a message. He had the super-long shift and was coming off, but I waved at him to stay on the ice. He's thinking the coach loves him. I said to the guys on the bench, "Don't let him in the doors. He's going to try to step over the boards, don't let him." He was out for seven faceoffs and seven minutes. He scored a goal towards the end of the shift and thought he was a hero. I said to him and the rest of the team, "Do you understand the math? If you have 20 shifts at one minute each, you'll play 20 minutes. If you have 40 shifts at 30 seconds each, you still play 20 minutes. But they will be 20 more intense minutes." He was overextending his shifts to the point where the guys behind him were missing shifts. I asked Mess to have a word with him and make sure the message was understood.

Behind the bench, I always knew who I was going to call for the next shift. Some coaches go 1-2-3-4 lines, roll them out. I would wait until the last possible second to call their names. It makes them pay attention, be engaged every second and stay ready. My coaching philosophy was to be predictably unpredictable, particularly on the road, so the other coach couldn't match lines. In the Canada Cup, I used 27 different line combinations in one game, including on the winning goal in 1987 when I had three centres—Wayne Gretzky, Mario Lemieux and Dale Hawerchuk—out in the final minutes. That line had never played together. It was probably an adjustment for players new to my way of coaching, but I had a great feel for which players were revved up and ready to go.

There were times, however, when I couldn't help myself when it came to pushing and confronting players. I did some irrational things; I would fly off the handle. One day, I called Graves, who played so hard, into the office and barked, "What have you won?" He calmly said, "A Stanley Cup in Edmonton, a Calder Cup in Adirondack, an OHL junior championship in Windsor." Oops. I scrambled and said, "Yeah, but what have you won in the NHL without Messier? Get out." I could have used a mulligan there.

After we picked up Larms, I put him on a line with Messier and Graves and he scored a goal in his first game. We were 7–5–1 at the time but went on a 19–3–2 run after that. Still, we weren't good enough. And even though we were sitting in first place overall as the March 21 trade deadline approached, I firmly believed we needed to make more changes, to get tougher and grittier. We had a 2–4–1 slump heading up to the deadline, including a 7–3 home loss to Chicago. I called Rob Campbell and asked him to call Gutkowski to push Neil into making some trades. With a change in ownership, from Paramount to Viacom, pending, I lost my ally Stan Jaffe in January. I understood Neil didn't want to be told by the coach what to do, but I also knew if we didn't make the changes we wouldn't win the Stanley Cup, so I had Rob make the call.

Gutkowski got Neil and me to meet to discuss our working relationship. I assured Neil I wasn't interested in his job and again told him, "We're in first place, but we're not big enough, tough enough, experienced enough to win the Stanley Cup." I had been to the final three times, I knew. Neil said he was going to look like he was panicking, making these trades with a first-place team. I said, "I don't care, we need a bigger team, a more physical team." I knew we weren't big enough to play against New Jersey, and I convinced Neil to make a few more moves. The first was a big one in terms of who we gave up—Tony Amonte. I liked him a lot, though I was frustrated by his play. I scouted him a lot as GM in Chicago. I saw him a lot at Boston University, and I talked a lot to Pulford about him. He was on my radar.

Neil didn't want to give up Tony, but was kind of told to. And to get something, you have to give something. Amonte was a younger player and the asset Chicago wanted. We got back hard-nosed wingers Stéphane Matteau and Brian Noonan, who had both played for me. It was a great trade for Chicago, and it worked out pretty darn well for us. Next, we traded winger Mike Gartner, who was really good playing for me in the '87 Canada Cup, to the Maple Leafs for Glenn Anderson, who had won Cups in Edmonton and played for me in the Canada Cup. Gartner was a very good player, a future Hall of Famer, but he didn't play the way I wanted or needed, and if he wasn't on the first line he wasn't as effective. Anderson had a history of winning and coming up big in the playoffs.

I said to Neil, "We need guys who have been there." Andy was playoff experienced, a good fit with Mess over the years. We had a bunch of the Oilers, who had won, but other guys like Larms, Matteau, Noonan and Gilbert were still hungry. We needed maturity and experience, because the pressure in New York to win was unbelievable with the Cup drought. We picked up another of the champion Oilers, centre Craig MacTavish, giving up young Todd Marchant in the process. But it was win now. And the moves were seamless. I knew MacT, and we had a whole new line with Matteau and Noonan, a necessary line we needed. I moved Kovy to centre because we needed a second centre at that level. I put him between Tik and Larms, and moved Andy on a line with Mess and Graves.

We were in Calgary for a game the next night (the joke was Collie wouldn't hand out the meal money until after the deadline), and we got on the bus in the morning to head into the rink and it was kind of empty, waiting for the new guys to arrive. But I remember Kevin Lowe saying to me, after we made all those trades, "Well, high risk, high return." A lot of people were surprised I pushed for those deals with us sitting in first place, but this was now a really special team in many ways. There were no assholes, as I mentioned, although some days the players might question that. It was a well-grounded group. We finished the regular season with 52 wins and 112 points and another Presidents' Trophy. But that wasn't the hardware we wanted to win. We were on a mission.

16

1940 NO MORE: SLAYING THE DRAGON

WHEN THE PLAYOFFS started, I really felt good about our team. My neck was on the line, thanks to me pushing so hard at the trade deadline with an already first-place team, but that was fine. I thought this was a Stanley Cup team. We went 8–2–1 down the stretch after the deadline, including winning seven of eight. Some people were fearful it would take the new players time to mesh, that the trades would be disruptive, but Stéphane Matteau and Brian Noonan knew me and how I wanted them to play. Glenn Anderson also knew me, and he and Craig MacTavish were former Edmonton Oilers with winning pedigrees. We were ready to win.

And we had Mark Messier, who was 33 and incredibly fit and skilled and tough, and the owner of five Stanley Cup rings. He was a great leader and really important to the team, very important for me. He controlled the dressing room, and he wasn't afraid to get in my face when I needed it, but he also helped to get my message across to the players. I remember we had an older gentleman in the dressing room who would shine the players' shoes. Mess made him feel like he was the most important guy on the team. Our Black Aces—the guys who didn't play a lot, guys like Olczyk, Kypreos, Hudson, Hartman, Lidster and Mattias Norström—still felt like they were important to the team. That was Mess. He was so inclusive and respectful. We had other great leaders, guys like Kevin Lowe and Steve Larmer, but Mess was the guy. He made sure everyone felt a part of it. Mess was good, too, when I would get mad and say to guys—the likes of Brian Leetch, Mike Richter and others—"What have you won?" In my office, he would remind me that I hadn't won in the NHL, either, and he had five Stanley Cup rings. But I was very confident that could change that spring.

Every season, the Rangers were reminded by the fans and media that they hadn't won the Stanley Cup since 1940, when the Blueshirts beat the Maple Leafs in six games. Back then there were six teams in the league. In 1994, there were 26 teams. The odds of winning weren't quite the same. Today, of course, there are 32 teams. It keeps getting tougher to win. Whenever we played the Islanders, we would hear the chants—*1940, 1940*—especially if we were losing. But as much as you heard about the losing and the heartache—the fans were preoccupied with it—I certainly didn't feel the weight of those 53 years, now 54 seasons, since the last championship. It was my first year in New York and I didn't care when they'd last won. I was just here to win now.

We swept the Islanders in the first round. You don't ever expect to win four straight, but our team was well prepared and ready for the playoffs. And not overconfident, either, despite winning the Presidents' Trophy. The Isles had gone on a roll to finish the season to get into the final playoff spot, but we'd hit another gear. We won the first two games at home, both by scores of 6–0, and then won 5–1 and 5–2 on the island. That was 22–3. Pretty dominant. Our players were experienced enough to know that eliminating the opposition as quickly as possible was advantageous, especially with an older team that would benefit from rest, and that ultimately helped us. We played four games in seven days, which is a lot, but it was over before they knew it, and we had six days until we played again.

After that series, legendary Islanders coach Al Arbour, who I admired and respected, told the media he thought the Rangers would win it all. Al referenced Mess and the determination he showed in the series as one of the reasons why. Al knew the ingredients it took to win, so it was nice hearing it from him. Next up was the Washington Capitals, who'd upset the Pittsburgh Penguins in the first round. We won in five games and would have swept again had we not slipped up in the second period of Game 4, allowing three goals in seven minutes. I remained calm and the team responded with a win in the fifth game. It's interesting, but Greg Gilbert, who had played for me in Chicago, told me later that I was a lot different in New York than I'd been with the Blackhawks, that I was really quiet. I'm sure there would have been some Rangers wondering about that. If I was quiet in New York, what the hell had I been like in Chicago?

When I pushed for all those trades, the team I was concerned about playing against was the New Jersey Devils. I watched and studied that Jacques Lemaire–coached team and realized we needed that same size, strength and experience to beat them.

They had finished second overall in the league, just six points behind us. We had motored through the first two rounds, but they'd had a much more difficult path, although that may have hardened them for the series against us. In the first round, they went up 3–2 against the Buffalo Sabres but lost an incredible sixth game, 1–0, in four overtime periods. They rallied and won the seventh game, 2–1. In the second round against Boston, they lost the first two games at home, but recovered and won the next four. So, they had played 13 games; we had played nine. We had six days between games; they had four. But we were in for a battle.

That Devils team had 21-year-old rookie Martin Brodeur in goal. Along with Chris Terreri, that was a great tandem. They had Scott Stevens on defence. He, of course, was an incredible physical force, but he also led the team in scoring that season with 78 points. Stéphane Richer and John MacLean were big scorers. Bill Guerin, who later would be one of my favourites in Boston, was a terrific player. They had Claude Lemieux, who was a pain in the ass but an effective player, a difference-maker. Scott Niedermayer was a great puck carrier on defence. It was a rock-solid roster.

Just prior to the series, there was an article in one of the New York papers, trumpeting "How Neil Smith Put the Rangers on the Road to the Cup." Bad timing, interesting spin. Quite amusing. We all shared in how that roster was put together. Anyway, in the series opener against the Devils we scored early and had the lead three times, but we couldn't hold them and ended up losing, 4–3, in double overtime. Lemieux had scored with 43 seconds left in regulation time, and Richer scored the winner 35-plus minutes later. Our defence, Leetch and Beukeboom, got caught, and Richer was able to muscle his way past Graves. It was not our finest effort. Not sure if it was the layoff, but our best players weren't our best players on that night, and I shared that sentiment with the media. Having said that, I knew the series would be really, really tight. Lemaire had the Devils playing the trap and we played an aggressive forechecking game. It was always going to be an interesting matchup.

We responded really well in the second game, led by Mess, who scored 1:13 into the first period, and cruised to a 4–0 victory. Mess had dominated my Blackhawks back in 1991 in Game 4 of the conference final, and he did the same to the Devils in this game. It was a great response by him and our team. We outshot the Devils 41–16. Some teams would have been rattled by losing the opener at home, but we were steady. In Game 3, in the Meadowlands, Lemaire was able to match lines, as much as I tried to finesse our changes. I wasn't happy with the officiating, but we persevered. Once again, we gave up two leads, but Matteau scored the winner at 6:13 of the second overtime, a 3–2 victory. That wouldn't be the last of his heroics. After the game, at my press conference, I called for the suspension of Devils centre Bernie Nicholls, who had laid a cross-checking beating on Kovalev. The league listened and Nicholls was suspended for a game.

In Game 4, we fell behind by a couple of goals in the first period, and Dr. Hook pulled Richter. I was trying to kick-start the team, although it probably wasn't my smartest move. When you pull your top goalie, you risk getting him upset, but I felt the team could have responded more. I also benched, at various times, Mess, MacT, Noonan and Leetch. What people didn't know was that there was some method to my apparent madness. For starters, Leetch had hurt his shoulder the previous game, which I wasn't informed of until the morning of Game 4. He had a painkiller injected into the shoulder and didn't have his usual strength. He also had a badly infected elbow, both injuries the result of Lemieux hits earlier in the series. Leetch was hit hard by Lemieux and split open his elbow, which became infected because of his equipment. He had to soak the elbow in brine. Nobody knew about it. All the others I sat were banged up, too. I was trying to nurse them along, not lose them for the series. Beyond that, the Devils took it to us from the start and we weren't good enough. I had hoped others would step up. Maybe I should have kept them all playing, who knows? I probably should have communicated better with the players about what I was thinking, and heard from them what they thought their bodies could endure. We lost, 3–1.

With the series now even, we returned home across the Hudson River. Between games, Mess visited my office. He was emotional. He asked me to ease off. He told me what the players were feeling: that my benchings had not given them the best chance to win. I understood. I had identified the issues I was upset with, too—how some of the players without playoff experience and success were preparing—and I asked him to take care of it. He said he would. It wasn't a disagreement. As a team, we had deviated from the things we were trying to implement. I made some mistakes with the goalie change and the benchings in the previous game, no question. It was a good talk, and that's why he is such a great leader. Mess cried when we talked—we were both emotional—but we got back on the same page, and he conveyed that message to the team. I apologized to the team before the fifth game. I also shared some of the injury information with the media, but I didn't have much support from the press. Neil had that market cornered.

Despite that conversation and all of the mending, we lost Game 5 at home, 4–1, and were trailing in the series. For the first time, we were facing elimination, and we weren't playing very well. I tried to stay positive with the group, and Mess certainly took charge in the dressing room. The day before Game 6, Mess made what became known as his "guaranteed win" statement. He said it to reinforce the confidence in the group; he wasn't making a bold statement guaranteeing the win himself. What he said was, "We're going to go in and win Game 6. That was the focus this morning and it's the way we feel right now. We've done that all year, we've won all the games we've had to win. I know we're going to go in and win Game 6 and bring it back here for Game 7. We have enough talent and experience to turn the tide. That's exactly what we're going to do." Well, the next day the headlines read that Mess had guaranteed a win.

We made the bus ride to the Meadowlands, in New Jersey, and I was told that Neil was in the hallway outside the dressing room before the game, talking to the media and others about how he didn't want to make all the changes at the trade deadline, but that I had pushed him to make them. He was questioning those decisions and blaming me. Not a surprise. Going into that game, we'd had to make some roster moves. Noonan's shoulder was too bad to play, so I asked Eddie Olczyk if he could make a difference, and he assured me he could. Eddie had been a helluva player. He just didn't play a lot on this team, just 37 games that season. But as I'd said on day one, he would be a good teammate, and he was. Beukeboom was suspended for a hit on Richer, so we replaced him with Lidster, who was a solid, experienced player. Neither he nor Eddie had played for months, but both stepped up, ready to play.

As the game unfolded, we might have been a little bit nervous, anxious, and New Jersey was in full throttle. We were down 2–0 in the first period, and I think virtually everyone was wondering if I would pull Richter. He was praying I wouldn't pull him to shake up the team. No way; it would have been punishment. We were badly outplayed in the first period; we could have been down by four or five. I had pulled him a few times during the season—11, I believe—but it never crossed my mind in Game 6. He had kept us in the game. He was outstanding in that first period and the rest of the way. Early in the second period, with the team still not gelling, I called a time out. I never said a word. The players gathered at the bench, expecting me to say something, but I kept quiet. I looked at Mess, gave him a nod, and he knew what to do. I can't say exactly what he said next, but it was Mess who addressed the team at that crucial moment, and he kept things positive.

I made some adjustments. The team was no doubt relieved I didn't pull Richter. I double-shifted Kovalev, who seemed to have limitless energy. I put him on right wing with Mess and at centre between Larmer and Tikkanen. That's when I sat Anderson for a while, but all he said was, "Whatever it takes, boys, whatever it takes." Great teammate.

We responded. Kovy scored late in the second period, on a set-up from Mess, and the momentum seemed to change. Hockey is a game of momentum. Of course, just 36 seconds later Tikkanen took a tripping penalty, but we got to the intermission, killed it off and took charge. That was the momentum changing again. Mess certainly took charge, scoring three times, including an empty netter to lead us to a 4–2 win. Talk about a big-game player. A hat trick in the guaranteed-win game. It speaks volumes about him as a leader, how he stepped forward under the most critical, intense situation, a must-win game, and came through. It speaks to the relationship we had that I didn't have to be the guy to inspire the team or refocus them during that time out. I left it to their leader, the captain. After the game, I called it the most impressive performance by any player in the history of the NHL. Richter deserves a ton of credit too, because he shut the door after those first two goals, kept us in the game and gave us a chance.

The seventh game was something else—the atmosphere in Madison Square Garden was unbelievable, a mix of tension and excitement in the air. Remember, this was year 54 since the last championship, and we were teetering on the brink. Talk about drama. Talk about nothing that is worthwhile coming easy. We took the lead midway through the second period, with Leetch scoring a beauty. Mess won the faceoff, Leetch carried the puck in deep, did a spin-o-rama and beat Brodeur. That lead held until the final seconds of the third period. I shortened the bench, and we didn't allow a shot on goal for six minutes, leading into the final minute of the third. With Brodeur on the bench for an extra attacker, with 7.7 seconds left, Valeri Zelepukin jammed the puck past Richter to tie the game.

The fans, obviously, were distraught. The New Jersey fans were chanting "1940," and all the speculation about the ghosts of the past, the curse, had instantly resurfaced. We had played really well. The team was down, understandably. We were *that* close. I walked into the dressing room and I remember saying, "As tough as this moment is, think about how great it will feel when we win this game." Some of the veterans, guys like Mess and Lowe, who was hurt in the third, spoke up. The guys felt positive, so I left the room.

In overtime, I know the Devils had a couple of good chances, but it felt like the ice was tilted in our favour. We were dominant. We weren't going to sit back; we were going for it. Having said that, there's always that one scoring chance, they come down and . . . almost score. Even in the second overtime, it felt tilted in our favour, which is not to say Richter didn't save it for us a few times. I was feeling super-confident.

It's funny how things work out. Matteau was late getting to the bench for the second overtime because he was getting his skates worked on between periods. The Prince of Wales Trophy was sitting in the corridor, and Steph touched it for good luck. And then he ends up scoring one of the biggest goals in franchise history. There was discussion prior to the series about how Brodeur, when he went right to left, post to post, always put the paddle of his stick down on the ice. Well, Matteau got to the puck ahead of Niedermayer, circled the net, hit Brodeur's paddle with the puck, and it goes between his legs at 4:24 of the second overtime. Series over.

At that moment, the feeling wasn't relief; it was joy. I remember saying to the coaches on the bench, "Now we've got a shot at the Cup." One of the greatest feelings when you coach in the Stanley Cup final is looking up at the out-of-town scoreboard and seeing that there are no other games. You're the only two teams left. There is a superstition among teams about touching the Wales or Campbell Trophies when you win the conference final. To me, pick up the trophy—you won it, it's part of the journey to get the big prize. Mess picked it up, allowed a few pictures, and then put it back down. We were still on a mission.

There was a feeling among the media and the fans that the Stanley Cup final was going to be an easy series, but our players weren't buying it, and neither was I. We were playing the Vancouver Canucks, who were an 85-point team—basically a .500 team—that had finished with 27 fewer points than the Rangers. But they were a team of destiny of sorts. Pat Quinn was a great coach, and they were on a run. They had been down 3–1 in the first round to Calgary, but won three straight overtime games, the final in double overtime, to beat the Flames. They beat Dallas in five games, then trailed the Maple Leafs by a game in the next round and ran the table to beat them in five. They were a fast, skilled, dangerous team with Pavel Bure, a two-time 60-goal scorer, playing with house money—meaning they had nothing to lose, while the Rangers were still chasing away ghosts and curses.

The Canucks arrived in New York very confident. Even though we outplayed them in Game 1, outshooting them 54–31, they found a way to win. They twice erased leads and beat us, 3–2, on a Greg Adams goal, set up by Bure, in the final minute of the first overtime period. Now they had won six of seven overtime games. That's a really dangerous team. The second game wasn't technically a must-win, but being on home ice, having lost the opener, it felt like a must-win. And the team was aware of just how critical it was. But the composure was there. All our experience came through and we won, 3–1, with Leetch securing it with an empty-net goal. This wasn't going to be easy.

On the flight to Vancouver, I made a point of delivering a message to our Russian contingent, who were frustrating me. I cornered them on the plane and I said, "I don't know if you guys know what it means to win the Stanley Cup, but it's fucking huge." That's when Sarge, centre Sergei Nemchinov, lit into them. I remember Mess was standing by laughing. Sarge saved him from having to do it.

In Game 3, Bure scored just 63 seconds in. Leetch, who was playing great, as good as I had ever seen him, tied it later in the period. A big moment came when it was 2–1 and Bure was awarded a penalty shot. Richter made an amazing save. It was a turning point, and then we caught a break of sorts when Bure was called for high-sticking defenceman Jay Wells and was given a game misconduct for drawing blood. We went on to win 5–1, and despite falling behind by a couple in the fourth game, bounced back to win 4–2 and head home one victory away from winning the Stanley Cup. *1940.*

So now we have the Canucks down 3–1 in the series, but they had faced this scenario before, in the first round versus Calgary. And we have half of New York fearing a collapse and the other half planning a parade. Maybe more than half were planning a parade. We got home and vendors had already printed T-shirts—*1994 Stanley Cup champions*, with a picture of the Cup. They were selling them before the fifth game. I was so pissed off. I'm sure one of the Canucks players bought one, put it up in the dressing room. It fuelled their fire. Too many people felt we had already slayed the dragon, that the ghosts of 1940 were gone. Not so fast.

Another distraction surfaced before the fifth game. A story appeared in the press saying that I was going to be the next coach and GM of the Detroit Red Wings. Mike Ilitch, who had put me on the $150,000 retainer a year and some earlier, had fired Bryan Murray as GM, and there were rumours Scotty Bowman was going to be fired as coach after an early-round exit to San Jose. A radio station in Prince Edward Island reported that I was headed to Detroit after the final. I thought Murray's assistant GM, Doug MacLean, who was from PEI, had fuelled the report, but Doug has denied it. More about this later, but the distraction was not what my Rangers needed just one victory away from the Stanley Cup.

We lost that fifth game. We were down only 1–0 entering the third period, but then it was quickly 3–0. There were probably more distractions—the media hype, the fans—than around any game in the playoffs. Despite all that, we battled back to tie it, but 29 seconds later we were trailing again and never recovered. We lost 6–3. I don't think we were overconfident; we just couldn't put them away. And the toughest game to win in any series is always the fourth. I was pissed off with referee Andy Van Hellemond (again) and the officiating crew. They had given Beukeboom the boot for intervening in an altercation involving Leetch, and then called back a goal with a bogus offside call. I called NHL commissioner Gary Bettman in the middle of the night and told him what I thought, and I had Matt Loughran, our director of team services, type up a letter of complaint to send to Gary's lieutenant, Brian Burke. It took the entire flight to Vancouver the next morning for me to calm down.

But when we arrived in Vancouver, we faced a Canucks team firing on all cylinders, and they beat us again, 4–1. They were living off the built-in confidence of coming back in the Calgary series, and they believed they could do it again. I wondered if I would ever win the Stanley Cup. I hadn't lost my own confidence in our team, but damn, nothing comes easy. We had two days off before Game 7 and stayed the night in Vancouver, where there were riots after the game. We were staying in the Westin Bayshore and we could hear it all. The city was going crazy. Cars were on fire; there was looting; the fans went berserk. We were flying home the next day and I discussed with Mess, Lowe and Larms the idea of taking the team to Lake Placid, to avoid some of the distractions and the bulk of the media. They thought about it and said no. Mess said, "We don't want to go anywhere, we don't want to look like we're running away from what's ahead of us, let's face it head on." Mess said, "We want to slay the dragon." Great leadership. I said, "No problem."

THE DAY BEFORE Game 7, I addressed the team. We had our practice, and then we gathered in the dressing room. I spoke of my belief in the team, of how we had started this mission in London, from day one, with the parade video. I said to them, "If anyone had guaranteed in our first meeting that we would be able to play one game, in Madison Square Garden, to win the Stanley Cup, would you have taken it? The answer would be yes." I talked about how much they had accomplished and how proud they should be, how proud I was of them, regardless of the outcome. I told them to enjoy the moment. Mess said it was one of the greatest speeches he had heard from a coach. We showed that parade video again, and Collie and Dick did a great job putting together a game-prep video on how the Canucks had taken over the series by having their defence jump into the rush. It was, "Boys, let's refocus and get ready for Game 7." And whatever my future was, the players didn't care about the rumours at that moment, or maybe ever. It was all about Game 7. Mess did a great job of keeping the team focused on the game, not next year, not the curse.

I will never forget the ride to Madison Square Garden on June 14. I had re-energized, and I think the two days off had re-energized the team too. I had a driver named Ricky, who drove us to every home game. Ricky picked up Gayla and me, Collie, Dick, Rob Campbell and my pal Tom Greenaway. Maybe Tommy anticipated there would be traffic issues, because he brought along the red flashing light from his secret security vehicle. As we got closer to the Garden, the roads were blocked with traffic. Tommy put the light on the roof and we were going down one-way streets the wrong way, Tommy was flashing his badge, and we were dodging the traffic chaos. The Garden had been surrounded with fans and traffic all day long. I liked to listen to music, and I remember Mary Chapin Carpenter was singing, "I take my chances, every chance I take." How fitting for the occasion. Still one of my favourites. I was so confident and so jacked up. I don't know if the team could feel it, or sense it, but I was supremely confident. I never thought for a second that we might lose that game.

Looking back, that was a tough game. It was vicious. As confident as I was, there's still the fear in a Game 7 that anything can happen. We started strong and led 2–0 after the first period on goals by Leetch and Graves. Now we were 40 minutes away from the big prize. Five minutes into the second period we found ourselves on the power play, but Trevor Linden scored short-handed to cut the lead to one. Then we were ahead again by two when Mess scored on the power play leading into the third period. Now we are 20 minutes away. Mess said to me before that third period, "Mike, let's not be afraid to slay the dragon." So we didn't change a thing, and we stuck with our game plan and strong forecheck.

Linden cut the lead again early in the third period on a power play, and now, I think more for the fans than us, it was white-knuckle time. There was no shortage of close calls. We barely missed restoring the two-goal lead when Lowe hit the post, and the Canucks had a couple of posts and crossbars themselves, with Nathan LaFayette coming the closest. And then, in the final minute, it got really tense. Of course, the fans, and maybe me and the players, remembered some of our final-seconds heartbreaks from earlier in the playoffs. We were so close. There were a couple of suspect icing calls against us, in my opinion, one with 28.2 seconds left that we survived, and another with 1.1 seconds remaining. Kevin Collins, the linesman, made a bad call on the icing and it was painfully obvious Bure had stopped skating. They put another half second on the clock. I put MacT in as the initial faceoff guy. Mess had taken the previous two. But crucial moments like this were why we'd traded for MacT and his experience and winning pedigree. Pat Quinn put in Bure. With so little time left on the clock, Pat was looking for Bure on the one-time side to shoot off the draw. Mess was our backup on the faceoff. As soon as the puck dropped, MacT swiped at it and Mess came in and cross-checked Pavel in the chest. The puck got pushed into the corner. Series over, dream realized. Unbelievable.

I will never forget seeing a fan, who I later learned was named Steve Zaretsky—a long-time Rangers fan, along with his whole family—hold up a sign that read: NOW I CAN DIE IN PEACE.

Amen to that.

When the final buzzer sounded, it was like the roof was going to blow off the Garden. It was like an explosion; the noise was incredible. The team raced out onto the ice, I hugged Collie and

Dick and the trainers, and then I walked off the bench, looking for Gayla. I had Tom Greenaway bring her and Rob down from the seats. She was taking photos of me. I went out on the ice to hug the players, and then I came back to the bench. Directly across from us in the crowd was Stanley Jaffe. I waved to him and said thank you. He'd been fired in January by Viacom, the new owners, and there he was sitting in the stands. He helped make this happen; he was responsible for putting the team together. He should have been in a VIP box. I also had a long hug with Bob Gutkowski, who had helped keep things together, especially with Neil and me, and was there when I asked to make the trade changes.

When Bettman came out to present the Cup, he said, "Well, New York, after 54 years your long wait is over." The arena was playing the Tina Turner song "The Best," which we had played in the dressing room before the game. What a feeling. What a journey it had been. After Bettman had given Mess the Cup and the players had skated around the rink, passing the trophy to each other, Mess got it back and he skated to the bench and handed it off to me. That had never happened in the history of the NHL. I couldn't believe it. I lifted it over my head. It felt as light as a feather. Mission accomplished. Dragon slayed!

17

ALL GOOD THINGS END: FAREWELL TO BROADWAY

THE CELEBRATION AFTER that Stanley Cup win was incredible, as you would expect. And it went on for days. That night, in the dressing room, the guys were drinking champagne out of the Cup, beer was flowing. After a while I got to bring the Cup to my office. I had a few of my old university teammates visiting. Gayla was there, too, and my agent Rob Campbell.

One of the old teammates there that night was Paul Patrick. When I arrived at St. Lawrence, Paul was the first guy I met. He was six foot three and I asked him if he played basketball. He said no, hockey. His grandfather was Muzz Patrick, who played on the 1940 New York Rangers Stanley Cup–winning team, and he was a member of the famous Patrick family. Muzz Patrick died in 1998, so he lived long enough to see the Rangers win again.

I remember Mess saying afterwards that he had won those five cups with the Edmonton Oilers and each win had its own personality, but this one truly was incredible. Maybe it was the 54 years, the curse, the history and finally the drama, literally going down to the last second. I'll never forget seeing him jumping up and down on the ice when the buzzer finally sounded.

Being New York, there were a lot of celebrities in the building that night: movie stars, Broadway actors, singers and the like. One was Donald Trump. Esa Tikkanen poured champagne over his head and his famous mane. I found Gayla, who was just a week shy of turning 15, in the hallway outside the dressing room enjoying her first (I believe) beer. I think our team dentist handed it to her, saying, "You've got to celebrate with your old man." One of the best moments came later, when it was just the players and myself in the dressing room. We were all sitting on the floor, in puddles of champagne and beer, and we talked about the journey and toasted our win with a beer. I had been a hard coach, no question, but we achieved our goal and it was a moment—for a short period of time I was the only one there who wasn't a player—to reflect and enjoy. It was a helluva journey. We couldn't get out of that building until three, maybe it was four, in the morning. The fans outside didn't want to leave. They had waited so long to celebrate, and the Rangers meant so much to New York.

There was one special fan who was brought into my office to meet me and the Stanley Cup. The gentleman was blind, but he asked if he could touch the Cup. Of course. Because of all the Detroit rumours that had surfaced, he also asked me not to leave. I doubt my general manager, Neil Smith, who I don't recall seeing during the celebration, shared that sentiment. Many years later, I found out that a few minutes after the game ended, Neil was privately saying "I'm getting rid of that fucker." Meaning me. That's how bad our relationship was.

Anyway, the victory party went on all night. When I finally got to bed, the sun was already up. We had a day to catch our breath, and then the partying resumed. We gathered at MSG two days later for a team photo.

And then there was the parade on June 17. What an amazing experience. It was a hot day, 89 degrees, and an estimated 1.5 million people lined the Canyon of Heroes as we went past on flat-bed trucks. I was later told that almost 20 tons of tickertape fell along the parade route.

On my truck were my assistants Collie Campbell and Dick Todd, along with Glenn Healy, Craig MacTavish, Greg Gilbert and our families. Late in the season, my dad, Ted, had asked if he could come visit for a couple of weeks. He had a strong Irish personality. I got him a room across from MSG for the nights he didn't want to commute back to Greenwich. Well, he endeared himself to the police, who gave him a card to call if he needed a ride to his next destination. He ended up staying six weeks, and I finally had to send him home so I could concentrate on the play-offs. I made a deal with him. I said, "If we win the Cup you'll be on a flight the next day." I got my father, mother and two sisters to come celebrate, and they were there for the parade. I remember, as we were riding along, the crowd was chanting "Keenan, Keenan," and Dad was waving his arms like they were cheering for him. I'm so glad my family could enjoy that moment together.

It was also a great moment for New York. The parade ended at City Hall, where we were presented with keys to the city by mayor Rudy Giuliani. When I spoke, the crowd chanted "four more years, four more years . . ." I guess they knew I had a five-year contract. Then we went to Gracie Mansion, where the mayor resided, for a barbecue, and I sang "My Way" and "New York, New York." That night, a bunch of us, my family included, went to a restaurant for a quiet dinner, but then Tik came in with the Cup. The next thing you know, all the tables are pushed together and there are people, including me, standing on the tables singing and dancing. Gayla had another beer, this one courtesy of Glenn Healy as they shared stories of living in Pickering, and another late night!

The next day, I attended a World Cup soccer game at Giants Stadium between Ireland and Italy, as a guest of the mayor. That night, we had a team celebration at the famous Waldorf Astoria hotel. We had a live band; the champagne was flowing. Next thing, we're on top of the tables singing and dancing again. We drank every bottle of Dom Pérignon the hotel had, then another brand of champagne. The champagne bill alone was thousands of dollars, and the night cost in the neighbourhood of $200,000, I'm sure. At one point, Neil was asked what the budget was for this. He said, "There is no budget tonight." In the midst of all that, our Russian players threw an amazing party in Brighton Beach, which was a fantastic night with music, dinner, a red-carpet welcome and a lot of singing and dancing.

As with anything in life, all good things must come to end. And so it was with all the parties, and my time with the Rangers. As mentioned, word had leaked in the media during the Stanley Cup final that I was "heading" to Detroit as coach and GM. There are all sorts of theories as to how the rumours started, including that Red Wings executive Jimmy Devellano—who didn't like me for some reason, and certainly despised Neil—was trying to create a distraction and derail our Cup run.

Whatever. Truth is, my agent, Rob Campbell, did talk with Mike Ilitch's lawyer, Jay Bielfield. After another disappointing spring, Mr. Ilitch fired GM Bryan Murray and his assistant Doug MacLean on June 3. Scotty Bowman remained as coach, but that was going to change if they hired me. Anyway, Rob and Bielfield met in New York at the Essex House Hotel midway through the final. Mr. Ilitch wanted Rob to know they were interested if I left New York, and Rob wanted to make sure he talked with them because he knew just how contentious my relationship with Neil was. Rob was thinking that if Neil had his way, I wouldn't be back. Remember, five minutes after winning the Cup, he'd told at least one person he was getting rid of me, or wanted to.

I remember telling Rob, when the Detroit rumours surfaced, "I don't want to talk about it, I don't want to think about it. You handle it any way you want, I'm completely focused on winning the Stanley Cup." I denied to the media any knowledge of a deal being done because there wasn't a deal. And I denied knowing about any talks because I left everything to Rob. I didn't want that distraction for me and the team when we were so close to winning.

Six days after we won the Cup, Rob and Neil talked on the phone about how to end my relationship with the Rangers. A few days later, Rob and I met with MSG president Bob Gutkowski at a New York hotel. He asked me a question: If a change happened, would John Davidson, the former Rangers goalie who was working on the television broadcasts, be a good fit as GM? I said, "I like John very much. The relationship between Neil and me is contentious, and I understand why. He didn't want to get instructions from the coach." JD never conspired to overthrow Neil, but clearly management was considering options, because late in the season Gutkowski had called—I put it on speaker-phone, with my friend Tom Greenaway listening—and asked the same questions about my relationship with Neil and about JD.

Despite all the back and forth and rumours, the exit strategy wasn't going to be as simple as just giving me permission to accept a GM job elsewhere. Viacom, who were about to become the new owners, had been clear with Gutkowski: he'd been told that the coach and GM were to stay, find a way to make it work. We'd just won a Cup together, so how bad could it be, right? But it was bad. Viacom was looking to sell off some assets, including the Rangers, and didn't need any bad press on the heels of a Cup win. But Neil definitely didn't want me around. I reminded Gutkowski that I'd had to push for the trades we made at the deadline—the ones that ultimately got us over the top. I didn't want Neil's job, but I also didn't want him as GM. That said, as much as I didn't want to continue working with Neil, if I'd had to stay, I could have carried on as coach of the Rangers.

A few days or so later, Neil flew to Toronto and met with Rob at an airport hotel. He said he wouldn't stand in my way if I got a GM offer elsewhere, but Rob also remembers Neil making it clear that he could not tolerate working with me. Still, the Viacom problem remained. With ownership committed to keep-ing both of us around, that plan likely wouldn't fly.

Rob had figured out a way for me to get out of the contract, a material breach of contract—meaning if the Rangers missed the deadline for paying my bonuses, which was 30 days after winning the Cup, I could walk as a free agent. I didn't want to leave, but

I also knew that at some point, sooner rather than later, Neil would find a way to fire me.

I was owed roughly $650,000 in bonuses, and when I asked well before the deadline to see exactly what I was owed, the Rangers were coming up about $40,000 short. Rob and Neil had several conversations about that and about the idea of a breach of contract.

Two days before the bonuses were to be paid, Rob spoke with Neil to confirm the breach was going to happen, that the cheque would be late. And as planned, my cheque did not arrive on July 14. The next afternoon, Rob faxed a letter to Gutkowski and the MSG lawyer, Ken Munoz, informing them of the breach and stating that I no longer had any obligations to the team. The contract was over. Neil had disappeared; he was on vacation in Key West. Gutkowski replied to Rob, saying that they would get me the cheque the next day and that my employment agreement was not over. Nevertheless, I went ahead with a 4 p.m. press conference I had scheduled at TSN to announce I was leaving. On the ride to the studio with Rob, Gutkowski called, but as we pulled into the parking garage the call dropped off. That and the press conference pissed off the Rangers and MSG to no end—well, at least some of them. Gutkowski was totally blindsided.

Following the press conference, MSG issued a statement stating they were "stunned at the capricious actions of Mr. Keenan and his agent . . . and will take all necessary actions to preserve all of its rights."

Looking back, I realize I should not have left the way I did, and it bothers me to this day that Gutkowski was blindsided. I probably should have stayed and taken my chances and forced

Neil to fire me, or waited to see if he survived. But at the time, I was thinking, *How can I stay?* The man who'd pushed to hire me, Stanley Jaffe, was gone. Gutkowski, who until my departure was an ally, would soon be gone (he was given a one-year extension by the new owners). My support at the top had eroded, and I was dealing with a GM who'd made it no secret that he wanted me gone—despite the fact that I'd coached the team to its first Stanley Cup in 54 years.

It was only going to be a matter of time.

In the years between then and now, a lot of players have said that Neil and I couldn't have gone on for another season. It was an impossible situation. Having said that, it was stupid of me to announce on national TV in two countries that I was leaving. But I was. And as I said at the time, to go from the high of winning the Stanley Cup to leaving within a month was disappointing, no matter how it happened or why. I really felt we could win the Stanley Cup again with that team.

18

SINGING THE BLUES: ST. LOUIS, 1994–96

THIRTY-THREE DAYS AFTER Madison Square Garden went bonkers and Mark Messier skated to the bench to hand me the Stanley Cup, and two days after my press conference on TSN announcing my departure, the St. Louis Blues hired me. I was headed to the Gateway to the West as the team's new head coach and general manager. But it took some work to make it happen—and, as always, some controversy.

As I've mentioned, Detroit Red Wings owner Mike Ilitch was interested in me and had made a strong pitch. The day after I announced my departure from New York, Rob Campbell and I met with Mr. Ilitch in Detroit. It wasn't a great meeting. He was a little nervous about moving too fast, or at least before NHL commissioner Gary Bettman had ruled on whether I was legally able to leave the Rangers. And if I took the job—which, to be clear, he didn't offer—he wanted me to fire Scotty Bowman. I couldn't do that. It would have been like kicking your dad out of the house. Scotty gave me my first pro job in Rochester. There was also the issue of some of the management group in Detroit, such as Jimmy Devellano, not wanting me. My other concern was the perception, given the rumours that had been flying around during the final, of finally signing with Detroit.

Rob also reached out to St. Louis after I split with the Rangers. Rob and I met with Blues chairman Mike Shanahan and the club president, Jack Quinn. They wanted secrecy because Ron Caron was still the manager and Bob Berry was the coach. So, we booked a meeting room at the Cleveland Hopkins International Airport and, wouldn't you know it, we got recognized.

That first meeting was short. It lasted about five minutes. After we all greeted each other, they asked us for our demands. Rob said, "$20 million." They walked out. Quinn said, "If you had told us that earlier we wouldn't have wasted our time meeting." He called to get the private jet fired up.

They came right back, though. Rob went to St. Louis and hammered out a five-year, $10 million contract. As Rob put it, the contract was light years ahead of the market, and he structured it in such a way that it covered any money that would be lost when we settled with the Rangers and the league. Caron was made a senior advisor, and they asked if I would keep Bob Berry on as an assistant coach. I had no problem with that request. I respected Bob's ability and experience, particularly coaching in Montreal.

Now we had to deal with Detroit, who still thought a deal might happen with them. Rob went to Mr. Ilitch with a bunch of crazy requests, asking for a ton of money and a say in who would stay or go in the organization, things like that, and they agreed to everything. Rob said we would talk further, but we made the deal with St. Louis. In the end, while St. Louis and Detroit had in essence been tampering (because I was technically still under contract), the breach hadn't been confirmed by Bettman, the talks were initiated by us, and Neil was onside with everything. Reports surfaced in New York that Neil had helped orchestrate my departure, though he denied it, and the Rangers denied any collusion.

A week after the Blues announced my hiring, the Rangers filed a lawsuit against me. Submissions were written from both sides, but then the Rangers withdrew their suit, perhaps now knowing how everything unfolded, and asked Gary Bettman to mediate a settlement. There was a hearing on July 25 in Manhattan. The Red Wings also had to send representatives to the proceedings. As part of the deal reached, the Rangers were forced to pay me my bonuses ($608,000). I repaid them $400,000, four-fifths of the signing bonus for my five-year contract. I was fined $100,000 "for conduct detrimental to the league," suspended for 60 days and had to repay the house loan. At the time, it was the largest fine levied against a non-player in the history of the league.

The Blues also were fined $250,000 for signing me while I was under contract, and the Red Wings were dinged $25,000 for talking to me. The Rangers had to pony up $25,000 for filing their lawsuit against me, action detrimental to the league. The other part of the deal was a trade between the Blues and Rangers that would compensate the Rangers for the loss of my services and help resolve the dispute. The deal sent Petr Nedvěd to New York for Doug Lidster and Esa Tikkanen. That trade meant Bettman didn't have to decide the validity of my contract with the Rangers, although he did say he "did not accept that it was appropriate for Mr. Keenan to declare himself 'free' and negotiate with other clubs." As part of the settlement, because of the suspension, I couldn't go to work for St. Louis until September 24. Bettman would call me at the cottage to ensure I wasn't in St. Louis. He called so often that I finally told him to stop.

But none of that prevented Jack Quinn from phoning to update me on a situation involving Al MacInnis. In early July, about two weeks before I officially landed with the Blues, Caron signed Scott Stevens to a free-agent offer sheet and acquired the restricted free agent MacInnis for Phil Housley and a second-round pick. The Devils matched the Stevens offer, so he stayed in New Jersey. MacInnis signed a four-year, $13.7 million contract with the Blues, but the trade was in jeopardy of not happening because Housley threatened to not report to Calgary because of the tax hit he would take playing in Alberta. Eventually, Housley backed off his stance, and MacInnis was a Blue.

Meantime, I had some remodelling to do at the Blues brand new rink, then known as the Kiel Center. The dressing room was too big. It could have housed a football team. So I had some walls built. We turned the extra space into storage rooms. The trainers and equipment guys loved it.

As I did everywhere I coached in the NHL, I also hung a photo of the Stanley Cup in the hallway leading out to the ice surface, and added some other pictures to commemorate the team's historic highlights. This was a team with history, home to numerous Hall of Famers. The Blues also went to three straight Stanley Cup finals under Scotty Bowman from 1968 to 1970.

I hired Olympic training guru Bob Kersee, husband of world-class athlete Jackie Joyner-Kersee, a three-time Olympic gold medallist in the heptathlon and long jump. He would bring Jackie to the workouts sometimes, and she would kick the crap out of the players. I got hooked up with Bobby through Dr. Rick Lehman. He had been an understudy on the Flyers medical staff when I was in Philadelphia. But he and his wife, Michele Koo, also a doctor, had moved to St. Louis and worked with Bob. I hired Rick, an orthopedic surgeon, as the Blues' team doctor.

I also spent time that summer with Nola, who later would become my second wife. Nola was a nurse. She was from Maine, and we'd started dating earlier that year, when I was still with the Rangers. I lived in a condo my first year in St. Louis, and she would come visit with her sons, Reed and Grant. We moved in together in my second year. Gayla also visited, especially around the holidays.

Because I couldn't officially join the team until September 24, assistant coaches Bob Berry and Ted Sator ran the first two weeks of training camp. Then, a lockout delayed the start of the season until late January. When the 48-game season finally got underway, my first matter to deal with was Craig Janney's conditioning. He wasn't the only one out of shape, but he was the most noticeable. I sat him for two of the first ten games and then learned he was going through some personal problems. I sent him home. We wanted him to get out of town to gain a fresh start. It took me three weeks, but we found a place for him in San Jose in a trade for defenceman Jeff Norton.

I had beefs with Janney, Brendan Shanahan and Curtis Joseph that first year. In January, we took a breather in Vail, Colorado. I came down to the resort lobby for practice one morning to find Curtis sitting in a chair. I knew the team bus had left for the rink, so I asked him what he was doing. He said he'd missed the bus. I couldn't believe he didn't jump in a cab. So I gave him an earful and a lift to the rink. Curtis had been great in St. Louis, but I already felt he was one of the Blues who was out of shape, and he never gave us the kind of goaltending he had during his previous seasons in St. Louis.

Today, I have a great deal of respect for Curtis. As a backup a decade later, he was such a professional for me in Calgary, and overall he enjoyed an outstanding career.

With Shanahan, I was not too fond of his game early in that first year and berated him after a 6–0 loss at home to Chicago on February 9. I told him I was close to trading him. He didn't like it, but he needed to hear it, and he became a very good player.

Overall, though, the season was progressing nicely. Glenn Anderson signed as a free agent and contributed. Another of my favourites, Greg Gilbert, was added via the waiver wire, and we needed his grit.

We finished the lockout-shortened season at 28–15–5, just nine points behind the Presidents' Trophy–winning Red Wings. But we were beaten in the conference quarterfinals by the same fired-up Vancouver Canucks club that my Rangers had defeated in Game 7 of the Stanley Cup final less than a year before. Canucks goalie Kirk McLean was outstanding, while Curtis struggled. Consider his save percentage in the playoffs: .865 compared to .902 in the regular season. Making things worse for us in that series was Shanahan breaking his leg in Game 5. We won Game 6, but lost 5–3 in Game 7 to lose the series. Losing Shanny was huge.

The fallout, unfortunately, was losing another Shanahan. That would be Mike Shanahan, who was removed in mid-June as chairman of the board. He was my guy. Jerry Ritter, a former executive with the Budweiser-owned St. Louis Cardinals, replaced him as chairman. And then things turned bad. I had a clause in my contract that stipulated that if either Shanahan or Jack Quinn or both were given their marching orders after the first year, I could opt out or I received $1 million. They gave me $1 million to stay in St. Louis and added an extra year to my contract. Rob Campbell had learned well from the shenanigans and our troubles with the Rangers.

Before Ritter took the helm, I had a good run during free agency. I spent $25 million to sign Grant Fuhr, Dale Hawerchuk, Geoff Courtnall and Shayne Corson. But with Ritter taking over as chairman, the board wanted the payroll cut. I remember an accountant coming to me and saying he wanted Brett Hull, Brendan Shanahan and Al MacInnis traded. Shanahan was the most tradable because he was the youngest. I warned Blues owner-ship that these guys were the most popular players on the team. I told them we would be blasted if we made those trades. They told me I wouldn't be living in St. Louis forever, but they would be.

I traded Shanahan to Hartford for Chris Pronger on July 27. The Blues ownership left me alone at the podium to explain the deal to the media. It was not a popular move, to say the least. Shanahan was voted St. Louis Sportsman of the Year, and, as I understand it, the voting took place after the trade. So you can imagine the feedback. The furor against me grew when I traded Curtis Joseph. To be clear, the ownership didn't order me to deal Curtis. But he was a restricted free agent, and our payroll was a concern to them. So we unloaded his rights to the Oilers with Mike Grier for first-round selections in 1996 and 1997.

How we signed Fuhr is a story. That summer, Bob Berry and I were in New York for some reason and were having lunch at an outdoor café. All of a sudden, this car comes to a screeching halt on the street in front of us. Out jumps Wayne Gretzky. He asked us how long we would be there; he had to be somewhere, but he wanted to catch up with us. We said we would be in that spot as long as he wanted us to be. He returned an hour later with his wife, Janet. The four of us talked about all kinds of things. I told Wayne we need a goalie and asked him for a recommendation. He said he couldn't think of one on the spot, but then Janet piped up with, "What about Grant Fuhr?"

Fuhr had played with Wayne for years in Edmonton, and on the Kings the previous season. I followed up and, not long after, we signed him. I knew him well from the '87 Canada Cup and two Stanley Cup finals. But Grant, who was 33, showed up to Blues training camp in terrible condition. I told him, "I put a lot of faith in signing you, and you show up 20 pounds overweight." I sent him home and told him to return when he was in shape. Bob Kersee put Grant on a rigorous two-week program, and Grant returned at his fighting weight, ready to prove himself.

Just before the season began, I made a move I regret. I can't remember why I traded Guy Carbonneau to the Dallas Stars for Paul Broten. Just the previous summer, I'd helped to engineer the trade to bring him to St. Louis from Montreal for Jim Montgomery. Guy was a leader. He kept Brett Hull in check as a teammate. With Guy gone, Brett became a handful.

At the beginning of my second season in St. Louis, I needed to figure out what to do with Dale Hawerchuk. I loved the Hall of Famer. Our relationship went back to my first brush with coaching, with the Oshawa Legionaires. I knew and respected his family. His family liked me. We won the 1987 Canada Cup together. I had so much faith in him that I put him in to take the critical last-minute faceoff in our end that led to that magical Gretzky-to-Lemieux championship-clinching goal. But he struggled in St. Louis. I don't think his agent, Pat Morris, disclosed how badly Dale was suffering from his hip problems. Dale could not keep up with our tempo.

I received plenty of criticism when I scratched Dale for his return game in Buffalo on October 22. Before signing with the Blues, he'd played five seasons with the Sabres. His family, including his ailing grandmother, and friends had tickets for his first game back. It's something I shouldn't have done. But after starting the season with three wins in four games, we lost the next three. Dale had a meagre three assists in the first seven games. We needed a spark. I put Basil McRae in for Dale. It didn't work. We lost 5–2. I wasn't trying to be mean to Dale. Like I said, I loved Dale. I just wanted to put out the best lineup possible. In hindsight, I can see that maybe Dale would have dug deeper that night, back in Buffalo, with his family and friends in the stands.

Three nights later, in Hartford, Dale was rested and back in. He scored a goal and three assists in our 4–2 win. Before that outing, however, Brett Hull spoke out. He didn't like that I'd sat out Dale in Buffalo. I didn't appreciate the public criticism. So, I stripped him of the captaincy and gave it to Shayne Corson.

We continued to struggle through the first half of that 1995–96 season. Pronger needed time to get in better shape and to adapt to his new surroundings. It was tough for him, with the trade not being very popular. The fans booed him a lot. I brought his parents from Dryden, Ontario, to St. Louis and had a meeting with them and my coaching staff. We talked about Chris needing to focus. He was just a young, distracted kid. After that conversation, he was a different player. But there were still many nights when I would call him into my office after a game and threaten to trade him.

December ended poorly. In five starts, we lost by a goal four times. The speculation that I was trying to trade Brett started to amp up. But ownership wasn't as keen to sell him off as they had been in the summer. He was a popular player in St. Louis, and ownership felt he was loyal to the Blues and the city. Brett had two more seasons left on his contract. I asked ownership if they thought that loyalty would still be there when he became a free agent. I argued that he was a great asset, and we might as well get something for him while we could. We didn't trade Brett. Guess what? He signed with Dallas in 1998, won a Stanley Cup in that first year and scored the controversial toe-in-the-crease title-clinching goal in triple OT. And, to rub salt in the wound, Guy Carbonneau won praise from the team for his leadership, and in particular for keeping Brett focused on playing winning hockey.

I wonder if Hully got along with any of his coaches. He was difficult to coach. I know he clashed with Ken Hitchcock in Dallas. I found him to be a very bright guy. He was an artist, like Denis Savard, and those players are different. Brett didn't want structure; he wanted to play his game, his way. I was unable to convince him that he had to be a complete team player to win a Stanley Cup. Great players have needs that have to be satisfied, but the needs of the team have to be first. And he could be brutal with his teammates, not just me. One time, we were playing in Dallas and Brett was on with Craig Johnson. The kid could skate, but he was young and had not developed a pro's hockey sense. The rink got quiet.

Johnson made a bad pass to Brett and, all of a sudden, you could hear, "You're a lousy excuse for an NHL hockey player." All the players looked back at me behind the bench. I didn't say a thing at the time but waited until the intermission. I told Brett, "Don't you ever say or treat a teammate like that on this team. You can't say things like that. We're not all as gifted as you are."

Brett was a superstar player, an incredible goal scorer. I wish I could have been a better coach for him and gotten even more out of him. But he was pigheaded and stubborn, perhaps a little like me, and he refused to take direction. He admitted as much on my February 2020 "Iron Mike Keenan Podcast."

"You had two headstrong people that had a difference in opinion," Brett explained. "A lot of it was media-driven. They would go to him, ask me for a response, and then return to him. It went back and forth like that."

Amid all of the speculation about Brett's future with the team, St. Louis played the Rangers in New York on January 14, 1996. It was my first trip back to Madison Square Garden, a year-and-a-half after that wonderful Game 7 championship-clinching evening with the Rangers. We tied the game 3–3, but the MSG faithful were merciless. They called me everything from a weasel to a traitor to a liar. There were also rumours (of course!) that I was talking to the Rangers about a trade for Brett.

Later that week, the NHL schedule took a break for the All-Star Game weekend in Boston. The big story in the media was all about where Brett Hull would wind up. But he remained with the Blues. As it turned out, we were working on a bigger move— landing Wayne Gretzky. Since December, I had been badgering Los Angeles Kings GM Sam McMaster to trade Gretzky to the

Blues. He would be an unrestricted free agent that summer, and the Kings wanted a return. Wayne had to give his permission for the trade. St. Louis appeared to be the perfect destination, mainly because Janet was from the area, and we had history together in the Canada Cup. Finally, on February 27, we made the deal. We acquired No. 99 for Roman Vopat, Craig Johnson, Patrice Tardif, a first-round pick and a fifth-rounder. It was a great deal, in my opinion, and I thought Wayne could put us over the top.

Our first game with Wayne was in Vancouver two nights later. He scored late in the first period to give us a 2–0 lead in a game that eventually ended in a 2–2 tie. I played him for about 26 minutes. After the game, he went for dinner with his new team-mates. When the waiter asked for his order, he replied: "I'll take a bottle of oxygen, please." Even he admitted that his condition-ing was not at the level I demanded from our team. So, he worked hard to get ready for the playoffs.

Not even the Great One could escape my wrath. Craig MacTavish tells the story of the night I went around the room going after each guy. When I got to Gretz, I asked, "When was the last time anyone gave you shit?" After I left the room, he said to the guys, "I didn't think it was appropriate to say 'Janet, this morning!'"

Not long after Gretz joined the team, I finally traded Dale Hawerchuk, sending him to Philadelphia for MacTavish on March 15. Even though we finished 6–10–5 after the Gretzky trade, I thought the team was taking shape. The Blues ownership was concerned with a drop-off in attendance, just as I'd predicted would happen if we traded Shanahan. But after Gretzky arrived you couldn't find a seat in our 20,000-capacity building. Our top line of Gretzky, Corson and Hull looked good. We called them the Wayner, the Shayner and the Complainer. Wayne would often come into my office and say I had to talk with Brett, but I said Wayne should be talking to Brett—he was the only one he would listen to. Brett was a pain in the ass, but a good player. I could have managed him better, I suppose, got more out of him. I did it my way; I can't do it any other way.

In the first round of the playoffs, we took a 3–1 series lead against the Maple Leafs. Wayne set up eight goals in the first four games. But we suffered a significant blow in Game 2 when Toronto's Nick Kypreos accidentally-on-purpose fell on Grant Fuhr in the goal crease. Grant's knee was shot. Even though we won the series with Jon Casey in goal, we weren't the same team. We played a nervous game instead of the free-flowing offensive display we put on when Fuhr was back there. In the sixth game, leading the series 3–2, we were down by a goal after two periods. That's when, between periods, I challenged the players to deliver and give something back to the organization. They did.

In the next round, we fell behind the Presidents' Trophy–winning Detroit Red Wings two games to none, but we fought back to take a 3–2 series lead. Game 6 was in St. Louis. We fell behind 3–0 only to make it a one-goal game on Hull's sixth goal of the playoffs. But Nicklas Lidström scored late, leaving us with a 4–2 loss. In the series finale, we were gutted by Steve Yzerman's slapshot goal from just inside the blue line early in the second overtime period, a 1–0 game. Poor Jon Casey. He couldn't make a 40th save that game. Hully and Gretz have often said they felt we had a Stanley Cup–contending team and could have won that year if Grant wasn't hurt. Even the Red Wings said after the next round that we had tired them out, and they didn't have much left in their six-game conference final loss to the Colorado Avalanche.

After the season, our focus was on re-signing Wayne. When he arrived following the trade, we offered him a three-year $23 million extension. I then excused myself from contract talks, partly because I wanted to focus on coaching and partly because I was too close to Wayne, having gotten to know him in the two Canada Cup tournaments. Hanging in my home are two prized possessions he gave me. One is a photo of Wayne lighting the torch at the Vancouver Winter Olympics; the other is his jersey from the Nagano Olympics. Jack Quinn was the Blues' point man in negotiations with Gretzky's agent, Mike Barnett, my old teammate at St. Lawrence University. The Blues took the initial offer off the table after the Red Wings grabbed a 2–0 series lead in the second round, but later came back with a three-year $15 million offer that called for $12 million to be paid out over the first two seasons. Gretzky had all the leverage. He was Wayne Gretzky, after all. He wanted a lot of his salary up front. Quinn wasn't keen on that. Unfortunately, he wound up signing with the Rangers to reunite with Mark Messier for a two-year $8 million contract that included incentives that, if reached, elevated the deal to $11 million.

There were stories that Wayne wasn't happy with me at times in St. Louis. I had called out my best players at various points, though not always by name. It wasn't the first time. There were occasions when I wasn't happy with his play. That's coaching. I had nothing but respect for him then and now. And I didn't handle those contract negotiations.

Without Wayne, we started my third season in St. Louis by winning three of four, including a win at home against the

Stanley Cup–champion Avalanche and road victories in Calgary and Edmonton. But troubled times were ahead. We were back at Madison Square Garden on October 18, 1996. We lost 2–1 after the timekeeper allowed an extra 2.3 seconds to unwind after Brian Leetch was called for a late-game hooking penalty. We failed to score, and the Rangers hung on for the win.

Two weeks later, I acquired a number-one centre in Hall of Famer Pierre Turgeon from the Montreal Canadiens in a trade for Corson and Murray Baron. We also added Craig Conroy and Rory Fitzpatrick in that deal. In late November, we added Pavol Demitra from the Ottawa Senators for defenceman Christer Olsson. Despite those moves, we lost three straight in early December to fall to 13–14–0. Brett tossed more verbal volleys in my direction after a 3–0 loss against Phoenix at home for the third of those losses. He blamed himself but took veiled shots at me and our power-play prep.

"It's my fault for letting it happen," Hull said. "I'm so much smarter than that. I'm quite embarrassed by letting it happen from someone not nearly as smart as me. I don't know what our power play is since we never practise it. We never do it. We have to keep shooting it and hope it goes in."

Roger Neilson, one of my assistant coaches, was in charge of the power play. One time, Brett walked into the video room and was expressing his displeasure to Roger. Jay Wells, one of our big defencemen, walked in, grabbed Brett's sweater by the collar and dragged him back to the dressing room, telling him, "You will never talk to those guys like that again."

I benched him the next game, at Colorado. That was stupid of me. If there's a regret I have in dealing with players, it's that I didn't always follow that adage about the coach being the teacher and the players the students. He'd pissed me off, but I should have been the adult in the room. I was upset with myself then, and I still am—for not finding a better way to handle Brett. I'd hired Jimmy Pappin in St. Louis as one of my pro scouts. He advised me to give Brett a day off rather than bench him. I didn't. I wish I had listened.

We won that game against the Avalanche, 4–3, and with Brett back in the lineup, we won again in Edmonton, 3–2. Of course, Hully scored the winner midway through the third period.

But then, after a 5–5 tie in Dallas, I questioned our team's pride. I was pushing hard again. We responded with losses at home to Chicago, Vancouver and Hartford. The Vancouver game was an 8–0 drubbing, and I just stood behind the bench and let the players change lines in the third period. Two days after the 5–3 loss to Hartford, I was fired. Jack Quinn was also let go as president. I was disappointed we didn't perform better that year, and I couldn't help but feel that I'd "lost the room"; the results certainly indicate that I had. But I also left the organization with key players such as Pierre Turgeon, Al MacInnis, Chris Pronger and Pavol Demitra. Turgeon, MacInnis and Pronger all went to the Hall of Fame. Pronger was a Hart Trophy winner with the Blues, and Al won a Norris Trophy in St. Louis.

In January 2014, Brett Hull did a one-on-one interview with Fox Sports St. Louis. He said, "I will never forgive [Keenan] for what he did while he was here and what he did to this organization." That hurt. Of course, I've often wondered why, if he cared so much about the Blues, he left as a free agent for Dallas in the summer of 1998.

Hull and I had certainly had our issues, but I never questioned his abilities. After the loss to Hartford, Blues chairman Jerry Ritter met with all the coaches individually, finishing up with me. He said to me, "Of all the coaches"—Roger, Bob Berry and Bobby Plager—"you like Hull the best." I said, "He's an exceptional talent." Despite that, he said, he was going to fire me.

He offered me a $1 million lump-sum payment. What a joke. I still had millions remaining on my contract, close to $8 million. I said, "I don't think so." They threatened to take me to court, drag it out and exhaust my finances. But Rob Campbell and I knew we could call Gary Bettman. We told him about the dispute and asked if he would rule on it. He agreed to do so. I arrived in New York with Rob and a feisty St. Louis lawyer, Merle "Ruffy" Silverstein, who had represented everyone from former Blues owner Harry Ornest to rock legend Chuck Berry to Teamsters' boss Jimmy Hoffa. Bettman urged both sides to come to a settlement. But that wasn't going to happen. The Blues had at least a half-dozen lawyers in the hearing, and none of the Blues people would even sit in the same room as me. After Bettman heard everyone's arguments, he ruled: the Blues owed me $4 million, to be paid in two $2 million instalments. I got fifty cents on the dollar.

I later asked Gary, "Why do we have contracts?"

He didn't have an answer.

19

A CURIOUS 14 MONTHS: VANCOUVER, 1997–99

THE 1997 OFF-SEASON began with 10 of the 26 NHL teams—almost one-third—having a head-coaching vacancy and no shortage of rumours about who would fill the positions. I interviewed in the spring with Harry Sinden for the Boston Bruins job but lost out to Pat Burns, who was a friend and had worked with me in the 1991 Canada Cup. Harry walked away from the negotiations with my agent, pissed about money, no doubt. It was very disappointing.

I didn't consider Montreal a landing spot because it was widely thought that the Canadiens wanted to hire a French Canadian. But then I read that the team had interviewed Dave King. So I contacted Habs general manager Réjean Houle, but it was too late. They'd already decided to give the job to Alain Vigneault. There was interest from the Phoenix Coyotes and the Washington Capitals—we had good discussions—and a query from the

Buffalo Sabres about replacing John Muckler as their general manager. But when the season began, there was no job for me, even though I was only three seasons removed from winning a Stanley Cup championship on Broadway and freshly departed from the St. Louis Blues. No doubt my exits from New York and St. Louis scared off some teams.

Burns and Vigneault weren't the only ones to find jobs. Kevin Constantine was hired in Pittsburgh, Wayne Cashman in Philadelphia, Brian Sutter in Calgary, Darryl Sutter in San Jose, Ron Wilson in Washington, Jim Schoenfeld in Phoenix, Lindy Ruff in Buffalo, and Pierre Pagé in Anaheim. Darcy Regier had been named the Sabres' new GM.

I didn't stress about being unemployed. I went to the cottage and enjoyed my time there. I travelled; I took Gayla to the University of Michigan for her freshman year. I was confident I would work again. And sure enough, the Vancouver Canucks— with a bunch of the same players my New York Rangers had beaten in the 1994 Stanley Cup final—stumbled out of the gate that 1997–98 season. On Mark Messier's suggestion, the Canucks ownership called. Messier, of course, had played a significant role on the two championship Canada Cup teams that I coached, as well as on the Stanley Cup–winning Rangers. After the Canucks lost in the final in '94, they were eliminated in the second round the following season and in the opening round in 1996. Pat Quinn, who had decided to step down as coach to focus on his GM duties, brought in Tom Renney to coach. But Vancouver missed the playoffs in his first season behind the bench. That's when, in the summer of 1997, they decided to sign Messier to a three-year, $20 million free-agent contract.

Canucks billionaire owner John McCaw Jr. purchased a majority stake in the Canucks in November 1996. John was based in Seattle and, after Mess told him he wanted me to coach the team, he invited me to dinner at his favourite restaurant in the city. He ordered an expensive bottle of Opus One, but the red wine remained untouched as he looked across the table and told me: "This will be the worst negotiation of my life. You are the coach. How much money would you like and what's the term?" That was the first time—and thank you, Mess—I was ever in a negotiation where the owner asked me to tell him what I wanted. He basically said, "I have to pay you because I've already told Mark you're going to coach."

The franchise was in a desperate situation, and John had played his hand by letting me know that he wanted to bring me in to reconstruct the Canucks. It took us only a short time to agree on a three-year, $2.25 million contract. Then we had a chat and enjoyed that expensive bottle of wine. I went to his office the next day to meet Orca Bay deputy chairman Stan McCammon, who had just returned from Washington, DC, where he had fired Quinn. Orca Bay was the company John owned that owned the Canucks and other assets.

The Canucks had lost 10 in a row between late October and early November. Quinn was sacked on November 4, after the eighth straight loss. Renney was fired three games after that, on November 13, following a win at San Jose that had ended the losing streak, leaving Vancouver with a 4–13–2 start.

We started well, getting a point in my debut in Anaheim thanks to a late second-period tying goal from one of my old reliable players, Brian Noonan, and a couple of assists from Pavel

Bure in a 3–3 tie. But my first home game behind the bench two nights later did not come without a mini-crisis. About 90 minutes before the game, Vancouver's long-time and popular equipment manager, Pat O'Neill, informed me that my best player, Bure, had just called to say he was stuck in traffic. All I could think was that the rest of the team would quickly jump to the wrong conclusion—that Pavel was unhappy with the coaching change and refused to play for me. He was unhappy, all right, but not with me. He was disgruntled with the Canucks and past contract negotiations and other issues, and had gone public with a trade request in the off-season, before I was hired. I called a meeting with the players to tell them about the situation, that Pavel was stuck in traffic but would arrive in time for the game. And I told them that if word got out about him arriving late, there would be repercussions.

We then won five of the next six, with the only loss at home to the Blackhawks. The game after the loss to Chicago, we went to Manhattan to play the Rangers. It was Messier's first game at Madison Square Garden since he'd departed. Mess scored in the second period to put us ahead 2–0, and we beat the Rangers 4–2.

We were in Boston three nights later, where I had almost ended up coaching. We won again, 5–2, and then extended our win streak to three with a win in Toronto the next day. It was always enjoyable to win at Maple Leaf Gardens. We returned home to play the defending Stanley Cup–champion Detroit Red Wings and my old mentor Scotty Bowman. We blew a 3–1 lead after two periods and settled for a 3–3 tie. But the roof caved in on our season after that. We won just three of the next 23 and overall just 16 more times in the final 55 games. It wasn't pretty.

For the first few weeks of my time with Vancouver, there always seemed to be some sidebar story hanging over me or the team. Part of that early stretch of games was a trip to St. Louis on December 8—my first game back since I'd been let go. The St. Louis media whipped up a frenzy and ensured that the fans would not let me enjoy my return trip. So, I avoided the local press and only granted interviews to national reporters and columnists. I also didn't allow local reporters to attend our practice the day before the game.

Of course, one of the reasons my time in St. Louis ended was because of my perceived feud with Brett Hull. But Brett was out with a gluteus maximus injury during my return game. There was still a reunion, though. Hully asked to meet with me to clear the air. Our encounter was full of smiles and goodwill. I even signed a stick for him, writing, "To Brett, all the best to you and your family, Mike Keenan."

None of that mattered, though, when the teams hit the ice. The capacity crowd let me have it. The signs some fans brought to the Kiel Center included: "All I want for Christmas is Keenan's two front teeth," "The Rat Is Back" and "Welcome Back Mike, Not." A family held up three signs that read, "Keenan's a Canuck, That's Their Tough Luck, Frankly, They Can Keep the Schmuck." I appeared five times on the scoreboard, and I was brutally booed each time. The last time, I stood on the bench and sarcastically waved my arms up and down, which seemed to quiet the crowd. I guess they knew at that point that they'd gotten my attention.

The Blues were 18–9–3, fourth overall in the standings when we arrived, but they beat us 5–1. I can't help but think our team was overwhelmed and distracted by the negative vibes in the rink that night.

That loss was the third of five in a row. We were in trouble. The players hadn't responded to my scolding them in the first and second intermissions, and I could clearly sense that something had changed. Not uncoincidentally, it also happened to be Trevor Linden's first game back after a nine-game absence due to a groin strain.

A bit of background: When I arrived in Vancouver, we had some great players, including two superstar Russians in Bure and Alexander Mogilny. But expectations were too high and that team was not ready to win, and I felt there were two significant issues. First, the dressing room was divided by a conflict among its leaders—Trevor and Mess. Trevor had stripped himself of the captaincy when the Canucks signed Messier, but some on the team were still very loyal to Linden, and every once in a while, this could cause a problem. Around the time of the St. Louis game, for example, I called out Trevor in an intermission for his play and we had a real shouting match. Gino Odjick stood up and defended his former captain, who was still the most popular player with the Canucks fan base, a terrific player. Trevor had also been named to the Canadian Olympic team, which only increased his popularity. I had to fix this, and that meant deciding what to do with Trevor. We had hoped having Mess and his resumé would pull the group together, bridge the gap with Trevor, but that didn't happen.

The second issue was that most of this group was too comfortable. They were not in good shape compared to elite NHLers and in terms of the levels I demanded for my teams. And the atmosphere was far too relaxed, like they still were living off the accomplishment of losing in Game 7 of the Stanley Cup final a few years earlier.

I knew I had a reputation for picking on popular players when I arrived at a new team—whether it was Denis Savard in Chicago or Brendan Shanahan, Al MacInnis and Brett Hull in St. Louis, or now Linden in Vancouver. But each was a unique situation. Savard sometimes sulked on the bench if things didn't go his way. He didn't buy into the team philosophy. The Blues ownership wanted me to trade all the high-salaried players. And now Linden's presence as a representative of the old-guard Canucks simply wasn't meshing with the addition of Mark Messier.

When I was hired, and with Quinn gone, the Canucks already had put together a three-person management team to make the personnel decisions: president Steve Bellringer; vice-president of hockey operations Steve Tambellini; and assistant GM Mike Penny. But now I also had a say and the right to make personnel changes. Pat Quinn, who was a terrific coach and manager, was very loyal to his players, to the point where I thought he overextended their time as Vancouver Canucks. You can't hang on to players forever.

We finally made a trade on January 2, 1998, moving goalie Kirk McLean and Martin Gélinas to the Carolina Hurricanes for goalie Sean Burke, Geoff Sanderson and Enrico Ciccone.

A couple of weeks later, the Canucks' situation became even more confusing. Local reports surfaced that John Muckler had been in town to interview for the vacated GM position. When reporters asked me, I told them I knew nothing about it. I reaffirmed that I was in control. The reports were later confirmed by Muckler's agent, Gil Scott. But then, on January 23, I was given complete control of personnel decisions, putting an end to any controversy. Muckler, by the way, ended up being hired as the Rangers' head coach during the Olympic break.

The next trade was moving out Mike Sillinger to the Flyers for a draft pick. Sanderson went to Buffalo for Brad May and a third-round choice. Peter Zezel was brought in from New Jersey for a fifth-rounder. But everybody was waiting to see what I would do with Linden, who had just seven goals and 21 points in 42 games. Finally, on February 6, Trevor was dealt to the Islanders for defenceman Bryan McCabe, winger Todd Bertuzzi and a third-round pick, which turned into Jarkko Ruutu.

It was a very unpopular trade. Steve Tambellini was supposed to be involved, but he had stepped away from this decision because he didn't think it was going to go over well, and he was correct. But Mark's arrival changed the franchise, and Trevor wasn't playing up to my expectations. There had to be a decision made, a way to end the conflict created by the presence of both of them in the dressing room. And, of course, Mark was the guy who brought me in and who I trusted after so much success together. I was going to go with the man who won with me.

The trade happened just a week before Canada's first game at the Winter Olympics in Nagano, Japan. It was a tough decision, but I would do it again for sure. I wished Trevor well and hoped he would have a great career in New York. There was a funny quote from Islanders GM Mike Milbury at the time. When asked about me being critical of Trevor, he said, "Mike's pretty critical of his mother!"

Anyway, we were delighted to get Bertuzzi, who was 23, and McCabe, who was 22 and showed a capability to log a lot of ice time. He could have been a cornerstone piece on our defence. Both were big men.

And we weren't done yet. Burke went to Philly for Garth Snow in a goalie swap, and Ciccone went to Tampa for defenceman

Jamie Huscroft. Montreal-born Ciccone had opened up to the francophone media, criticizing me after I made him a healthy scratch in a 2–2 tie in Montreal on March 11. So I scratched him again the next night, in Philly, a 3–2 loss. I was talking to the players in the dressing room when Ciccone walked in, and I asked him if he wanted to apologize to his teammates. He refused the invitation, was sent home, and was traded two days later.

Around this time, we visited Long Island for a reunion game against Linden. We won 6–2. Before we played him again, 10 days later, we dealt Odjick, reuniting him with Trevor on Long Island for defenceman Jason Strudwick, who has told the story of a game when I told to him to sit at the end of the bench—on the other side of the backup goalie. Anyway, we beat the Islanders again, 4–3, in their return game in Vancouver. Gino talked to Vancouver *Province* columnist Tony Gallagher, criticizing Messier for a lack of leadership.

We missed the playoffs that year with the third-worst record in the league. But the culture change was underway. One bright spot about the season's final six weeks was Bure. I told Pavel he could play as much as he wanted. I knew he had a bonus for scoring 50 goals and I wanted him to get it. He scored 15 times in the final 21 games to finish with 51 goals. But he reiterated his wish to be traded after the season. Some cited the trading of Odjick, his good buddy. But his desire to depart had more to do with a feud with the Canucks' past management.

Pavel's trade request was the least of my problems. Missing back-to-back playoffs had ownership concerned about the team's financial outlook. Orca Bay claimed it lost $21 million in 1996–97 and $36 million after my first season in Vancouver. Did this prompt the hiring of Brian Burke as GM? The financial losses probably did play a role. Burke came aboard on June 22, 1998, two days before the NHL draft in Buffalo. Immediately, the speculation started: How long would we co-exist in Vancouver?

I actually knew Brian from way back. There may have been some initial interaction when I was coaching in Rochester, but the first interaction I actually remember with him was when I was coach/GM of the Blackhawks. He had taken over the Hartford Whalers and made a point of visiting rival GMs around the league to introduce himself. When I traded Shanahan to Hartford for Pronger, Burke had already left to work for the league, and Jimmy Rutherford was in charge of the Whalers.

In my first meeting with Burke in Vancouver, I asked him if he'd had time to read my contract and had seen the clause that said I had a say in player personnel decisions. As he wrote in his book *Burke's Law: A Life in Hockey*, he asked me if I had read his contract: "It says that I fire and hire the coach."

The Canucks ownership asked Burke to work with me, but everybody knew we were a combination that was doomed to fail. We were two strong personalities, and my input into personnel decisions was going to be reduced, or eliminated. Early in our time together, Burke ran into me outside the dressing room and was actually empathetic about us losing. I told him to get me some players who could score. Next thing you know we're having a loud confrontation. He took off down the hallway, past my wife, Nola. She asked me what that was all about. I said it was the beginning of a battle.

In the off-season, I urged Burke not to let the Bure situation linger. Bure had promised not to play another game for the Canucks. He was done, and we needed to trade him. There was no point letting a stalemate hang over the team's head. I also wanted Burke to take a crack at signing free agent Mike Richter, my Stanley Cup–winning goalie from the Rangers. As promised, come fall, Bure stayed home in Moscow, and improvements to the roster did not happen in the first few months. With some injuries and no Pavel, the Canucks were an ordinary 9–10–1. On November 25, we were in Toronto, down 3–1 midway through the third period. I pulled Garth Snow while we were on the power play. We hit the post, but Maple Leafs defenceman Dmitri Yushkevich scored a short-handed, empty-net goal. We lost the game, 5–1.

Burke was livid. Again, my retort was that the team had no offence, and we needed a spark. Get me some players. I asked him what was happening with the possibility of a Bure trade. Finally, on January 17, 1999, Bure had a new home. He was dealt to the Florida Panthers with defencemen Bret Hedican, Brad Ference and a third-round pick. In return, the Canucks received Ed Jovanovski, Dave Gagner, Kevin Weekes, Mike Brown and a first-round pick. Two nights later, with the new players aboard, we dropped a 4–1 decision in Nashville heading into the All-Star break in Florida. I needed more time to incorporate the new complement of players, but I wasn't going to get it.

I used the All-Star break to take a getaway to Whistler. My phone rang at midnight on the Friday night. It was Canucks media relations man Chris Brumwell. He informed me that a story was going to run in the next morning's *Vancouver Sun*, written by columnist Gary Mason, stating that I was going to be fired and replaced by Marc Crawford. I thought it was gutless that Burke didn't have the decency to tell me himself. I tried to track him down by phone in his Florida hotel room to confront him, but we didn't connect. I called Stan McCammon and asked what the hell was going on. He said he would call Burke. Crawford was with Burke in Florida. I phoned Crawford, too, and told him to ask for more money because the word was already out in Vancouver that he was the new coach of the Canucks.

In his book, Burke said he regretted how I found out I had been fired. He also denied telling Mason, which is difficult to believe. Burke wrote that I was a bully, and by the time I coached the Canucks, I "was no good." He told people he didn't like the style of play with my teams. He wanted more offence. Yet, whenever I asked, he failed to get me some offensive players. He also wanted me to fire Stan Smyl. I didn't understand it. Stan worked hard and was a good assistant coach. He also was well regarded in Vancouver. It was just one more strange situation in my curious 14 months with the Canucks.

I'll let you decide whether it was a good decision for Burke not to allow me to finish the season, and whether it was worth waiting more than three months to unload a 51-goal scorer in Bure. The Canucks finished 8–23–6 under Marc Crawford, good for last place in the Western Conference and six points below the prior season— although, in fairness, after a few seasons and some personnel moves they did get better. They just didn't go deep in the playoffs.

And, as it turned out, Bertuzzi turned out to become a terrific player on those good Canucks teams, and Burke later traded McCabe, who became a good defenceman, to get the picks to draft the Sedin twins, centrepieces of Vancouver's next run to the final. That would be a decade later, against Boston. As it turned out, Boston was in my future, too.

20

BACK BEHIND THE BENCH: BOSTON, 2000–01

WHEN THE 2000–01 NHL season started, more than 21 months had elapsed since my Vancouver Canucks gig had come to an end. This was only the second time I had sat out an entire season since I started my coaching career back in 1978 with the Oshawa Legionaires. The other was the year off between being fired in Chicago and taking the New York Rangers job.

I spent most of that time working as a studio analyst for Sportsnet television in Canada and as a colour analyst on their regional game coverage of the Ottawa Senators. Nola and I also travelled to Europe. We spent time in the Florida Keys and at the cottage north of Toronto. But I was itching to make a return as an NHL coach. You always wonder when you get fired whether you'll get another opportunity, especially when you've had a few stops already. I wasn't nervous, but I was anxious to get back behind the bench.

The NHL can be a copycat league. But in the 1999 off-season, I watched clubs opt for first-time NHL coaches in Andy Murray (Los Angeles Kings), Steve Ludzik (Tampa Bay Lightning), Curt Fraser (Atlanta Thrashers), Bobby Francis (Arizona Coyotes) and Kevin Lowe (Edmonton Oilers). There were expansion teams in Columbus and Minnesota coming into the league in 2000. But the Blue Jackets handed the coaching reins to Dave King for their first year, and Jacques Lemaire received the call from the Wild.

Although there was speculation that I was a contender to return to the Rangers when Glen Sather took over as president and GM in the summer of 2000, I didn't talk with Sather. Instead, Ron Low, a former Oilers assistant and head coach under Sather, got the job. But I'd soon have my eye on another Original Six franchise.

In late October 2000, I was working in studio at Sportsnet. After an evening slate of games, a bunch of us retired to a nearby establishment for wings and beverages. I had been negotiating a contract with the Boston Bruins but had kept quiet about it. I excused myself earlier than usual from the Sportsnet gang to prepare for an early morning flight to Boston. I remember a few of the crew were surprised I was leaving so early, and that I hugged a few on the way out, but no one knew why. Some weren't very happy the next morning when rival TSN broke the news. But it didn't come from me.

I'd come within a whisker of being hired by the Bruins in 1997. In fact, I'd thought I had the job. But after leaving Rob Campbell and Bruins GM Harry Sinden to finish up the contract talks, I went off to do my television work. Later that night, I discovered the negotiations had fallen through. I figure my side had pushed demands too far, and Harry, who could be tight with money, got pissed off. Instead, he hired Pat Burns, who was a good choice. He took the team to the playoffs in 1997–98 and 1998–99, but lost in the first round both times. Then, after trading Raymond Bourque to the Colorado Avalanche in March 2000, the Bruins struggled and missed the playoffs. Burns had relied heavily on Raymond's leadership and his presence on the ice. Pat and Raymond talked in French on the bench and in front of the team. That pissed off Harry—and things were about to get worse.

Pat's fourth season in Boston began with a 3–0–1 run, but then concluded with four losses in a five-game Western swing. Sinden fired Burns on October 25.

When Harry turned to me, he was upfront. He was 68 years old and wanted me to know he planned to step down as the Bruins GM but would be remaining as team president, an arrangement that would allow his assistant Mike O'Connell to take over. There was one key item to note, however: O'Connell would be free to hire his own coach if he saw fit. True to his word, Harry did step down as GM on November 1, eight days after I was hired, maintaining his role as president after 28 years as the Bruins' GM.

I accepted the job anyway, agreeing to a $600,000 contract for the remaining 74 games. It was far less money than I had been making, but I wanted to return to the game. The other part of the deal was that the Bruins and O'Connell had 10 days from the end of the season to decide if the contract would be extended for two more years.

Harry and I had a history. Before he became a Bruins icon, before he coached Team Canada to its epic victory in the 1972 Summit Series against the Soviet Union, he was a defenceman and captain of the Whitby Dunlops, who won the 1956–57 Allan Cup and the 1958 World Championship. Of course, I lived in Oshawa and later moved to nearby Whitby. Harry played on the Dunlops with two brothers, Tom and Ted O'Connor. My dad was a first cousin of the O'Connor brothers, and sometimes we would entertain the Whitby Dunlops at our house. They'd come over for a beer or two. As a result, I became the Dunlops' stick boy.

From the beginning in Boston, though, I sensed O'Connell was uneasy with me. I think he worried I was going to take his job, but I'm not sure. I didn't let that stop me from getting to work, though. I kept Peter Laviolette and Jacques Laperrière on as assistant coaches. Laviolette had won the AHL Calder Cup with the Providence Bruins in 1998–99, and this was his first year as an assistant coach in the NHL. Coaching wasn't the problem with this team, but Pat took the fall.

When I arrived in Boston, I was shocked about two things. First, I couldn't believe how out of shape the team was, especially playing for a coach like Pat Burns, who worked his teams hard. And second, I was surprised about the state of the practice facility. There were no stationary bikes and no gym equipment, and the head coach had to share an office with the assistant coaches.

I wasn't used to this. In Philadelphia, everything was state of the art. In Chicago, we'd had nothing when I got there, but we built the same sort of facilities we'd had in Philly. I guess we were going to start over in Boston, too.

I remember calling in Joe Thornton in the early-going. The big, talented centre was in his fourth NHL year. He'd been a first-overall pick in 1997, but he was struggling. The previous two seasons he'd had 41 and 60 points. I told him, "You're a wonderful young player, but look at you—you have a belly. You're not giving yourself a chance to be the best player you can be. So I will put you on the bike and give you some extra work."

Before his first session he asked me how long he should ride. I said, "I'll let you know." An hour later, the trainer entered my office and said, "Joe wants to know how much longer he has to ride." I had completely forgotten that I'd put him on the bike!

These Bruins weren't the tough Bruins I'd thought they would be. They were soft. And the environment in the dressing room wasn't good. This group needed a culture change. When I arrived on the scene, there was a contract dispute with Anson Carter. I also sensed a problem with my assistant coach Laviolette. He was ambitious, and I had to tell him he was a good coach and would one day be a head coach in the NHL, but for now, he had to step back, get behind me and wait for his opportunity.

And then there was a player revolt. The Bruins won my first game, 4–1, against Washington at home, but then lost five of the next six, including an embarrassing 7–1 beating in Toronto on November 5.

The players, led by Jason Allison, Don Sweeney, Peter Popovic, Hal Gill—a whole pile of them—went to Harry's office and complained that I couldn't coach. They were pissed because I'd called them soft. They had already taken down a very good coach in Pat Burns, and now they were looking for an easy way out again. Harry told them, "If he can't coach, how did he win a Stanley Cup in New York? How did he take Philadelphia to two Stanley Cup finals and Chicago to another?" They tried to pull a coup. I don't know if Laviolette had a part in it. Rob Campbell always told me that when I entered a new situation, I should bring my own staff with me. But I never did—at least not a full staff. I think about all the good people I inherited, like in Vancouver with Glen Hanlon and Stan Smyl, or in St. Louis with Bob Berry, or in Philly with Ted Sator. If I'd brought my own staff all the time, I never would have had the opportunity to work with those guys.

Anyway, Harry told this group of disgruntled players to go back downstairs because I wasn't going anywhere. I called Allison into my office and asked him why he hadn't come to me to share his concerns to my face.

He told me, "I made a mistake. I should have come in and talked to you first."

Allison played well the rest of the way, and we got along fine. And, of course, there were the guys I knew weren't part of the attempted coup—like Paul Coffey and Joe Thornton (Joe came to my office and told me as much). When it came to player relations during those early weeks in Boston, it was a real mixed bag.

I did eventually gain the respect of the players, but the big shift in the room came with the arrival of Bill Guerin—who joined the team about three weeks after I did, as part of the trade that sent the disgruntled Carter to Edmonton. He took Thornton under his wing, and he sent a clear message to the team about his expectations. Following a loss at home, just after his arrival, Bill destroyed a stationary bike in the dressing room and told the others they had to work harder.

In early December, I lost Coffey. He was 39 and felt he couldn't play anymore. I'd had him on both of my Canada Cup teams and thought the world of him. I told him he still was better than most. But he had lost his passion. After 18 games, we waived him to see if there was a better fit with another team. But there were no takers. He played his last game on December 4 in Atlanta. He

was a minus-one and played 20:54 in a 5–4 defeat. Not bad minutes under the circumstances.

We began the new year well with a 5–1–1 run to put us in the
playoff picture, but then lost three in a row in mid-January to
Carolina, Nashville and Florida. I unloaded on the team the day
before a game in Toronto on January 23. "I'm at a loss for words,"
I told reporters. "I can't tell what the hell is going on. They play
when they feel like it." The Bruins responded with a gutsy comeback 2–1 win over my old buddy Curtis Joseph and the Maple
Leafs. Allison scored the winner in the third period.

A hamstring injury to goalie Byron Dafoe hurt our playoff push.
He missed 13 games in February and March, and we struggled in his
absence, going 4–9–0. We used five different goalies that year because
our backup, Peter Skudra, also got hurt. A 20-year-old, Andrew
Raycroft, played 15 games. John Grahame and Kay Whitmore were
also summoned from Providence at different times to fill in.

Dafoe returned on March 15 with a 2–2 tie at home against
Vancouver—my first game against the Canucks since my bush-
league dismissal. I was still pissed that Brian Burke hadn't called me
to let me know I had been fired. When reporters surrounded me
in the lead-up to that game, asking about my history with
Vancouver, I told them, "I'm not saying I'm bitter, but I'm still
upset with the fact I was fired for no real reason. For about a year,
the team played worse after I left. The way it was handled was
unprofessional. But, that being said, I set myself up for that anyway.
I don't blame Brian. He was entitled to his own coach, but ownership should have hired a manager before hiring a coach."

A 3–0 Dafoe shutout in Toronto on March 28 put us in a tie
with Carolina for the final playoff spot with six games remaining.

For some reason, before Game 79 in Montreal, O'Connell flew in to address the team in the dressing room. It was an X's and O's talk: he went over the system we were playing. I was standing in the back of the room in wonderment. He was out of line. We still won, 3–2 in overtime, but I wasn't sure why he'd felt the need to do that.

We lost 5–2 in New Jersey in our second-last game of the year to mathematically eliminate ourselves from the playoff chase, only to win our season finale at home against the Islanders, 4–2. In our last 13 games, we lost twice in regulation, going 8–2–3. We finished 33–26–7–8 (36–30–8–8 overall) and in a tie with the Hurricanes with 88 points, but we lost the tiebreaker because we had fewer wins. They had 38, two more than we did.

We just ran out of time. We'd had a good year and overcame many issues, like the attempted player coup. Thornton improved his game (37 goals and 71 points, career highs at the time) and his fitness, and we came *that* close to the playoffs. I actually coached well that season, considering we had to use 41 players because of injuries and indifferent play and all the other stuff happening. But I knew the writing was on the wall with O'Connell, especially after he made that appearance in the dressing room. It wasn't a good relationship. I didn't let that bother me, and I focused on coaching and trying to get the most out of the team. It wasn't enough. Five days after the season ended, I was fired by O'Connell. I remember a phone conversation I'd had with Pat Burns just after I got the job. He told me that he did not like O'Connell and to watch my back. He was right.

In the media, Laviolette was considered the favourite as my replacement, but after the player coup Sinden had said Laviolette would never coach the Bruins. He left to coach the Islanders and

O'Connell hired Robbie Ftorek, who didn't quite last two full seasons, with O'Connell himself coaching nine games to end the 2002–03 season. A few years later, in late March 2006, O'Connell got fired as GM after making a few trades that didn't work out— including moving Thornton, who was becoming the star everyone projected, to San Jose.

With the Bruins, I'd had five core players. There was Bill Guerin, Joe Thornton and Jason Allison. Sergei Samsonov was a scooter on left wing, playing with Thornton and Guerin. And there was Brian Rolston. Mike Knuble was also an excellent person to have with the group, but he didn't have a good year.

One of those players was involved in a cool thing that brought my Boston experience to a more positive close. When free agency opened in the summer of 2002, at midnight on July 1, Guerin bolted Boston to sign a five-year, $45 million contract with the Dallas Stars. Afterwards, he called to thank me for our time together in Boston.

I guess not everyone disliked Iron.

21

SUNBURN: FLORIDA, 2001–06

IT'S FUNNY HOW your career path connects and intersects. In 1993, before the New York Rangers hired me, I had been contacted by the ownership of the two expansion franchises: the Mighty Ducks of Anaheim, as they were known then, and the Florida Panthers. I particularly recall the Panthers' courtship. I flew into the Fort Lauderdale airport and, from there, was whisked into a helicopter that landed on the top of an office building not too far away.

The majority owner of the Panthers was the late Wayne Huizenga, who had made his fortune by founding AutoNation and Waste Management, and at the time owned the Blockbuster video chain as well. Mr. Huizenga made his pitch, and then I flew to Anaheim to meet with Walt Disney chairman Michael Eisner. It turned out his wife, Jane, went to St. Lawrence University a few years before I had.

I told both ownership groups that after coaching the
Philadelphia Flyers to two Stanley Cup finals and the Chicago
Blackhawks to the final in 1992, I was looking to take over a team
that was ready to challenge for a championship. As it turned out,
my good friend Roger Neilson became the Panthers' first coach
and Bobby Clarke the first GM. Small world. And under the
direction of new GM Bryan Murray and new coach Doug
MacLean, they made it to the Stanley Cup final in just their third
season, losing to Colorado. But success had dried up after that.

Eight years later, I found myself interviewing in Florida again.
The team was under a new ownership consortium led by Alan
Cohen, who had bought the team from Huizenga for $101 million
in June 2001. The Panthers went from a playoff spot and a first-
round loss in 1999–2000, to 12th out of 15 teams in the Eastern
Conference the following year, to a poor start in 2001–02.

I began that season working as a network analyst on the
nightly *NHL On The Fly* show. There were rumours that fall that
the Rangers and Devils were interested in me after enduring slow
starts themselves, but nothing was serious until the Panthers
called in early December. Florida had lost four in a row and were
29th in the league at 6–15–5 under head coach Duane Sutter, who
I had coached in Chicago. Injuries to Pavel Bure and his brother
Valeri, as well as to defenceman Bret Hedican and goalie Roberto
Luongo, contributed to the sluggish start. But that didn't save
Sutter's job. Veteran general manager Bill Torrey, who had been
team president but took over as GM after firing Murray, was also
given the boot.

At a press conference on December 3, 2001, I was introduced
as the new head coach, and Chuck Fletcher was elevated from

assistant GM to interim GM. Alan Cohen, a New Yorker, reached across the table in the presser, grabbed my right hand and showed off my Stanley Cup ring to those in the room. "I want one of those without the 'Rangers' on it," he said.

As it turns out, Iron Mike had a champion in Miami just as he'd had in Vancouver when Mark Messier told the owner he wanted me to coach the Canucks. This time, it was Pavel Bure doing the work with Cohen and the Panthers. Pavel had plenty of influence on the Panthers' ownership because he was a great player with a big salary. One of the inducements for me to take the job came when I asked Cohen how much he was willing to spend in salaries. He promised a $60 million, maybe even $65 million payroll, which was a big number, and I probably should have known it wasn't realistic given that the top-spending teams had payrolls of $50-plus million. But I was in.

Alan Cohen was a clever person. I liked him very much. He went to the University of Florida for a degree in pharmacology but quickly discovered a need for a drug distribution company. So he started his own company, sold that and founded another called Andrx Pharmaceuticals. He thought outside of the box. Just look at what he did before the 2003 NHL draft.

We had the first-overall pick that year. At a scouting meeting, Cohen had overheard a conversation about up-and-coming star Alex Ovechkin. The scout was frustrated by the fact that Ovechkin's birthday was September 17, which meant he'd turn 18 two days *after* the cut-off date for that year's draft. "Too bad Alex Ovechkin wasn't born two days earlier," he said.

Immediately, the wheels in Cohen's brain started turning. Cohen claimed the NHL's Collective Bargaining Agreement

(CBA) needed to be more explicit, since there was no mention of what type of calendar the league considered as its measuring stick for a player's age. Cohen pointed out that it was not specified that a "tropical calendar" was being followed, and that if leap years were taken into account, Ovechkin would turn 18 four days before the cut-off date. Poor Rick Dudley, now the team's GM, went back and forth with the league, attempting to make Cohen's argument. But the NHL stood firm and finally warned Dudley that if he selected Ovechkin first overall, the Panthers would lose the pick.

But Cohen kept pressing Dudley to take Ovechkin with a later pick. In the ninth and final round, the league actually turned off the Panthers' microphone to dissuade them from trying. Dudley called a timeout, and the Panthers eventually drafted Tanner Glass, 265th overall. Crazy.

But back to that first season behind Florida's bench. We won my first game as coach, 2–0 at home against Columbus, but then won only 15 more times that season. We were a young team and lost a lot of close games—including eight of nine games to finish off February and begin March. All eight defeats were by one goal, including two in overtime.

With the team missing the playoffs three years in a row, attendance had dwindled in South Florida. Cohen became concerned about the bottom line. He asked interim GM Chuck Fletcher to trade Bure and his contract. Shortly after Pavel arrived from Vancouver in January 1999, just before I was fired by the Canucks, he signed a five-year, $47.5 million contract extension with an option for a sixth season at $10.5 million. Pavel was a guy who produced. In his first two full seasons with the Panthers, he checked in with 58 and 59 goals.

But Cohen wanted to unload his salary. I said, "Alan, you told me the budget was going to be $60 million, now you're telling me, all in, including the minor league team, it's going to be $30 million." He said, "We're not drawing any fans, I'm losing a ton of money." He wasn't wrong. So, Pavel was dealt to the Rangers at the trade deadline with a second-round selection in return for Igor Ulanov, Filip Novák and first-, second- and fourth-round picks.

Later that season, I was sitting in my office talking to Cohen, who spent a lot of time in my office, when the phone rang. It was Pavel. Under GM Glen Sather, the Rangers were floundering, and he wondered if I could get out of my contract in Florida and was interested in coaching the Rangers—a team that also had Eric Lindros, Mark Messier and Brian Leetch. Bure had scored 12 times in his 12 games with his new team, but the Rangers stumbled with a 6–6–0 record in those final dozen games to miss the playoffs.

It was an awkward moment with Alan in the room. He asked me if that call was about what he thought it was about. "It's the Rangers, isn't it?" he said. "They want you to go?" He didn't know it was Pavel, but even though the call probably shouldn't have been made, I later followed up with Sather, thinking I had an out-clause in my contract. Sather quickly ended the call, knowing he would have to ask for permission to talk to me. The league looked into it and no tampering charges were laid.

Anyway, none of it mattered, because Alan told me that I wasn't going anywhere, that he was extending my contract. I said, "Alan, the budget is so reduced from what you told me when I signed. And we got rid of Pavel, our best player." It was a disaster, but I still liked Alan very much, and I couldn't lie to him. So, I stayed put, and, later that summer, he did give me an extension through the 2007–08 season.

Despite any awkwardness around that call, I still had a great relationship with Pavel. We were close. Only a few people know this story, which speaks to the relationship we shared, but when I arrived in South Florida to interview to coach the Panthers, and while I was waiting for the decision to be made, I stayed with Pavel in his penthouse in South Beach. I actually lived with him during my first couple of weeks of work, before I found my own place.

We had some laughs. On my first day in his penthouse, which overlooked the beach, the Panthers' massage therapist was also there. Pavel was downstairs working out—something he did every day before dinner. He'd practise in the morning, and then work out in the late afternoon, and then we'd have dinner and watch hockey. Anyway, when Pavel came back upstairs, I was sitting at the computer. The massage therapist, who was also Russian, asked Pavel, "Who's this guy?" Pavel told him, "He's my computer guy." The next day was the press conference announcing my hiring. The massage therapist, who had figured out what was happening, joked with Pavel, "Hey, the computer guy is here!"

After my first season with the team, Fletcher negotiated with the Panthers about getting the GM position full-time. He asked me for advice, and I'm sure he also asked his father, Cliff, a legendary GM himself, about the salary he should demand. Unfortunately, Chuck couldn't come to a new contract arrangement with Cohen. On May 10, on the recommendation of myself and Rob Campbell, Rick Dudley was hired. Cohen had first asked me to take over for Chuck as the team's new GM, but I said no. At the time, being a GM was way too involved with contract negotiations and other aspects of the portfolio. I needed more hours in the day to coach and manage, as I'd had in Chicago.

Six weeks after Dudley came on board, the guy I'd replaced as coach, Duane Sutter, was hired as the team's new director of player development. I didn't have a beef with the move. If there was one person with a history of getting along with all six NHL-playing Sutter brothers, it was me. I'd coached the twins, Rich and Ron, in Philly. Darryl was my assistant coach in Chicago, and I traded for Brent, who had been with me in the Canada Cup, to play for the Blackhawks when I was there. Brian was my assistant coach for the 1991 Canada Cup. And I coached Duane, who was a terrific addition in my second season in Chicago. There had been some big changes during the off-season, but I was looking forward to my second season with the team, and my first full season behind the Panthers bench.

MY SECOND SEASON with the Panthers turned out to be the most challenging of my coaching career because of the youth on the team. When I took over the Flyers in 1984, we had the youngest team in pro sports, with an average age of just over 25. The 2002–03 Panthers had an average age of 25, with 15 players under 25. It was a fun group to be around, because you were teaching skills, but it was a group I had to learn to be very patient with.

One player whose development I was proud of was Olli Jokinen. Olli was the Los Angeles Kings' third-overall selection in the 1997 draft. By the time I arrived on the scene in South Florida, he was 23, in his fourth full season in the NHL, and on his third team, after being traded from the Kings to the Islanders and then to the Panthers. I was eager to learn what Olli was all about. There were a lot of question marks regarding his ability to make the grade in the league. Had all the scouts made a mistake in his draft year, or was he an underachiever or a late bloomer? Either way, it was time for him to demonstrate whether he could play or not.

Jokinen checked in with just nine goals in the first year I was with the Panthers, a three-goal increase from his previous year, but a two-goal decrease from his career high at the time in his only season with the Islanders, 1999–00. He enjoyed a breakout year in my second season behind the Panthers bench, improving his production from nine goals to a whopping 36. One of the things I did with Olli was give him an A as one of the alternate captains. We didn't have a captain. So he joined Viktor Kozlov, Marcus Nilsson, Sandis Ozolinsh and Dmitri Yushkevich in the leadership group that wore an A. But Ozolinsh and Yushkevich were traded to Anaheim and Los Angeles, respectively, that season.

Florida happened to play host to the 2003 All-Star Game. I was pleased when Olli was added to the Eastern Conference team after Mats Sundin came down with an injury and Saku Koivu was undergoing cancer treatment for a form of non-Hodgkin lymphoma. Ozolinsh had been named the Panthers' representative for the game but was traded two days before the showcase. Olli scored a goal and two assists in the East's 6–5 shootout loss.

Led by Olli's fine play, the Panthers were in the hunt for a playoff spot in early January. We had back-to-back significant wins at New Jersey and Colorado, both good wins against top teams. But the Panthers would lose the next five, including a spirit-breaking 12–2 decision in Washington on January 11. We went 12–25–6 in the final 43 games that season to earn the first overall pick in that infamous "tropical calendar" 2003 draft.

After Alan Cohen failed to convince the league that Alex Ovechkin should be available, Dudley traded down with Pittsburgh and picked up some assets to land forward Nathan Horton with the third-overall selection. While we were going through our second-half swoon, Dudley had decided to fire Paul Baxter and George Kingston, the assistant coaches I'd inherited when I was hired by the Panthers. Dudley then installed Duane Sutter as one of the replacements and brought in his buddy John Torchetti as the other. I should have known something was up.

Despite the late-season coaching shuffle and the draft drama, our off-season was relatively quiet. It did, however, bring some sad news. On the first day of the draft in Nashville, word circulated about Roger Neilson's passing at age 69. Roger was such a loyal friend. He had helped me get hired as the coach of the Peterborough Petes and put in a good word for me with Scotty Bowman to become head coach with the AHL Rochester Americans. Roger was my associate coach in St. Louis and my assistant with Canada at the 1993 World Championship in Germany. He was a different coach, relying heavily on video before most coaches did. Not many know this, but he earned a Stanley Cup ring with the Oilers in 1984 when he was hired for the playoffs as the team's video analyst and advance scout. He'd been fired earlier that season after 48 games with the Canucks.

In August, I made a late move and hired Mike Pelino as an assistant coach. Mike had played for me at the University of Toronto and was on my staff for the 1991 Canada Cup tournament. He was very talented and loyal, and I knew I could trust

him. We are great friends to this day. At the end of training camp,
Olli was named captain, and I was looking forward to getting
down to business. But after a 5–8–2 start with the Panthers in that
2003–04 season, I was fired following a 2–0 loss in, of all places,
St. Louis. Dudley named himself as my replacement, but after a
13–15–12 run, he turned the interim coaching reins over to
Torchetti for the rest of the season.

I was actually fired at the private jet terminal in Fort
Lauderdale. When we got off the plane, Cohen, who had been
on the road trip, said, "I want to talk to you." He started crying
and then fired me. I remember that during the drive home—I
lived north of Fort Lauderdale—my phone rang and it was
Cohen. He said, "I fired the wrong guy, I want to hire you back."
I told him he couldn't do that. "Everyone knows you fired me—
you did it in a public space. Everyone knows, including Dudley.
You'll look foolish. You have to stick with your decision." Pelino
wanted to quit, but I said, "No, you're not quitting." He went
back to work, but shortly after, Dudley called him in and said,
"We have to fire one more guy, and it's you."

I knew that roster wasn't good enough. We needed more size
and experience, and I had been urging Dudley to make changes.
The Panthers finished only five points better in 2003–04 than
they had the previous season.

But once again, strange developments were on the horizon.
In the spring of 2004, I got a call from Rob Campbell, who said
the Panthers were wondering if I was interested in becoming
the team's GM. Campbell also represented Jacques Martin, my
old St. Lawrence University teammate and assistant coach in
Chicago. The Ottawa Senators had fired Jacques after a lengthy

eight-and-a-half-year stint as head coach. When Rob was negotiating Martin's contract with the Panthers, Alan Cohen repeated
his point that he'd made a mistake when he fired me, and that
he'd fired the wrong guy.

So, on May 26, 2004, I was hired as the Panthers GM—the
same day Jacques Martin was introduced as head coach. I brought
in Jack Birch as my assistant.

In the meantime, I had become the head coach and character
in a CBC Television reality show called *Making the Cut: Last Man
Standing*, shot in Vernon, BC. The premise of this 13-week program was that a group of about 6,000 wannabe NHLers would
attend training camps in seven Canadian cities. A final 68 would
attend a two-week training camp under me, Scotty Bowman
and a collection of scouts. Six players would be awarded training camp spots, one each for Vancouver, Edmonton, Calgary,
Toronto, Ottawa and Montreal. The show was successful and was
picked up for a second season. And even though I had a new
position in Florida, it turned out that I had plenty of time that
summer for *Making the Cut*. A lockout wiped out the entire
2004–05 season.

That didn't mean that I kept my name out of the news, however. Because of the lockout, most of the game's top teenagers
were available for the World Junior tournament in Grand Forks,
North Dakota. But I caught fire for not releasing Nathan Horton
to play for Canada. I wasn't the only coach to make this kind of
unpopular decision: the Minnesota Wild didn't allow Brent
Burns to play either. It came down to me wanting Horton to play
with our AHL affiliate, the San Antonio Rampage. He had shoulder problems in his rookie season in Florida, scoring 14 goals in

55 games. He also enjoyed the Fort Lauderdale nightlife too much. I wanted him to play in a better league that season, and the AHL was at its competitive best because a lot of good young players had been sent down due to the lockout.

Horton joined Jay Bouwmeester, Stephen Weiss, Gregory Campbell, Filip Novák and Lukas Krajicek, all from our team. We traded Novák to the Senators the following year, but the others all improved with the Panthers after the lockout. Horton doubled his goal total from his rookie season to 28. I was concerned about Weiss. He befriended the owner's son. It wasn't a good situation; you can't have the owner's son hanging out with the players. He was just an average player.

When the new CBA was agreed upon in the summer of 2005, we signed unrestricted free agents Joe Nieuwendyk and Gary Roberts away from the Maple Leafs, as well as Chris Gratton from Colorado and Martin Gélinas from Calgary. An ordinary 6–4–0 start was wiped out by a 12-game (0–8–4) winless streak. But I had a bigger problem on my hands with goalie Roberto Luongo. He was awarded a one-year, $3.2 million contract in his salary arbitration case in August.

Roberto was playing behind a poor team and there was no doubt that he faced a lot of shots. But the other thing going on in Florida at the time was a happy trigger finger on the shot counter; Roberto was the face of the franchise, and this was a way to pump his stats. Negotiations for a contract extension during the season hit a snag. In January 2006, ownership set an upper limit for Luongo at five years, $30 million. But Luongo's agent, Gilles Lupien, turned down the offer and insisted on talking directly to Cohen.

I told Lupien a meeting with the owner wouldn't solve the issue, and it didn't. Luongo's camp wanted five years, $35 million. With the low taxes in Florida, it was a fair offer. It was like getting $600,000 more a year than you would in some heavily taxed states or in Canada.

I phoned Roberto—he had sat in on the talks—and tried to get my point across. I also told him that if he didn't accept the $30 million, he would be traded. The owner had told me, "If he doesn't take it, trade him." I said to Roberto, "Do the math." He said no, he wanted the $7 million a year. The last thing he wanted, though, was to be traded. His wife was from the area; she had lots of family there and owned an Italian restaurant. I don't think Roberto or Lupien believed I would trade him. Well, he played the season in Florida and we traded him to the Canucks the day before the draft in Vancouver, along with Krajicek, for Todd Bertuzzi (who I had acquired in Vancouver), Alex Auld and Bryan Allen.

Roberto wound up signing a four-year, $27 million deal with Vancouver. Here's the kicker: I lived in Vancouver, and taxes were 52 percent. So, if you do the math, he actually took less money. Ours was a great offer. He didn't want to move, and his agent should have been smarter. He did play well in Vancouver. In 2009, he signed a 12-year, $64 million extension, and he eventually became a Hall of Famer. We knew how good he was, but we had limits to our spending. Maybe he was smarter than all of us; he knew the team was bad and got out. With Roberto gone, I signed Ed Belfour to a one-year, $750,000 free-agent contract a month later.

After the draft, I also had an issue with Gary Roberts that needed to be solved. He asked to be traded closer to his Toronto

home because his 16-year-old daughter was on her own at board-
ing school after his ex-wife had decided to move back to Calgary.
I tried to work out a trade with Maple Leafs GM John Ferguson
Jr., but no deal was to be made. I was in a tough spot. The previous summer, I'd gotten into hot water for signing Nieuwendyk
and Roberts. They signed identical contracts: $2.25 million a
season for two years. They came in and provided much-needed
leadership and supported the coaching staff, but Cohen thought
I overpaid them and he threatened to fire me. And now here I
was, working on trading Roberts. Jacques was upset about losing
a key player, so he complained to Cohen—who called me in to
talk about the situation. I reminded him that he'd wanted me to
trade one of them the year before.

I was making $1 million a year at the time and had three more
years left on my deal. Cohen told me he wouldn't pay me and
instead offered a take-it-or-leave-it $300,000 payout before train-
ing camp began. He also wanted the optics of me saying that I'd
resigned.

And that's how my time in Florida ended. Maybe I'm naive,
but I've always said it would be better if owners own, managers
manage, coaches coach, and players play. But if there was blessing
to being fired, it was that I was able to spend some time with Nola,
who had major back surgery, and with my mom in her final weeks
fighting pancreatic cancer. I was with her and my sisters, my
daughter and father at the end and after.

22

UP IN FLAMES: CALGARY, 2007–09

I KEPT A pretty low profile after my time with the Florida Panthers ended in early September 2006. I did some television spots, including the trade deadline show with TSN, and I also took a position as a senior advisor with the Swedish Ice Hockey Association. I would fly to Stockholm occasionally to participate in various camps and give lectures to coaches and officials. And then a rumour that Darryl Sutter wanted to hire me as coach of the Calgary Flames started making the rounds.

Darryl had coached the Flames to the 2004 Stanley Cup final, where they lost to Tampa Bay in seven games. He coached another year after the cancelled 2004–05 lockout season, and then replaced himself with Jim Playfair so he could focus on his general manager duties. Playfair had coached the Saint John Flames to the 2001 Calder Cup championship and was promoted to the big team as an assistant coach a couple of years later. Under Playfair in

2006–07, Calgary made the playoffs with a good record, but the top-seeded Detroit Red Wings eliminated the eighth-seeded Flames in six games. Darryl, who was my associate coach in Chicago for a couple of seasons, called after the playoffs to see if I could meet him at the Westin Harbour Castle hotel on the Toronto waterfront. He told me his plan was to replace Jim with me as head coach. I'd be lying if I said I wasn't interested. I had been getting on with life away from the NHL, but still wanted to coach.

I travelled to Calgary a few days later to meet with Darryl and Flames president Ken King at a ranch they co-owned. At the time, Jacques Lemaire was coaching the Minnesota Wild, and he might have been the highest-paid coach in the NHL at $1.2 million or $ 1.3 million annually. King and Sutter asked me about my salary demands. I told them, "The same as Jacques." We negotiated back and forth and finally settled on $900,000 a season for three years with bonuses for playoffs and so on.

My hiring was announced in the middle of June, and the Calgary press immediately started grilling me. I was 13-plus years removed from winning the Stanley Cup with the New York Rangers, and I had made four more stops along the way, but I made my case: "If you want to scrutinize my coaching reputation, demeanour, approach, and if you want to really examine it closely, I have changed. If I hadn't changed, I wouldn't have coached in the league as long as I did."

I was 57 years old when I took over the Flames. Darryl asked if I wanted to keep assistant coaches Jimmy Playfair, Rich Preston and Rob Cookson on my staff. I had no problem keeping them all. They knew the players, and I knew them. I'd coached Jimmy in Chicago, and Rich was my assistant coach with the Blackhawks.

Darryl hired me because he felt the Flames needed a firmer hand than Jimmy had exhibited. Darryl knew me well.

Calgary had plenty of players I was familiar with. I'd had Craig Conroy in St. Louis, and Kristian Huselius in Florida. Alex Tanguay was a difficult player to coach because he wanted to do his own thing. But I really enjoyed coaching Owen Nolan. He was an impact player on and off the ice, an old-school type. There were good leaders in Jarome Iginla, who was our best player, and Robyn Regehr. And we had some good young talent, such as Dion Phaneuf, who had a career-best 60 points during my first season in Calgary.

The big concern was in goal. I inherited one of the game's best in Miikka Kiprusoff—he'd won the Vezina Trophy in 2006–07. But we needed a reliable backup. Curtis McElhinney began the year as Miikka's backup, but McElhinney was 24 and had yet to play a game in the NHL when he arrived. In my opinion, he wasn't ready. And there was too big of a difference between the two. Kiprusoff was so much better. As a result, our number-one goalie started the first 23 games that season.

We started the season with a decent run, but November greeted us with a five-game losing streak, including back-to-back losses in Vancouver and Edmonton. The first controversy of the season happened when my remarks about the team's penalty killing were misinterpreted. Local reporters felt I had lashed out at Kiprusoff. I had to clarify the next day.

"First of all, the media has misconstrued the comments," I said. "The question was, 'What about the penalty killing?' So you didn't ask me about Miikka Kiprusoff, you asked me about the penalty killing, and I said that he missed a shot that he'd like to have back and he's part of the penalty killing. So that addressed the question, 'What happened to your penalty killing tonight?' So it wasn't talking about the goaltender."

After that drama died down, the Flames went on to win 20 of the next 34 games to comfortably move into a playoff position. Part of this run included my 600th career win, a 5–3 victory in St. Louis. At the time, only Scott Bowman (1,244), Al Arbour (781), Dick Irvin (692), Pat Quinn (657) and Bryan Murray (607) were ahead of me.

I remember reading that only Bowman and Arbour had reached the 600-win mark at a younger age than my 57 years. But I didn't pay much attention to the milestone then, and it didn't mean any more to me that I accomplished the feat in St. Louis, a city that had turned on me. When I look back at my time there, I blame the local St. Louis media for being very critical of me; I believe they turned the fan base against me. All these years later, I still feel I put together a heck of a Blues team in 1995–96. We could have won the Stanley Cup had Kypreos not put Grant Fuhr out for the playoffs.

Speaking of goalies . . . Darryl made a good move in mid-January, signing Curtis Joseph as our backup. Curtis was 40 years old at the time, but he could still play. He chose the Flames over several teams that were interested in him. There was no awkwardness on my part with Curtis. I hadn't disliked him in St. Louis. Yes, I questioned his fitness level after he seemed to tire out in the playoffs, and then there was a contract dispute. But Curtis was a real professional in Calgary. He was exactly what we needed, with his experience and how he fit into our dressing room.

Jarome went on to score 50 goals in our first season together. It would be the second and final time he would reach that mark in his career (he'd scored 52 goals in his breakout 2001–02 season). Jarome was as tough as they come. And he was stubborn. We didn't want him to fight, but he did anyway. For some reason, I particularly remember a game in Columbus that season. Jarome fought their tough guy, Jared Boll, late in the first period and then scored for us a couple of shifts after the Blue Jackets came within one in the third period. We ended up winning 3–1. It was a vintage Jarome effort.

When Jarome was inducted into the Hockey Hall of Fame in 2020, he thanked Darryl and me for coaching him. I only had him for two seasons, but you appreciate thoughtful words like that, especially from a player and person of his calibre. Ed Belfour called me a few minutes after he received his Hall of Fame phone call, saying, "Thanks for putting me in the Hall." And Chris Pronger thanked me for helping develop him as a player in his Hart Trophy acceptance speech in 2000. These were all uplifting moments for me.

Even Chris Chelios recently called, inviting me to Chicago when the Blackhawks retired his No. 7 in February 2024. I told him I hadn't had anything to do with the Blackhawks for a long time. He said, "You made the trade for me to come to Chicago. Clear your schedule and plan on being there two days before the ceremony, because there will be a party, and I want you to be there." That meant a lot. I had a blast with other guests that included Wayne Gretzky, Mark Messier, Jeremy Roenick, John McEnroe, Cindy Crawford and Pearl Jam frontman Eddie Vedder.

The Flames finished the 2007–08 regular season sitting seventh in the Western Conference with 94 points—good enough to earn a first-round matchup with the San Jose Sharks. They'd finished second in the conference, 14 points ahead of us. We won the opener in San Jose, but we split the first four games. Except for a 2–0 loss in Game 2, four of the first five games were decided by a goal. In Game 3, we allowed three goals in the first three and a half minutes. I pulled Kiprusoff, and Curtis came in to stop 22 shots in a 4–3 come-from-behind win. San Jose won Game 5 at home, and we won our potential elimination game 2–0 back home to force Game 7. Miikka made 21 saves for the shutout, with Owen Nolan and Daymond Langkow scoring goals in the first and second periods.

Nolan put us ahead 2–1 early in the second period in the deciding game. But then Miikka stumbled. He allowed three goals in an eight-minute span, and Doctor Hook went to work. With Joseph now in goal, we fell behind 5–2 and wound up losing 5–3 after Wayne Primeau scored for us early in the final period. Joseph stopped 10 of 11 shots, while Kiprusoff faced 30 shots, making 26 saves. A lot was made about me pulling Miikka in the season-ending media post-mortems, but I'd lifted him to give our team a spark.

Miikka went back to Finland for the summer without talking to reporters. This led to speculation that there was a rift between us, but I didn't perceive any problems. In the off-season, former Flames goalie Jamie McLennan was added as the organization's director of goaltending development. I had him in St. Louis; he was a good guy. And even though I didn't think there was a problem between Miikka and me, Jamie suggested we go to Finland to bond with him. Jamie had been Miikka's backup for a few seasons in Calgary, and they knew each other well. We had a great time there. Miikka had a beautiful place overlooking the Gulf of Finland. We took saunas and jumped in the water.

I know I had a reputation for being hard on my goalies and pulling them often, but I had a good rapport with my goalies. I was fortunate to work with many Vezina Trophy winners: Pelle Lindbergh, Ron Hextall, Ed Belfour, Dominik Hašek, Grant Fuhr and Miikka Kiprusoff. Curtis Joseph and Mike Richter were also deserving of the honour. It's too bad that some of their best years coincided with Dominik being at the top of his game. When Miikka returned to Calgary for my second season behind the Flames bench, he ensured the reporters knew that all was good between us.

Darryl Sutter had a busy off-season. Mike Cammalleri joined us, and Tanguay was moved in a three-way trade with the Kings and Canadiens. The Flames also acquired Rene Bourque in a deal with the Blackhawks. Unrestricted free agents Todd Bertuzzi, Mark Giordano, Curtis Glencross, Jamie Lundmark and André Roy signed. At the same time, Joseph, Huselius, Nolan and David Hale left through free agency.

A six-game win streak wiped out a rough 1–3–1 start to the 2008–09 season. Then, we caught fire with an 11–1–1 run between December 16 and January 15 to pretty much solidify a playoff spot. Our roster was further fortified at the trade deadline, when we acquired my old buddy from Florida Olli Jokinen, and defenceman Jordan Leopold from Colorado. When Olli became available, I told Darryl he would be a good player for the Flames, especially on the power play. Darryl trusted me.

As an aside, one highlight of that season was a meeting with singer Michael Bublé. He was in Calgary for the Juno Awards, and one day there was a knock on my office door and the security guard asked if Michael and his family could have a tour of the dressing room. I showed them around the room, and afterwards, Michael asked if we could hang out for a while. We had a good talk, mostly about music. Not long after that, we were playing in Los Angeles. A security guard comes into the dressing room and says, "Some guy named Bubbles wants to talk to you." I knew it was Michael. I brought him in and walked him through the room. The players are looking like *Holy crap, where did he come from?* That was a great memory.

The Flames limped into the playoffs that season, going 8–11–0 after the trade deadline. We squandered a 13-point lead for the top spot in the division. We were dealing with some injuries; Rhett Warrener, Robyn Regehr and Mark Giordano would miss the entire playoffs. Still, we finished fifth in the Western Conference, four points better than my first season in Calgary. We had a post-season matchup with the fourth-seeded Blackhawks. They were a young and talented team on the rise, with Jonathan Toews and Patrick Kane leading the way. Of course, they would go on the next season to win their first of three Stanley Cups in six seasons.

We lost the first two games in Chicago by scores of 3–2, the first of which was decided in overtime. But then we rallied at the Saddledome to tie the series. They tried to pester Jarome as much as possible. He responded with a two-goal outing in Game 4 to send the series back to Chicago all even. In the pre-game warm-up before Game 4, our tough guy André Roy bumped one of their extra defencemen, Aaron Johnson. As a result, Roy was suspended for Game 5.

The Blackhawks outscored us 9–2 in the final two games to end our season. Those injuries really hurt us, and the toll mounted during the playoffs. Phaneuf missed the final game of the series with broken ribs. Bourque, who broke his jaw after an Adam Burish high stick earlier in the series, also sat out a game. Craig Conroy and Cory Sarich also played hurt, Sarich with a broken ankle.

When I met with reporters a few days after the series, I told them I had another year on my contract and expected to be back for a third year. We were eliminated on April 27, and on May 22 I was fired. In his presser that day, Darryl said, "It's a business, right? It's like explaining, 'You just finished with 98 points and we want you do be better.' When you're in that top group, you want to be the top of that group." Darryl added, "Mike Keenan is one of the best coaches in the history of the game. He hit milestones this year that nobody's going to catch." About a month after they fired me, Brent Sutter resigned from the New Jersey Devils and became my replacement, working for his older brother in Calgary.

I remained silent about my disappointment about not getting a third season with the Flames. We improved that second season to 46 wins. We were 10th overall in the standings, seventh overall at 3.06 goals scored per game, and eighth overall with 3.00 goals allowed per game. I like those trade-offs. We didn't advance past the first round of the playoffs because we had a paper-thin roster with all the injuries. As I have often said, injuries can be an excuse, but they can also be a reason.

I suspected my dismissal wasn't Darryl's decision. I don't think he wanted to fire me. I held my tongue until I did a radio interview with AM640 in Toronto on October 1. I listed all our injuries and blamed the Flames for being too impatient. "They gave Bowman four years to get a Cup in Detroit, but we only had a two-year stint," I said in the interview. I was asked if Flames CEO and president Ken King had influenced Darryl's decision to sack me. At the time, I said I wasn't sure what role King or owner Murray Edwards had in the decision. But I think King wanted me gone.

The Flames didn't make the playoffs for the next five seasons.

THAT WAS THE end for me in the NHL. I didn't know it at the time, but on April 27, 2009, I had coached my final NHL game, a 4–1 loss at home to Chicago. I look back at my start with the Flyers: we made it to the final twice. Then, in Chicago, the team advanced to another final. I had had good runs in St. Louis, but then the ownership changed and they wanted me to get rid of our best players. I won the Stanley Cup with the Rangers in 1994. There was the Brian Burke scenario in Vancouver, which was similar to the Mike O'Connell situation in Boston. Florida certainly was a different experience, and I enjoyed my time in Calgary. I wish I'd had one more season there; it would have been nice to see what we could have done.

Given the chance, I think I probably could have coached for 10 more years. But after 672 wins and 20 seasons behind the bench, my time in the NHL was over. Still, there was a silver lining. That June, just after I was fired, my granddaughter, Maelle, was born. Grandson Connor followed the next year—two babies in under 19 months—and I was blessed to be able to spend time with them and Gayla and her husband Craig.

23

ONCE A COACH, ALWAYS A COACH: THE KHL AND ITALY

WHEN I LEFT Calgary, I was pretty sure, deep down, that that would be it for me behind the bench, not that I wanted it to be. Starting with the 1977–78 Oshawa Legionaires and ending with the 2008–09 Flames, I had a good thirty-year run, winning an OHL Robertson Cup, an AHL Calder Cup, a Canadian University Cup, two Canada Cups, and a Stanley Cup along the way. Was there one more Cup in my future?

Dallas Stars general manager Joe Nieuwendyk talked to me about his vacant head coach position in 2009, but he hired Marc Crawford. I was interested in the New Jersey Devils job when Jacques Lemaire retired in April 2011, but Peter DeBoer was hired. After returning to television work at Versus, MSG and Sportsnet, I did find myself behind the bench once again, this time on the afternoon of New Year's Eve 2011 at an outdoor game between alumni from the New York Rangers and the Philadelphia Flyers at a packed Citizens Bank Park, where the baseball Phillies play. It was a prelude to the Winter Classic between the two teams the next day.

I coached Mark Messier and the old Rangers. The game was full of storylines: Eric Lindros made a long-awaited return to play for the Flyers; a 66-year-old Bernie Parent strapped on the pads for a few shifts in goal for Philly; and there was me, who coached the Flyers to a pair of Stanley Cup finals and then won the big prize with the Rangers. The game was friendly. At one point, Ron Duguay had a breakaway on Parent but shot into his pads to keep the Hall of Famer in good spirits. There was a lot of kibitzing.

But when we fell behind, Messier stood up, turned to me and said, "Shorten the bench." I'm serious. I heeded Mark's orders, but we still lost 3–1 before a crowd of 45,808. Kris King wasn't happy with me—still isn't—because I put Nick Kypreos out in his spot late in the game on his line with Darren Turcotte and Paul Broten. Flyers owner Ed Snider, who had fired me years earlier, of course, dropped the ceremonial puck and shook hands with both teams. He stood on the Flyers bench. But he wouldn't talk to me. He still was pissed about what transpired back in 1993.

The outdoor alumni game was fun but also very emotional. Fifteen weeks earlier, former Flyers defenceman Brad McCrimmon had been killed in a tragic plane crash in Russia. The Beast was in his first year coaching Lokomotiv Yaroslavl. On September 7, 2011, his Kontinental Hockey League (KHL) team boarded a plane at the Tunoshna Airport to travel to Minsk for their season opener. The takeoff was botched, and 45 people were killed. The only survivor was a flight engineer.

I coached McCrimmon for three seasons in Philadelphia and loved him as a person and a player. He went on to win a

Stanley Cup with the 1989 Calgary Flames. His coaching staff with Lokomotiv included two more players I'd coached: Alex Karpovtsev and Igor Korolev. Karpovtsev was part of the Stanley Cup–winning Rangers team. I had Korolev in St. Louis for the Blues training camp in 1994–95, but he was picked up on the waiver wire by the Winnipeg Jets during the lockout. Also among the players who perished on that tragic flight was Pavol Demitra, who I acquired in a trade from the Ottawa Senators when I was in St. Louis. A lot of hockey talent was lost when the plane went down, a lot of really good people, and the memory of those players, especially Brad, was front and centre during that alumni game. Like I said, very emotional.

IN 2012, I was asked to coach a two-game exhibition series in Russia, with stops in St. Petersburg and Yaroslavl, to commemorate the 40th anniversary of the 1972 Summit Series and the first anniversary of the Lokomotiv Yaroslavl tragedy. Phil Esposito, Ken Dryden and many of the great Team Canada players made the trip but didn't play, just like their Russian counterparts. Instead, many members of my 1987 Canada Cup team suited up. Brett Hull joined Wayne Gretzky and Messier, and they played a Russian team that included Igor Larionov, Alex Mogilny and Alexei Yashin. Börje Salming, at 60, also played for us, and he was incredible.

That series turned competitive, too. In the first game in St. Petersburg, on September 5, we lost. During an intermission in the second game, two nights later, Messier told the guys in the dressing room, "We're not losing this game." And he was right: we ended up winning to tie the series. We had a wonderful time in Russia and were treated with superb hospitality. But there were intense moments. Phil Esposito was the hit of the trip with his stories about 1972. He also hadn't lost his competitiveness. I asked him to coach with me and I remember him yelling at the Russians during one of the games, "You fucking Commies." I had to tell him to chill, that this wasn't 1972. He laughed. The fans were incredible, as was the tribute to the 1972 and 1987 teams.

I ended up returning to Russia a year later, again to coach, but this time for real. At age 63, I was hired to coach Magnitogorsk Metallurg of the KHL. Metallurg had previously been coached by Dave King, and then, in 2012–13, by Paul Maurice. Tom Barrasso was one of his assistants. Paul and hockey broadcaster Darren Dreger, who I'd worked with at Sportsnet, visited me at my cottage in the summer of 2013 to see if I would be interested in the Magnitogorsk job. Paul had been hired by the Winnipeg Jets. Next thing I knew, I received an offer from Magnitogorsk; Paul had recommended me to ownership.

I had taken a call from a young agent named Rasty Saylo from Ukraine. I was on the NBC set then and had a break coming up during the playoffs on the May 24 weekend. So I told Saylo, "First of all, where is Magnitogorsk?" Second of all, "We can negotiate a deal, but I want to fly over there during my break to check out the facilities and the organization." I met the team's GM, Gennady Velichkin, and on the way home flew into Moscow to meet with the team owner, Russian billionaire oligarch Viktor Rashnikov. That was an experience.

His office was impressive, with luxurious wood panelling. He also had about 10 security people around him, all with guns, some with machine guns. As Rashnikov sat across from me at a beautiful conference table, dressed in a suit straight out of *GQ*, Gennady walked around the table to present the owner with a contract to sign star right winger Danis Zaripov. Gennady used my presence to get Rashnikov to approve without any fuss. At the time, I didn't know who Zaripov was, but he became a vital player on our team. He was one-third of the highest-scoring line in the league, along with a Czech named Jan Kovář and Sergei Mozyakin, a former Columbus pick (2002, ninth round). Mozyakin scored a league-leading 34 goals in 54 games during my first year in the KHL. Rashnikov didn't speak English, and I had yet to grasp Russian. But we hit it off.

Magnitogorsk is smack in the middle of Russia, at the foot of the Ural Mountains, a two-and-a-half-hour flight to Moscow. It reminded me of Gary, Indiana—a little rough around the edges. Rashnikov owned Magnitogorsk Iron and Steel Works, one of the world's leading steel producers, which employed 60,000 people. He got a kick out of it when I told him about the summer I spent as a spot welder on the assembly line at the GM plant in Oshawa. He also owned a ski resort outside of Magnitogorsk. He explained and hammered home just how critical the hockey team's success was to the morale of the town, especially his steel-workers. Production went up when the team was doing well.

When we assembled for our six-week training camp in Garmisch-Partenkirchen, Germany, near the Austrian border, my first impression of the team was unfavourable. We played our first exhibition game in Füssen, home of the castle that inspired Disney's iconic logo. I brought Mike Pelino along as one of my assistant coaches. I also inherited a wonderful guy in Ilya Vorobiev as my other assistant. His father, Pyotr, was a legendary Russian player and coach, who finished his playing career in Germany. That's where Ilya was born and had played most of his career, although he did finish with a championship in Magnitogorsk under Dave King in 2007 and worked for Maurice.

Ilya was invaluable because he could speak Russian, English and German. When I got to Russia, I told Pelino that our biggest responsibility was to understand, not be understood. I'd say 95 percent of the players couldn't speak English. I had to learn phrases. The players were respectful and responsive. They liked the firmness; maybe it goes back to their culture, upbringing. But coaching in Russia with the language issues made me think about all the foreign players I'd coached in the NHL. I was embarrassed that I'd never thrown them a lifeline, never told them how to bank, or find an apartment. I'd missed the boat. Most of us probably did back then.

Before that pre-season game in Füssen, Pelino said to me, "I think something's wrong. Ilya is out in the hallway pacing. I think he wants to talk to you." I guess Ilya had heard about my Iron Mike reputation and was nervous because he had to break some bad news to me. Ilya informed me that our new goalie, Vasily Koshechkin, had forgotten his equipment an hour away in Garmisch-Partenkirchen. Apparently, with his old team, Cherepovets, the trainers packed his goalie equipment. With Magnitogorsk, the players were responsible for putting their equipment on the bus. In the same game, another one of our players had his jersey ripped badly. I told the trainers to get him another jersey, but they informed me it was their only one. They had to find a practice jersey and put white tape on the back for his numbers. I thought, *So this is what Russia is all about.*

In Magnitogorsk, a couple of the younger players, including my backup goaltender Ilya Samsonov, lived in a complex called a baza. This was an old-school athletic residence in Eastern Europe, which was like a five-star university dorm. The other players lived in a nearby apartment building with their families. But the baza was a comfortable place with swimming pools, saunas and security. Pelino and I lived there the first year, but then moved downtown so we could enjoy restaurants and other amenities.

We had a rough start to that first season. In the KHL, you're allowed five imports, and I urged our general manager, Velichkin, to get some better players. He did. One of the Canadians he brought in was Tim Brent, who had played briefly for the Toronto Maple Leafs and proved to be a solid guy and a good character player. Another Canadian, Chris Lee of MacTier, Ontario, was one of our top defencemen. He would later play for Canada at the 2018 Olympic Games.

The new additions made a difference. We ended up finishing first in the Eastern Conference with a regular-season record of 35–11–8.

The KHL had teams in nine different countries back then: Russia, Belarus, Latvia, Finland, Kazakhstan, Ukraine, Croatia, Slovakia and the Czech Republic, now known as Czechia. Travel was far worse than the NHL teams experienced, even in the Western Conference with its infamously long flights. Sure enough, in the first round of the playoffs we matched up against Admiral Vladivostok, just about eight hours away by plane. Yes, eight hours. Oh well, we survived the travel and defeated Admiral Vladivostok (4–1) in the first round, HC Sibir Novosibirsk (4–0) in the conference semifinals, and Salavat Yulaev Ufa (4–1) in the

Eastern Conference final. Their goalie was a 19-year-old Andrei Vasilevskiy, who kept the games close. He, of course, went on to star with Tampa in the NHL.

We played HC Lev Praha in the Gagarin Cup final. They won the regular-season Western Conference and forced a seventh game against us with an overtime win in Game 6. In the final game, we overcame an extremely ardent crowd in Prague. Their arena had a capacity of about 18,000 and the fans stood the entire game. The energy was incredible. But we survived. We rallied to win the deciding game, 7–4, on April 30, 2014, two decades after my Rangers had won the Stanley Cup. I became the first coach to win both a Gagarin Cup and a Stanley Cup. I was also named the 2014 KHL coach of the year and coached in the KHL All-Star Game that January. Not bad for a guy my players in Magnitogorsk nicknamed "The Grandfather." Because the city revolved around the steel industry, they also loved my nickname, Iron Mike. What was also nice about winning the Gagarin Cup was that it happened prior to my dad passing, and my sisters, Gayla and Craig, Nola and her boys, and my niece all came to Prague that spring.

The championship parade in New York City to celebrate our Rangers' Stanley Cup drew more than a million people. The celebration in Magnitogorsk, a city of about 500,000, was just as memorable. The parade route veered close to the steel factory so the workers could come out and celebrate with us. It truly was a magical feeling for the players and me. I loved my time in that Russian Steel City.

Aside from that celebration, another unforgettable, and crucial, part of that championship season was taking the team to tour the memorial site honouring Brad McCrimmon and the

Yaroslavl team from the 2011 plane crash. It was an emotional day, to say the least, and it helped bring the group together.

WE PERFORMED EVEN better in my second season in Magnitogorsk, finishing with a regular-season record of 40–15–0–5, but late-season injuries hurt us in the playoffs. We were eliminated in the second round.

I turned 65 a few months into that second season. What a party. When you're a male in Russia and celebrate your 65th birthday, it's a celebration akin to a bar mitzvah or a wedding. I was presented with an unbelievable sword decorated with jewels, and some golden goblets.

In my third season, we weren't terrible, starting at 13–8–0, but management and ownership feared they were about to lose Ilya Vorobiev. Other teams were courting him, so Magnitogorsk felt the timing was right to pass the torch from me to him. I remained with the team as a consultant. I couldn't have been prouder of Ilya and Pelino when they coached Magnitogorsk to another KHL championship the year Ilya took over. The one thing I regret was the timing. I'd been ready to get my Russian citizenship so I could coach the Russian team at the 2016 World Cup of Hockey in Toronto. But that opportunity disappeared when I lost my head coaching job in Magnitogorsk.

But my time with the KHL wasn't quite done. The Russians would invite me back each Christmas. They had this massive hockey conference during the holiday season, and I would talk about coaching. About the time of my second appearance at this conference, Russian president Vladimir Putin was negotiating an oil and gas deal with China. As part of the deal, Putin urged China to have a KHL expansion franchise. They agreed, and the Chinese officials asked for suggestions as to who might coach the country's new hockey team. My name came up often. The team was based in Beijing, and Russian Vladimir Yurzinov became its first coach. I was hired as a consultant and helped them arrange training camps for Chinese North Americans in Vancouver and Toronto.

Eventually, Kunlun Red Star asked me to be their coach, and I accepted. I took over behind the bench to begin the 2017–18 season. Just about that time, my marriage with Nola ended, so China was a nice distraction. But even with NHLers on the roster whose names you may recognize—Wojtek Wolski, Alexei Ponikarovsky, Andrei Kostitsyn, Brandon Yip, Taylor Beck, Kyle Chipchura and Gilbert Brulé—we started with a 12–16–8 record and suffered a nine-game losing streak, which led to me being replaced by my assistant coach, former Washington Capitals centre Bobby Carpenter. I actually didn't mind. The experience in Russia was fantastic. The experience in China was a nightmare. The Chinese were starting from scratch. I was drawn into matters like how to flood the ice properly and how to construct the proper dressing room. Coaching took up enough time. All this extra stuff was too much, and anyway, I would soon have a different battle on my hands.

In May 2018, I was diagnosed with prostate cancer. I have always been good about my health, taking annual physicals. In Key West, Florida, I had a blood test that revealed my PSA count had gone from low to abnormally high. My first reaction was very matter of fact. I said, "Okay, I've got cancer. What are my options? What's the best course of action"?

My doctor, Julie Floyd, said I should get a biopsy. I drove up to Fort Lauderdale where I saw a surgeon, who was Russian and loved hockey. He confirmed the cancer diagnosis and wanted to perform surgery, but I said, "Hold on, I'd like to get another opinion and see a radiologist." The second doctor to look after me said, "I know you." I asked him how he knew me, and he said, "I'm a New Yorker."

Eventually, Dr. Hans Chung, a University of Toronto grad, oversaw my medical journey at Sunnybrook Hospital in Toronto. I underwent a procedure called brachytherapy, in which seeds are implanted into the prostate and gradually release radiation to kill the cancer cells. The procedure worked. My PSA blood count has been low ever since. I urge everyone to get checked annually. My particular situation was caught early, so the road to recovery went rather well.

This wasn't my first cancer scare. In 2011, Gayla was diagnosed with ocular melanoma. I have a theory about how she happened to contract this rare form of eye cancer. But it's only a theory, and it's only mine—so make of it what you will. Gayla went to the University of Michigan and then to Columbia University in New York City to complete her master's in education. One morning, while she was at Columbia, I received a phone call at the cottage. "Dad, what should I do?" I didn't know what she was talking about. I turned on the television, and then I knew right away. It was 9/11, the terrorist attacks.

Gayla was a block away from the World Trade Center that morning, giving a seminar at a high school. I told her to walk along the Hudson River away from the attacks, and that I was on my way. I made it as far as the Canada–US border near Kingston,

Ontario, but that was it. They wouldn't let me into the United States, even though I had an American passport. The cellphone towers in Manhattan were out. I waited for hours—some of the longest in my life—wondering what had happened to her. The towers had fallen by then, and the city was in a state of chaos. We later made contact, and I learned she had gotten to safety. But when she was diagnosed with eye cancer ten years later, I wondered if all the dust and everything else that had been set loose when the buildings collapsed had something to do with it.

After Gayla's diagnosis, my involvement and contacts in hockey really came through for us. The foremost eye cancer hospital in the United States happened to be in Philadelphia (Wills Eye Hospital), and they took such good care of her. Thank God, she recovered. I'm so proud of the way she attacked her setback. To this day, Gayla continues to raise money for research and awareness.

AS IT TURNS out, I wasn't quite done with coaching. Remember how my strong relationships with Mark Messier and Pavel Bure turned into coaching jobs in Vancouver and Florida, respectively? Well, in the fall of 2022, another player and a teammate from my past helped get me the head coaching job with the Italian national team. Many years ago, Ron Chipperfield was a highly touted NHL prospect, but he found himself playing for me in the minors in Rochester. One day, he knocked on my office door and said he couldn't play in the AHL anymore; he was about to leave to play in Italy. He signed with HC Bolzano. He played a few seasons there, coached for several years and became a player agent. He married a local woman.

When Milan and Cortina d'Ampezzo were awarded the 2026 Winter Olympics, Italy needed somebody to take over its hockey program. As hosts, the Italians receive a berth in the men's Olympic tournament, but the team was ranked 18th in the world at the time. The Italian Ice Sports Federation contacted my old St. Lawrence university teammate Mike Barnett and Chipperfield, who both suggested they call me. They courted Marc Crawford, too, but Marc was still hoping to get back into the NHL, with a fallback position in Switzerland. They asked me for some names, which I gave them, never thinking about it for myself. A week or so later I got a call from the Italians: "How busy are you? Would you move to Italy and become our coach?"

And so I did. Coaching was still in my blood. At age 72, I agreed to another head coaching stint. Mike Pelino, whose father is Italian, once again agreed to help as my associate coach and Dave Jamieson, who played for me back in Oshawa, came as my goalie coach. I had coached Canada at the World Junior tournament in Helsinki (1979–80), in two Canada Cups (1987 and 1991), and at a World Championship in Munich (1993). Now, I was getting a shot at the Olympics and would be coaching against Canada, which is in our group.

What a trip it's been. I wasn't ready to give up my NHL career, but look at what's happened since. First, I ended up in Russia, then I spent time in China, and then I landed in Italy, living in beautiful Bolzano with my partner, Gabrielle Juttner, a wonderful woman who I met in a restaurant on February 14, 2019, on vacation in Rome. She is originally from Costa Rica but was living in Miami at the time. I was living in Key West. We eventually came together and have been together since.

After heart surgery early in 2024, for health reasons it was mutually agreed with the Italian federation that it was best for me to step down as coach, which I did in June. It was disappointing, but Italy was another wonderful chapter in my coaching life, which started almost 50 years ago for Iron Mike. Not a bad run.

ACKNOWLEDGEMENTS

OVER THE YEARS, some of those players who called me a bastard (I am, as mentioned at the start of the book) no doubt questioned if I even had a heart. Well, I do—and Dr. Leonard Girardi, a heart surgeon at New York-Presbyterian Hospital, can prove it. On April 2, 2024, Dr. Girardi performed open-heart surgery on me to repair an aneurysm in my ascending aorta, the main artery that carries blood from the heart to the rest of the body. Another battle, and a big one. Seemed like a good idea to thank the good doctor first. I would also like to thank Dr. Fred Feuerbach, a cardiologist who works with the New York Rangers and referred me to Dr. Girardi.

But there are plenty of others to acknowledge and thank for my life, career and this book. First, though, a reflection on me and my coaching career.

I believed in my principles, but, with the benefit of hindsight, I might have adjusted my methodology. Having said that, though, looking through a 2024 lens reveals that this is a much different world than it was during my earlier coaching career. But I know I took everything to the extreme. I took losing very personally, and I had to learn to enjoy winning. I don't know why I was so driven to succeed and win, at times irrationally. But I was. Winning requires abnormal behaviour. I was focused to a distraction, my own, and it was difficult on my personal relationships. I made mistakes, but I always just wanted people to succeed, including myself. I know I had my flaws, but I also think I was a solid friend and a good coach. I enjoyed learning, and being a student for life. I had a lot of great opportunities in many great cities and countries. I was very lucky to be in the NHL, and I am grateful.

I know I was hard on a lot of players, but the goal was always to make them better for themselves, both to realize their potential and for the team to win. Again, perhaps the methodology could have been different, but there are many players who still stay in contact, who I count as friends, and many who thank me for the careers they had. More than 60 of my former players have gone on to become NHL coaches or general managers and many have been inducted into the Hockey Hall of Fame.

There are so many to thank in my life and my coaching career.

The arrival of my daughter, Gayla, was the most joyous moment of my life, even more so than winning the Stanley Cup. And she has blessed me with two wonderful grandchildren, Maelle and Connor. Maelle, who is autistic, has taught all of us so many life lessons, and Connor continues to be an exceptional young man. Their father, Craig, is also a wonderful part of our family.

I am fortunate to have Gabrielle in my life. I'm not the easiest person to live with, but she is special. My two ex-wives, Rita and Nola, are still friends. Hockey was difficult on the two marriages.

My mother, Thelma, and father, Ted, have both passed, but they had an enormous impact on my life and my story. My sisters, Marie and Cathy, remain very close and supportive, along with Peter and Dan, their husbands and partners, respectively. The same is true for my nieces, Kate and Kim, Nola's sons, Grant and Reed, and Gabrielle's loving family in Costa Rica.

I mentioned throughout the book so many of the great players I was privileged to coach, and I want to thank all of them. My assistant coaches at so many different stops were great, but a special shout-out goes to long-time friend and coach Mike Pelino, who played for me at the University of Toronto and has been a part of so many of the adventures since.

Sadly, in April 2011, we lost one of my first assistants, E.J. McGuire, to cancer. I was honoured to have had him in my life and to be able to call him friend. He was like a younger brother. Not long before he passed, I met up with him for a beer and we had a lot of laughs. The next day his wife, Terry, called to tell me E.J. had cancer. He couldn't tell me. He was a great man and had no expiration date on loyalty.

I want to acknowledge and thank all the support staff I had over the years, the public-relations folks, the team services people, the training, equipment and medical staff. There were so many that supported me and put up with some of my crazy demands. A couple of stories: Joe Kadlec was the first PR person and director of team services with the Flyers. He was with the team for 40 years. A great guy. I remember once, during my time in Philly, we were on the bus driving to Washington for a game. I asked Joe which hotel we were staying in and he told me. I said, "No way. We lost the last time we stayed there." I made the driver pull into a gas station, and Joe had to get on the payphone and book a different hotel.

Another great guy was Devin Smith, who was with me in Vancouver. His dad was Ron Smith, a terrific coach who has passed. I drove Devo crazy changing hotels on the road. I told him, "We're a professional hockey team, we can't be staying in a bus terminal, so upgrade the hotel." I was always changing the room list. One time, I made him change the room list while we were on a flight using the phone on the plane that needed a calling card. It was a disaster. I once asked him to fire the anthem singer because he was too slow and didn't get the team pumped.

There were so many good people—the likes of Matt Loughran, John Rosasco and Barry Watkins in New York; Steve Williams and Cindy Bodnarchuk in Chicago; Mike Caruso and Janeice Chambers in St. Louis; the legend Johnny Bucyk in Boston; Austin Guhl and Janine Shea in Florida; Peter Hanlon in Calgary and Kalli Quinn in Vancouver. I've missed a few folks, but I appreciate all they did. Likewise with all the trainers and medical folks—the list goes on.

I also want to acknowledge a couple of guys who gave me my most recent coaching position, and the leave required to have my medical issues dealt with: Andrea Gios, who is president of the Italian Ice Sport Federation, and my general manager, Stefan Zisser.

And a special thanks to my coaching mentors: Tom Watt, Roger Neilson and Scotty Bowman. They were inspiring. And my long-time friend and agent Rob Campbell—it has been a helluva ride. Thanks also to my long-time lawyers, Peter Chin and Doug Jovanovic, and my accountant Dave Yoshida. When I wasn't coaching, I worked mostly in television with a lot of great teammates there: Darren Dreger, Nick Kypreos, John Shannon and Bob Torrens at Sportsnet; James Duthie and Rod Black at TSN; Mike Milbury, Keith Jones, Jeremy Roenick and Liam McHugh at NBC; Ron Duguay, Al Trautwig, Ken Daneyko, Sam Rosen and Joe Micheletti at MSG. There were also members of the print media with whom I had a good relationship: Jay Greenberg and Al Morganti in Philadelphia; Al Strachan in

Toronto; Tony Gallagher in Vancouver; Eric Duhatschek in Calgary; Terry Jones in Edmonton. I know I've forgotten some good people, but thanks to all for the support.

As for the book, it was my friend, the late Jay Greenberg, who got this project going. Sadly, during the COVID-19 pandemic, Jay passed. My thanks to Scott Morrison, another Hall of Fame writer, for taking over and writing the book. We have known each other since 1979 and have had a great relationship. Thanks also to another terrific writer, Tim Wharnsby, who assisted Scott and was an incredible resource. A special thanks to my former captain, the great Mark Messier, for writing the foreword. He was a tremendous player, leader and teammate. A true champion and friend.

We were fortunate to have a great editorial team, starting with Craig Pyette, who did the first edit, and Linda Pruessen, who took over the edit and did the copyedit and was amazing to work with. Both have worked with Scott before and both did a tremendous job with this book. Thanks also to Deirdre Molina, managing editor at Random House Canada, Catherine Abes, who handled the photos and captions, and publisher, Sue Kuruvilla.

I know there are folks who impacted my life and career who haven't been mentioned by name—owners, presidents, managers, players, coaches, trainers, friends and family. A blanket thank-you to all.

INDEX